DAMNED IF YOU DO.
BORED IF YOU DON'T.

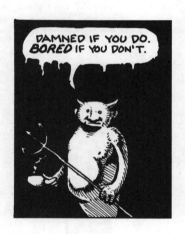

editor • DIANA SCHUTZ
assistant editor • JEREMY BARLOW
digital production • DAN JACKSON, RICH POWERS
book design • DARIN FABRICK, HOLLY CLEMMONS
art director, DH Maverick • CARY GRAZZINI
publisher • MIKE RICHARDSON

Special thanks to Dave Nestelle and Michael Ring for their assistance with the cover design.

This book collects issues 9 and 10 of *Too Much Coffee Man*, published by Adhesive Comics, along with sundry strips published in a miscellany of venues.

Address all correspondence to:
Adhesive Comics
P.O. Box 14549
Portland, OR 97293-1459
www.tmcm.com

Published by
Dark Horse Comics, Inc.
10956 SE Main Street
Milwaukie, Oregon 97222

First edition: December 2001
ISBN 1-56971-633-3

1 3 5 7 9 10 8 6 4 2
PRINTED IN CANADA

TOO MUCH COFFEE MAN'S™
amusing musings
notions, insights, ideas, theories, inklings, realizations, & thoughts

by SHANNON WHEELER

This book is dedicated to Austin and Berkeley, my children, not the cities.
It's also dedicated to Holly, my wife,
not the plant.

TABLE OF CONTENTS

TMCM's Amusing Musings book cover was argued over extensively. We decided on "Reflection in a Cup" as the cover image because of its balance of elegance and humor. The cover could front a styled work of urban socio-neo-pop fiction except for TMCM's peering reflection. He's a ridiculous, weird, and cartoony character. One should also notice that TMCM's eyes are unfocused. His mind is elsewhere. He's not spaced out. He looks worried, freaked out, or simply amped on coffee. He's thinking about something important. This look is the key to his character; TMCM is a thinker, always pondering, always musing. We wanted the cover to express this central theme of the book: ideas. We rejected the "Sexy Woman" cover, even though it had greater "Market Appeal." Please support our integrity by buying several copies of this book.

CHAPTER 6

CHAPTER 7

THE END

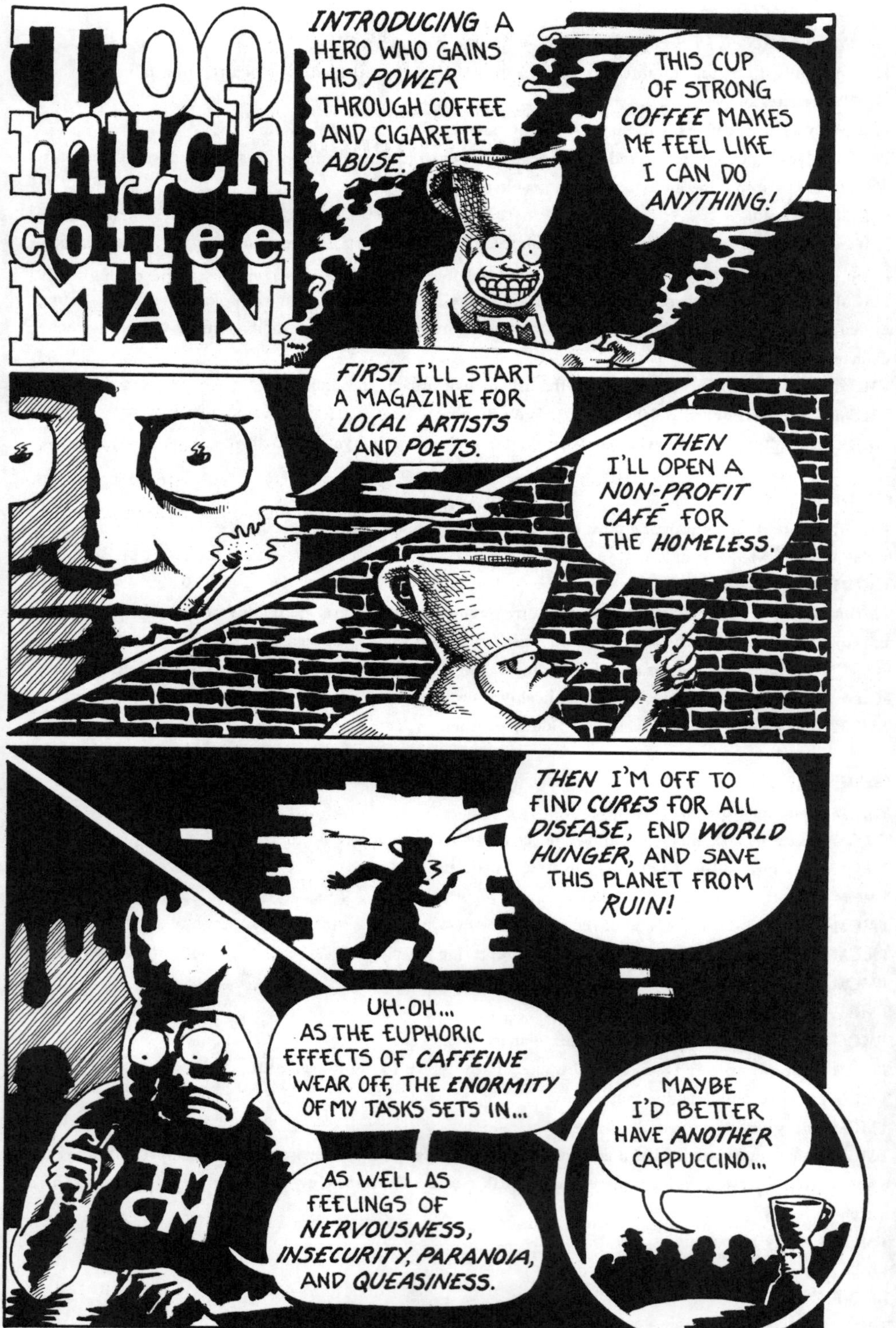

TOO much coffee MAN
INTRODUCING A HERO WHO GAINS HIS POWER THROUGH COFFEE AND CIGARETTE ABUSE.
THIS CUP OF STRONG COFFEE MAKES ME FEEL LIKE I CAN DO ANYTHING!
TM
FIRST I'LL START A MAGAZINE FOR LOCAL ARTISTS AND POETS.
THEN I'LL OPEN A NON-PROFIT CAFÉ FOR THE HOMELESS.
THEN I'M OFF TO FIND CURES FOR ALL DISEASE, END WORLD HUNGER, AND SAVE THIS PLANET FROM RUIN!
UH-OH... AS THE EUPHORIC EFFECTS OF CAFFEINE WEAR OFF, THE ENORMITY OF MY TASKS SETS IN...
AS WELL AS FEELINGS OF NERVOUSNESS, INSECURITY, PARANOIA, AND QUEASINESS.
TM CM
MAYBE I'D BETTER HAVE ANOTHER CAPPUCCINO...

INTRODUCTION

by TOM TOMORROW

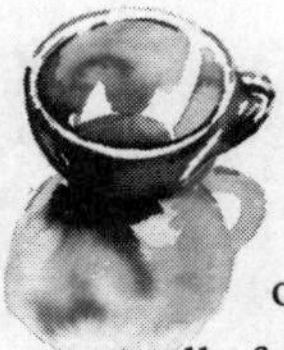

Shannon Wheeler and I went to a strip club in New Orleans last summer, along with a bunch of other cartoonists and an editor or two, all of us refugees from the Association of Alternative Newsweeklies conference. We drank to excess as we bantered with strippers trying to hustle us for lap dances, and if I were to embroider this anecdote slightly, perhaps stretch the truth just a little, to tell of the craziness which followed as we wandered through the bleary neon night of Bourbon Street, drinks in hand and strippers in tow, staggering from one mad jazz club to the next, spinning out crazy stories which would soon become the stuff of legend — if I were to do this, I could certainly make us all sound like devil-may-care raconteurs living life to its fullest, crazed artists to whom normal rules of conduct cannot and should not be applied, because creativity cannot be constrained, genius makes its own rules, blah blah blah.

In reality, most of us cowered uncomfortably, clustered in a dimly lit corner, sipping on our beers and declining the opportunity to pay topless women to wiggle around in our laps (though there were exceptions, and as long as the payoffs continue, I will not name names). Because the truth is, almost all the cartoonists I know are very mild people, for whom living life to the fullest entails time spent with their wives and kids, taking the dog for a walk, things like that. We're really just not very interesting, for the most part.

I've only hung out with Shannon a few times at conventions over the years, and while I can't state definitively that he doesn't have some insane secret life involving mistresses and illegitimate children and perhaps a room in the basement which is always kept padlocked, he seems like a pretty typical cartoonist, which is to say boring. But I mean that in a good way. There are exceptions to this, of course, but mostly cartoonists are too busy living in their head to worry too much about wacky affectations — an entire wardrobe of Edwardian clothing, say, or a hairstyle which requires far too much attention. It's not that you'd mistake us for salarymen — our wardrobes are too shabby, and there's often a stray piercing or a soul patch or some other small indication that we do not have office jobs — but mostly, and this is the point, our inner demons are purged on the drawing board and the computer. Mostly we are not compelled to wear our hearts on our sleeves, to declare to the world that we are, goddammit, individuals.

It wasn't always this way. I know a cartoonist from an earlier generation, whose working routine used to include a dalliance with a different prostitute every day at lunchtime. I don't know Shannon well, but I think it is safe to conclude that his working habits are rather more mundane than that. He does not burn brightly like a roman candle in the night, there is no inevitable rendezvous with a looming tree at the end of some dark whiskey-soaked evening of debauchery, neatly bookending the legend of his tortured genius and inspiring a critically acclaimed film in ten or fifteen years with a handsome young actor in the lead role as the doomed cartoonist for whom life itself was simply too much to bear. As far as I know, he's just a guy who lives out on the West Coast with his family and draws these really strange comics.

Ah, but those comics — this is where we get to the heart of the matter. If you are not familiar with the oeuvre of the man who drinks too much coffee, the alternately angry and perplexed and poignant world of the excessively caffeinated one, then you have a treat in store. There is a temptation to use the metaphors of coffee consumption here, to give Shannon that easily extracted blurb which he can plaster on his promotional materials — Too Much Coffee Man is a triple shot of espresso for the funny bone! TMCM is a caffeine-fueled journey through the dark heart of the sleepless American night! — but I will resist, because TMCM is not ultimately about coffee. Yes, that's right — you, the reader, the purchaser of this book, the lover of all things coffee-related, have been bamboozled. The coffee is just the pretty lure, the bright attractive colored plastic hiding the sharp steel hook which is, as we speak, protruding from your cheek.

Sure, the central character wears a large coffee cup on his head at all times — sometimes it seems to be a part of his anatomy, but in at least one of these cartoons, it's just a costume he can remove when he decides to take an office job. So who is this TMCM, exactly? Is he from another planet? Is he a superhero?

Is he driven by the death of his gentle uncle, a death he could have prevented if only he hadn't been wasting his time sitting around in the coffee shop all afternoon? Has he been taught a painful lesson, that with great amounts of coffee come great responsibilities? And if he is a superhero, doesn't that mean we are all superheroes, any of us who spend our time drinking too much coffee and thinking about the world? Is TMCM a metaphor for the cartoonist himself?

These are but a few of the questions to which you will find no easy answers in the pages ahead. But do not be frightened! TMCM can be enjoyed on many levels. He is, in one sense, consumer culture anthropomorphized, a satire on consumerism masquerading as a consumer icon. You need never to have read the work to enjoy drinking a fine hot cup of java from a cup featuring the screen-printed image of a man with a coffee cup for a head. Too much coffee, man! What more do you need to know? Everyone at the office is sure to enjoy a hearty chuckle. And let's not forget the TMCM T-shirts and sponges and god knows what else, because Shannon is an unparalleled master at coming up with weird shit to sell you, useless crap which parodies the very impulse to buy useless crap, even as it enriches his coffers. (Personally, I can't wait for the limited edition TMCM action figures. That sounds like a joke, but I am completely serious. What could be cooler? If Jesse Ventura can have an action figure, if the Flaming Carrot can have an action figure — and they both do — I don't see why TMCM can't have an action figure. But I digress.)

On another level, TMCM is a roving philosopher, an ambassador from the inner depths of Shannon's mind. You want good-natured, laff-filled comics about the foibles that make us all human, there's always *Garfield*. But TMCM will give you meditations on the economy as a placebo, on the simultaneous necessity and futility of voting, on the paradoxical relationship of expectation and experience. TMCM is like an onion, except that it probably won't make you cry, and if you keep peeling back layers, you find more rather than less — so scratch that, it's really nothing like an onion at all. Maybe it's more like an artichoke, at the heart of which lies a tasty reward for the work of navigating its thorny layers, even though those layers are themselves quite delicious, particularly with a buttery sauce.

TMCM is also, and this is where we get to my own level of expertise, a political cartoon. It may not be what you're used to thinking of as a political cartoon, in the sense that there are no donkeys and no elephants and no drawings of the Statue of Liberty shedding a tear of grief as the Twin Towers burn in the distance, or even any talking penguins, but the politics contained therein are quite astute, even if they don't always grab you by the lapel and spew saliva in your face as they rant about the shortcomings of the two-party system. "The Coffee Lawsuit" is a case in point — a look at the facts behind the famous story of the idiotic old woman who sued McDonald's because her coffee was too hot, for chrissakes — the story that shows everything that's wrong with our lawsuit-happy society. Except that there's more to the story — there's always more to the story — and Shannon lays out the difference between what really happened and the urban legend that sprang from it, the gulf between fact and oversimplification, and lets the smug commentators and editorialists of the chattering classes stand revealed as the morons they are by simply quoting them verbatim.

I write these words at a dark moment in history. There is a long night looming, and daybreak is but a distant hope. The gulf between fact and oversimplification has suddenly become very, very important, and our preference for one over the other will define the world we will live in for a very long time to come. Enjoy these cartoons and take their wisdom and their thoughtfulness to heart, because we may soon need all the wisdom and thoughtfulness we can muster.

And try not to drink quite so much coffee — it's bad for your health.

Tom Tomorrow
October 2001

9

chapter 1

REFLECTING ON EXCESS

Censorship through inclusion, and other notions

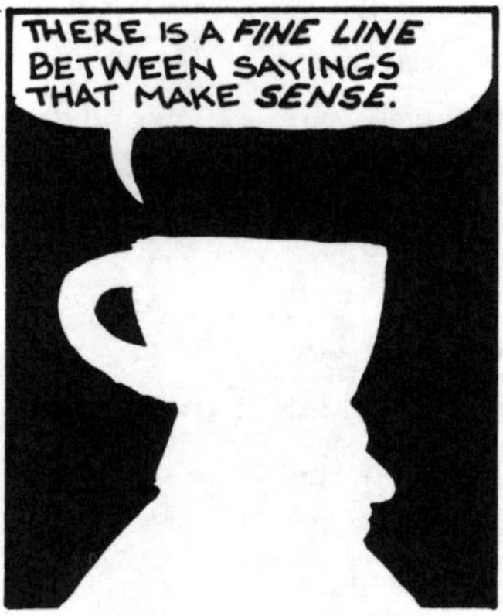
THERE IS A FINE LINE BETWEEN SAYINGS THAT MAKE SENSE.

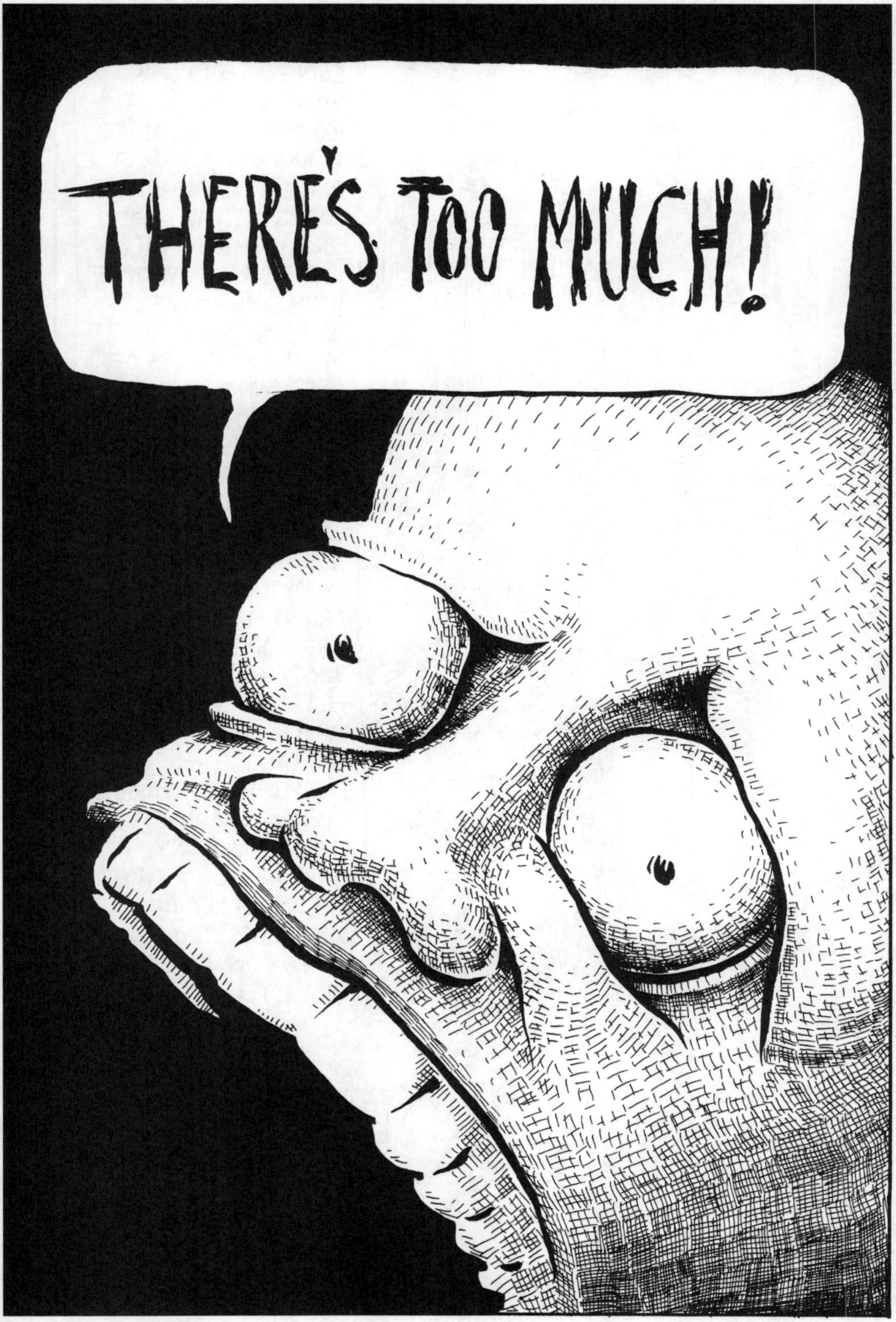
THERE'S TOO MUCH!

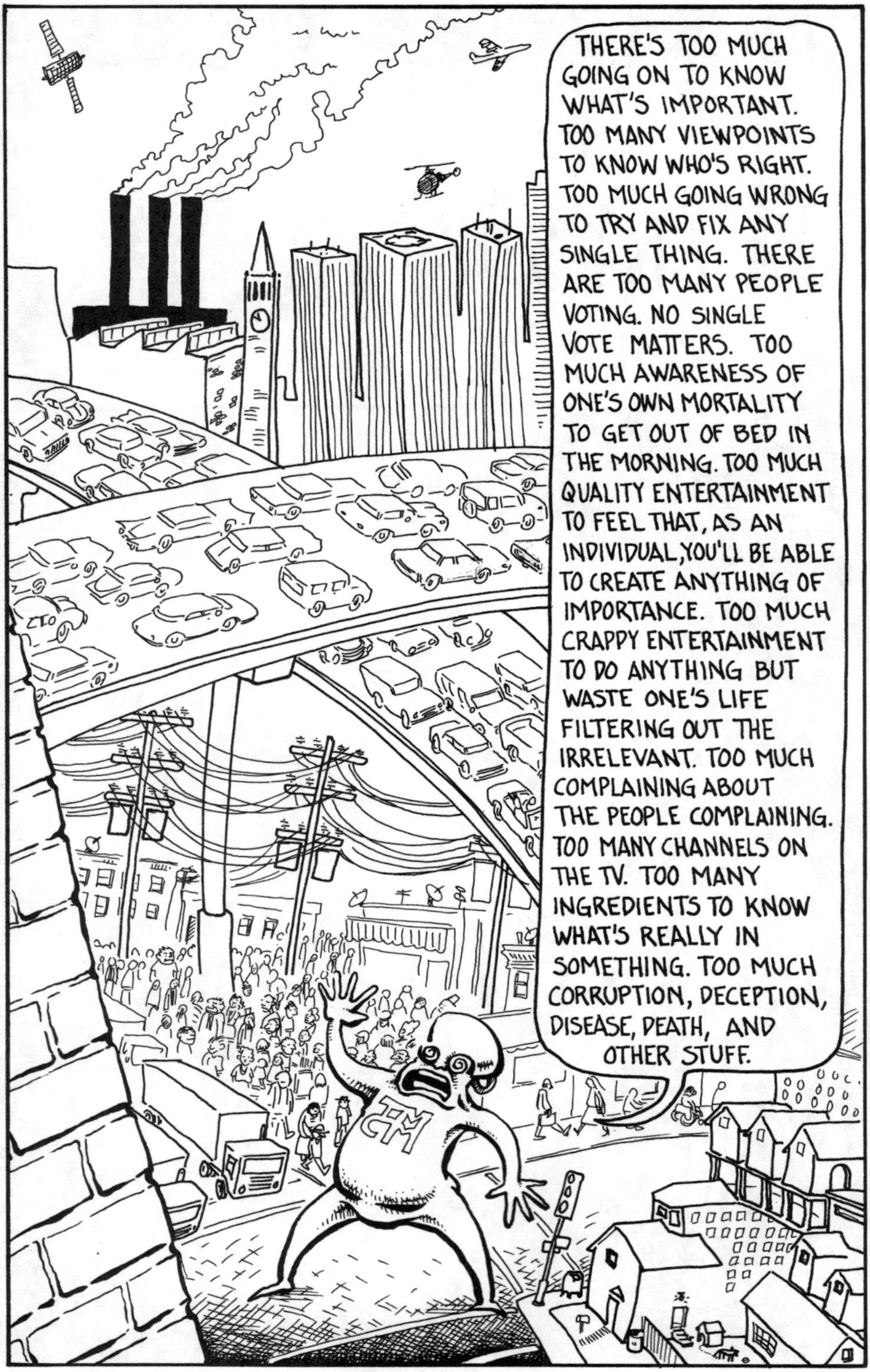
THERE'S TOO MUCH GOING ON TO KNOW WHAT'S IMPORTANT. TOO MANY VIEWPOINTS TO KNOW WHO'S RIGHT. TOO MUCH GOING WRONG TO TRY AND FIX ANY SINGLE THING. THERE ARE TOO MANY PEOPLE VOTING. NO SINGLE VOTE MATTERS. TOO MUCH AWARENESS OF ONE'S OWN MORTALITY TO GET OUT OF BED IN THE MORNING. TOO MUCH QUALITY ENTERTAINMENT TO FEEL THAT, AS AN INDIVIDUAL, YOU'LL BE ABLE TO CREATE ANYTHING OF IMPORTANCE. TOO MUCH CRAPPY ENTERTAINMENT TO DO ANYTHING BUT WASTE ONE'S LIFE FILTERING OUT THE IRRELEVANT. TOO MUCH COMPLAINING ABOUT THE PEOPLE COMPLAINING. TOO MANY CHANNELS ON THE TV. TOO MANY INGREDIENTS TO KNOW WHAT'S REALLY IN SOMETHING. TOO MUCH CORRUPTION, DECEPTION, DISEASE, DEATH, AND OTHER STUFF.

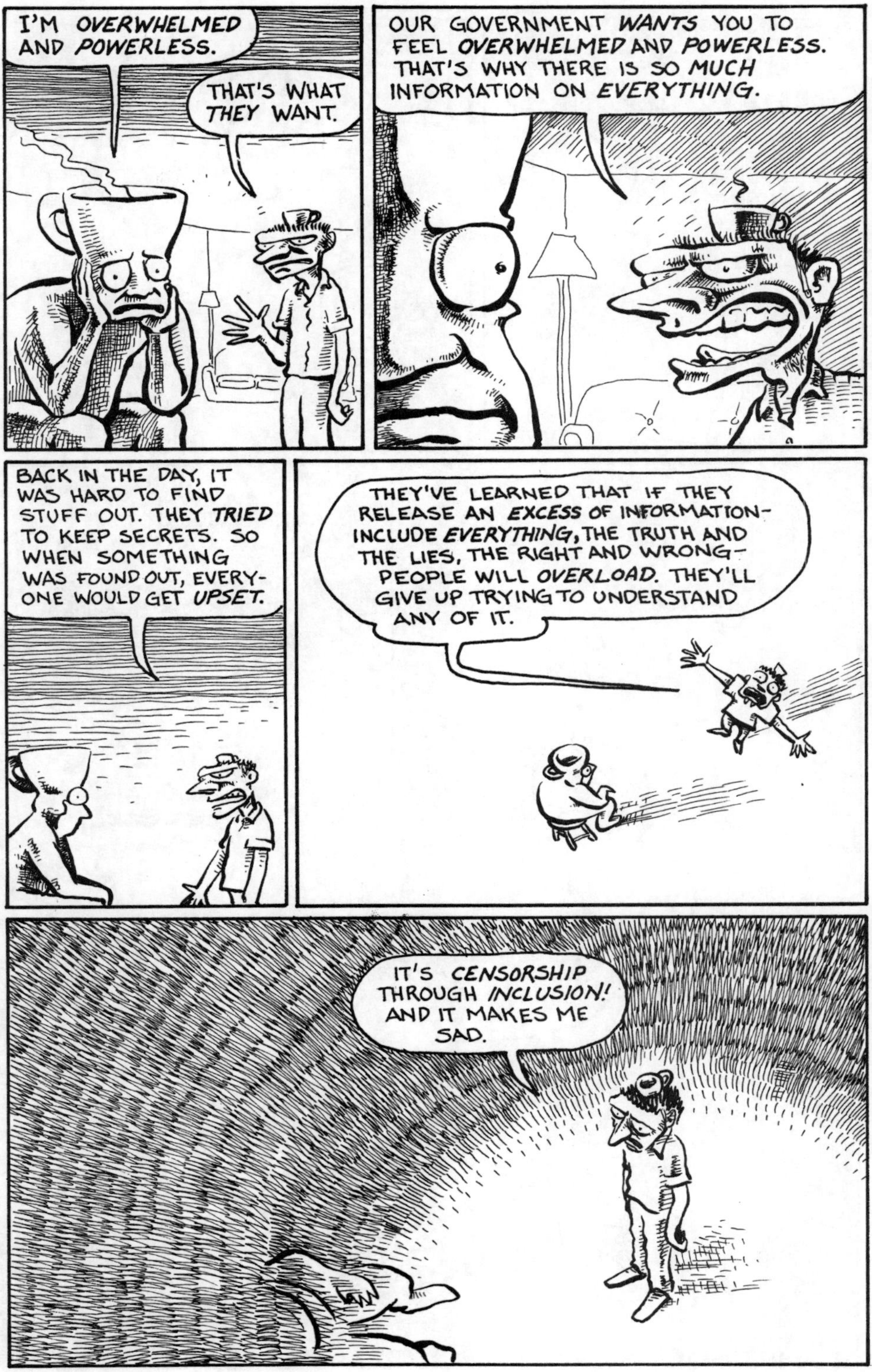
I'M OVERWHELMED AND POWERLESS.
THAT'S WHAT THEY WANT.
OUR GOVERNMENT WANTS YOU TO FEEL OVERWHELMED AND POWERLESS. THAT'S WHY THERE IS SO MUCH INFORMATION ON EVERYTHING.
BACK IN THE DAY, IT WAS HARD TO FIND STUFF OUT. THEY TRIED TO KEEP SECRETS. SO WHEN SOMETHING WAS FOUND OUT, EVERYONE WOULD GET UPSET.
THEY'VE LEARNED THAT IF THEY RELEASE AN EXCESS OF INFORMATION- INCLUDE EVERYTHING, THE TRUTH AND THE LIES, THE RIGHT AND WRONG- PEOPLE WILL OVERLOAD. THEY'LL GIVE UP TRYING TO UNDERSTAND ANY OF IT.
IT'S CENSORSHIP THROUGH INCLUSION! AND IT MAKES ME SAD.

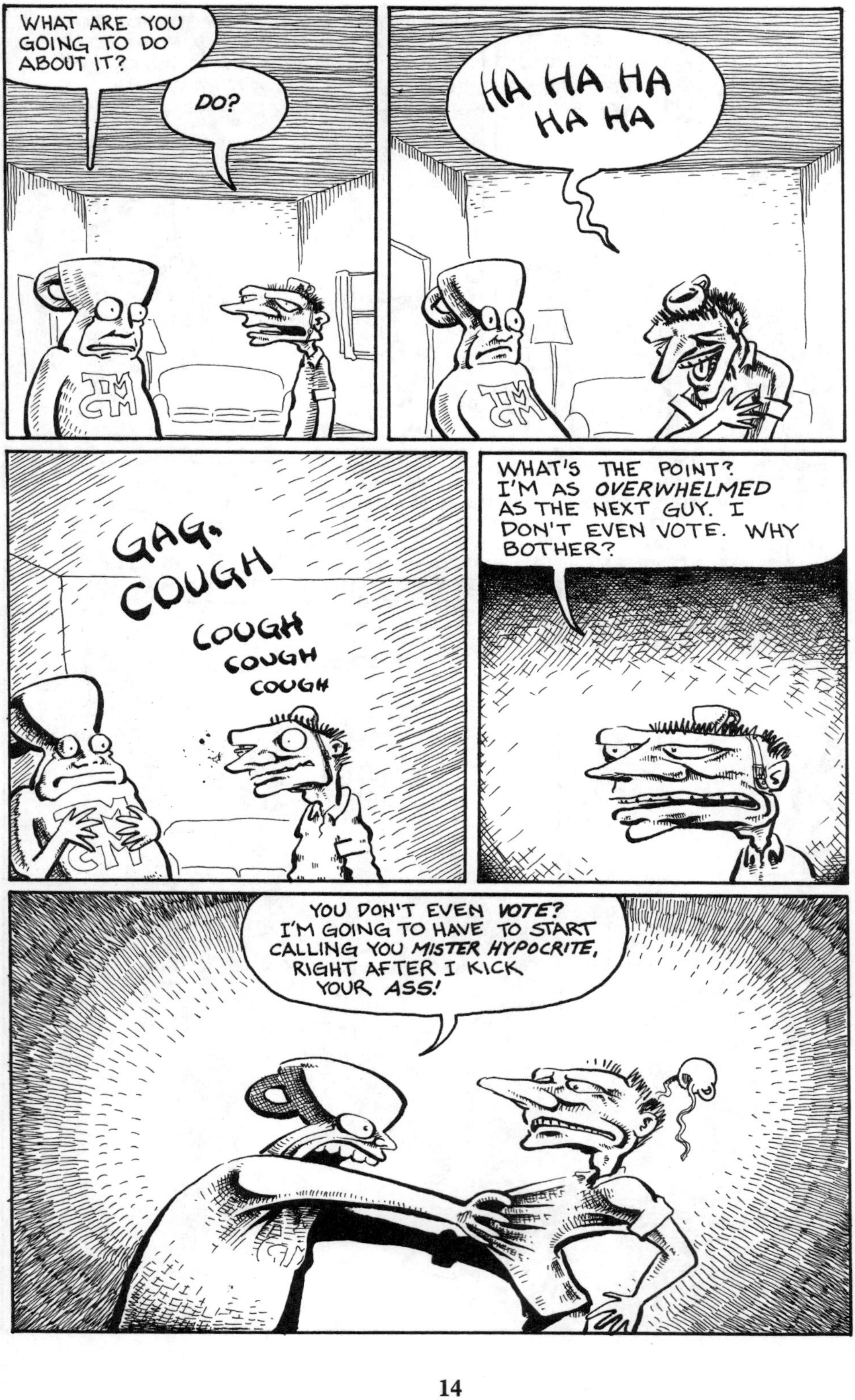
WHAT ARE YOU GOING TO DO ABOUT IT?
DO?
HA HA HA HA HA
GAG. COUGH
COUGH COUGH COUGH
WHAT'S THE POINT? I'M AS OVERWHELMED AS THE NEXT GUY. I DON'T EVEN VOTE. WHY BOTHER?
YOU DON'T EVEN VOTE? I'M GOING TO HAVE TO START CALLING YOU MISTER HYPOCRITE, RIGHT AFTER I KICK YOUR ASS!

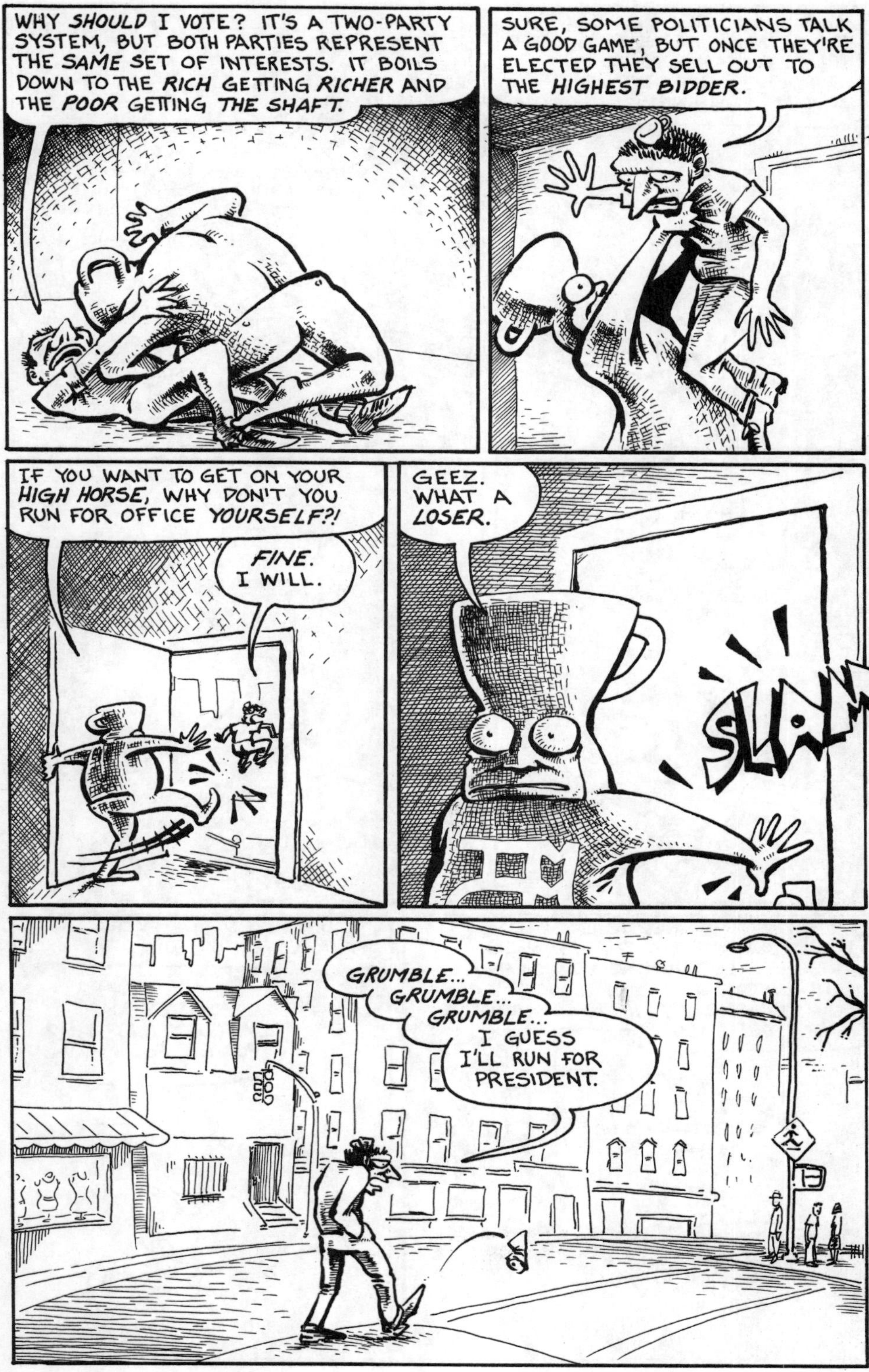

WHY SHOULD I VOTE? IT'S A TWO-PARTY SYSTEM, BUT BOTH PARTIES REPRESENT THE SAME SET OF INTERESTS. IT BOILS DOWN TO THE RICH GETTING RICHER AND THE POOR GETTING THE SHAFT.
SURE, SOME POLITICIANS TALK A GOOD GAME, BUT ONCE THEY'RE ELECTED THEY SELL OUT TO THE HIGHEST BIDDER.
IF YOU WANT TO GET ON YOUR HIGH HORSE, WHY DON'T YOU RUN FOR OFFICE YOURSELF?!
FINE. I WILL.
GEEZ. WHAT A LOSER.
SLAM
GRUMBLE... GRUMBLE... GRUMBLE... I GUESS I'LL RUN FOR PRESIDENT.

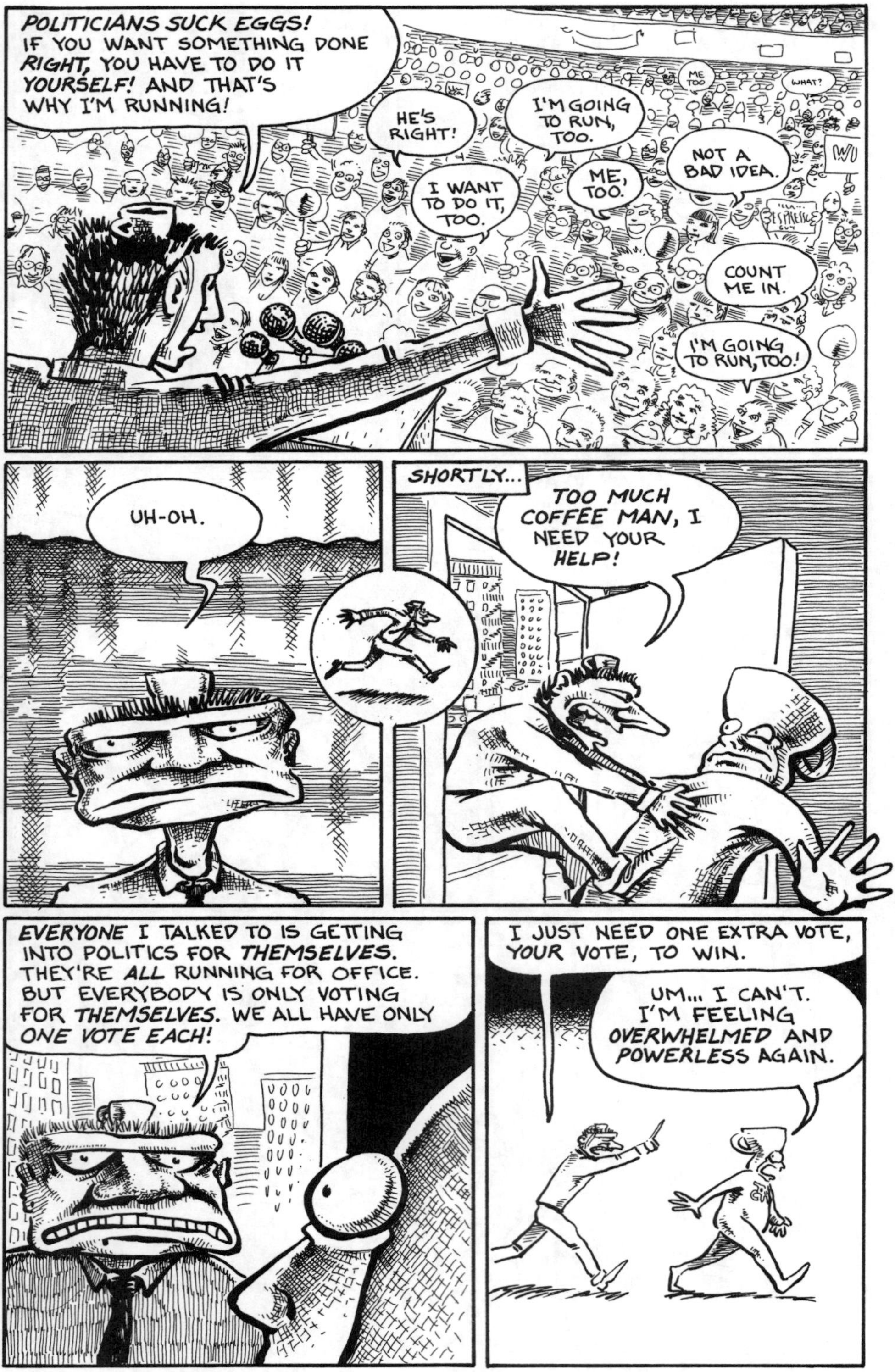
POLITICIANS SUCK EGGS! IF YOU WANT SOMETHING DONE RIGHT, YOU HAVE TO DO IT YOURSELF! AND THAT'S WHY I'M RUNNING!
HE'S RIGHT!
I'M GOING TO RUN, TOO.
ME TOO
WHAT?
I WANT TO DO IT, TOO.
ME, TOO.
NOT A BAD IDEA.
COUNT ME IN.
I'M GOING TO RUN, TOO!
UH-OH.
SHORTLY...
TOO MUCH COFFEE MAN, I NEED YOUR HELP!
EVERYONE I TALKED TO IS GETTING INTO POLITICS FOR THEMSELVES. THEY'RE ALL RUNNING FOR OFFICE. BUT EVERYBODY IS ONLY VOTING FOR THEMSELVES. WE ALL HAVE ONLY ONE VOTE EACH!
I JUST NEED ONE EXTRA VOTE, YOUR VOTE, TO WIN.
UM... I CAN'T. I'M FEELING OVERWHELMED AND POWERLESS AGAIN.

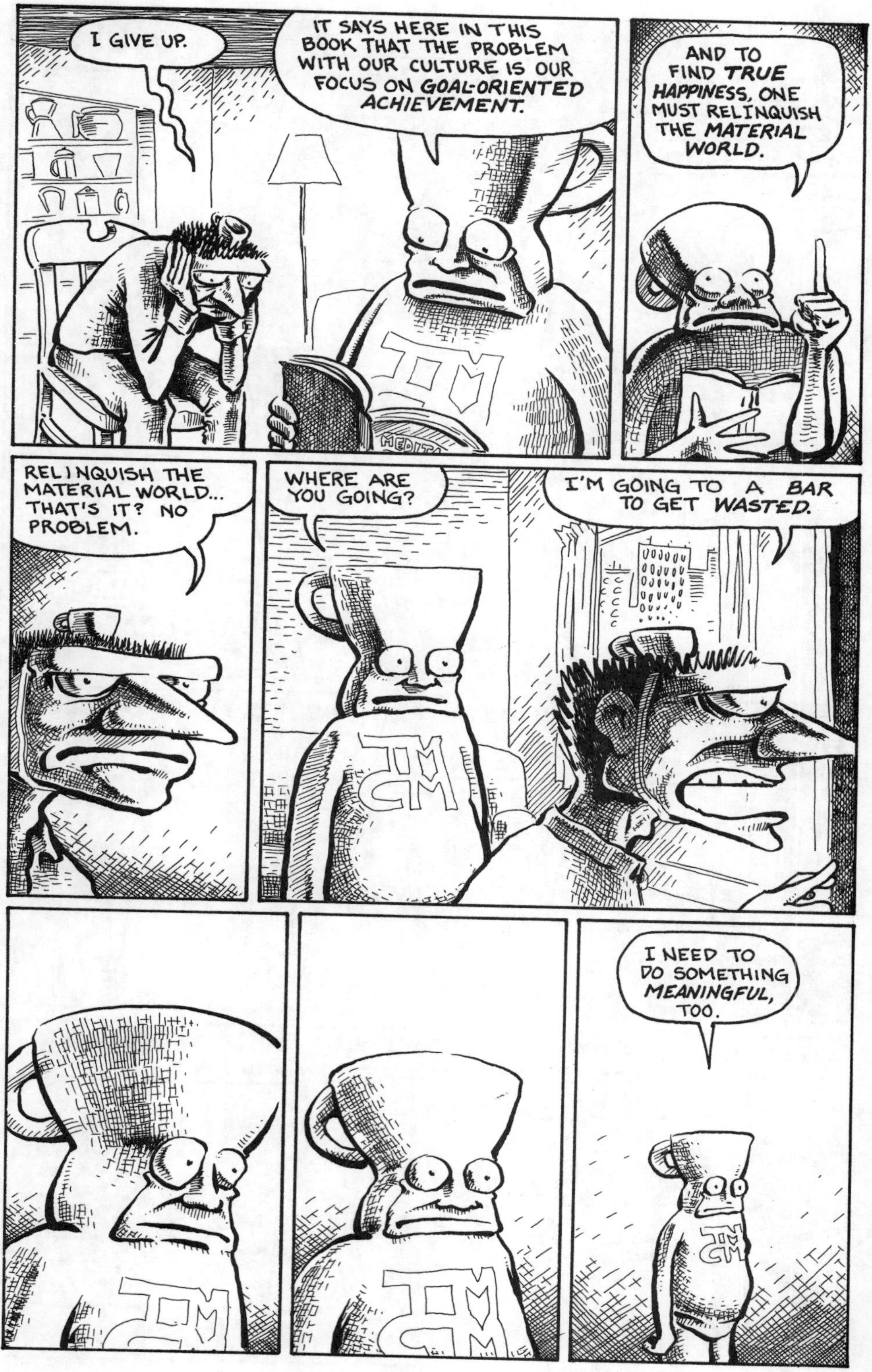
I GIVE UP.
IT SAYS HERE IN THIS BOOK THAT THE PROBLEM WITH OUR CULTURE IS OUR FOCUS ON GOAL-ORIENTED ACHIEVEMENT.
AND TO FIND TRUE HAPPINESS, ONE MUST RELINQUISH THE MATERIAL WORLD.
RELINQUISH THE MATERIAL WORLD... THAT'S IT? NO PROBLEM.
WHERE ARE YOU GOING?
I'M GOING TO A BAR TO GET WASTED.
I NEED TO DO SOMETHING MEANINGFUL, TOO.

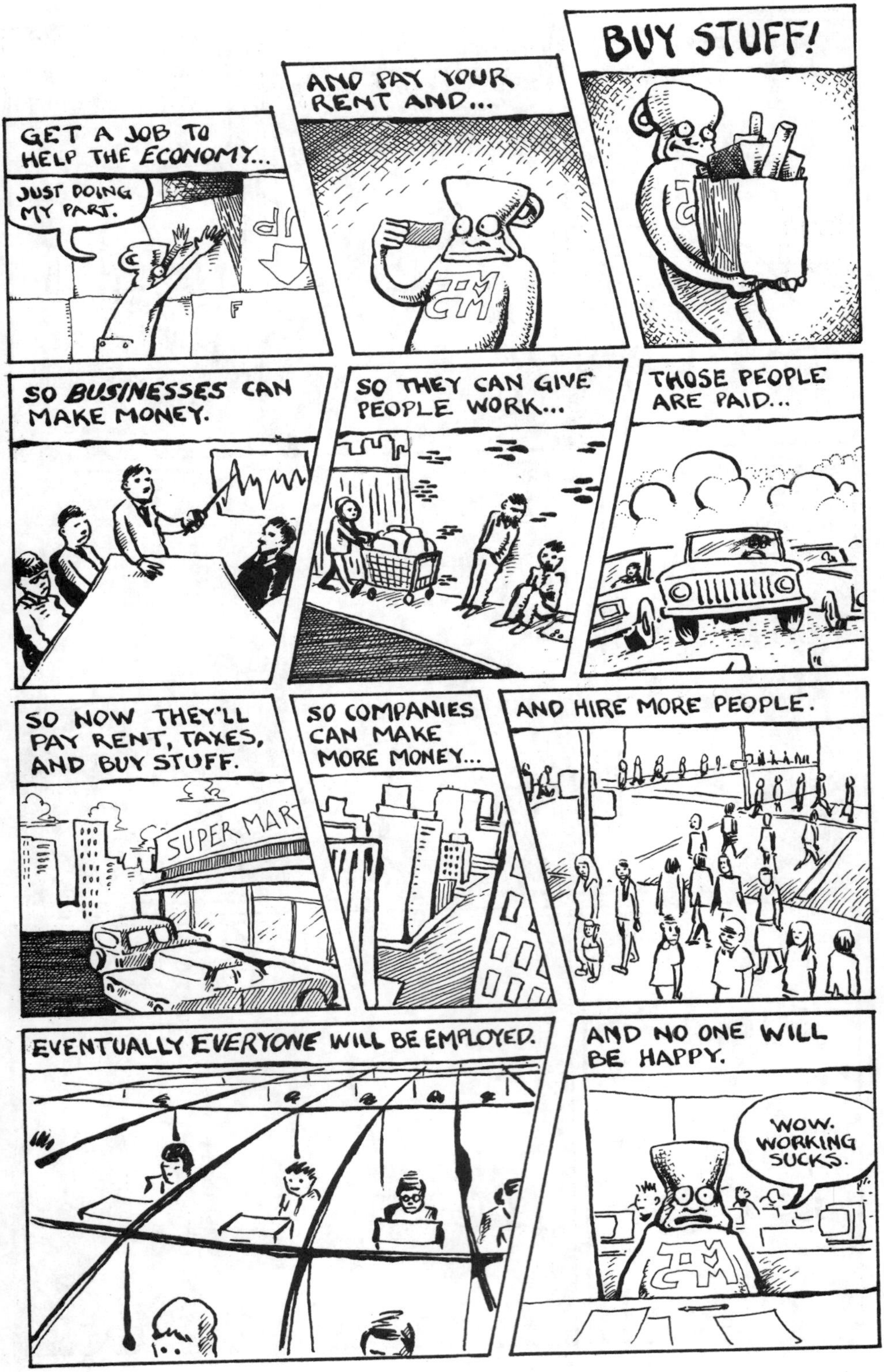
GET A JOB TO HELP THE ECONOMY...
JUST DOING MY PART.
AND PAY YOUR RENT AND...
BUY STUFF!
SO BUSINESSES CAN MAKE MONEY.
SO THEY CAN GIVE PEOPLE WORK...
THOSE PEOPLE ARE PAID...
SO NOW THEY'LL PAY RENT, TAXES, AND BUY STUFF.
SUPER MART
SO COMPANIES CAN MAKE MORE MONEY...
AND HIRE MORE PEOPLE.
EVENTUALLY EVERYONE WILL BE EMPLOYED.
AND NO ONE WILL BE HAPPY.
WOW. WORKING SUCKS.

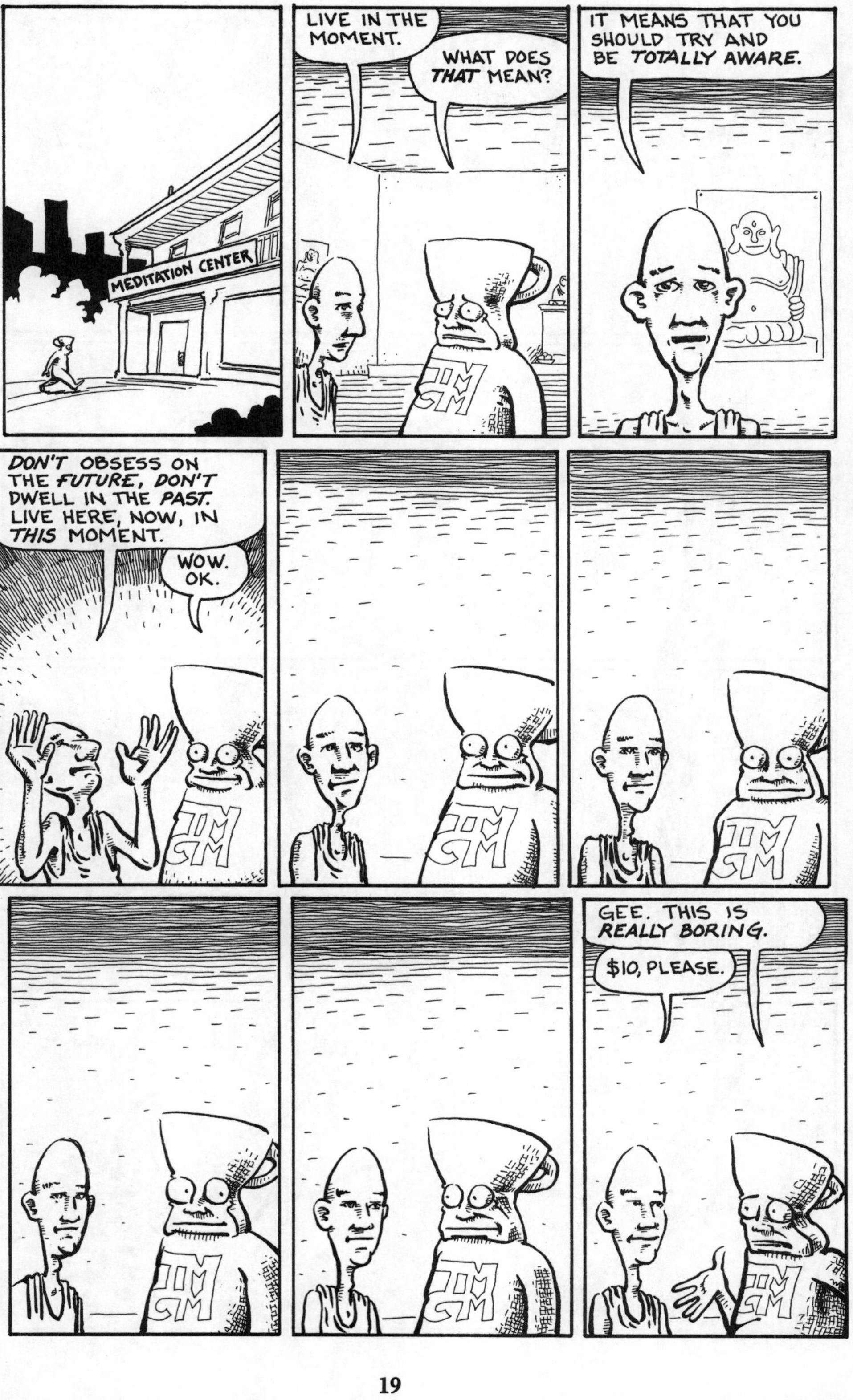
MEDITATION CENTER
LIVE IN THE MOMENT.
WHAT DOES THAT MEAN?
IT MEANS THAT YOU SHOULD TRY AND BE TOTALLY AWARE.
DON'T OBSESS ON THE FUTURE, DON'T DWELL IN THE PAST. LIVE HERE, NOW, IN THIS MOMENT.
WOW. OK.
GEE. THIS IS REALLY BORING.
$10, PLEASE.

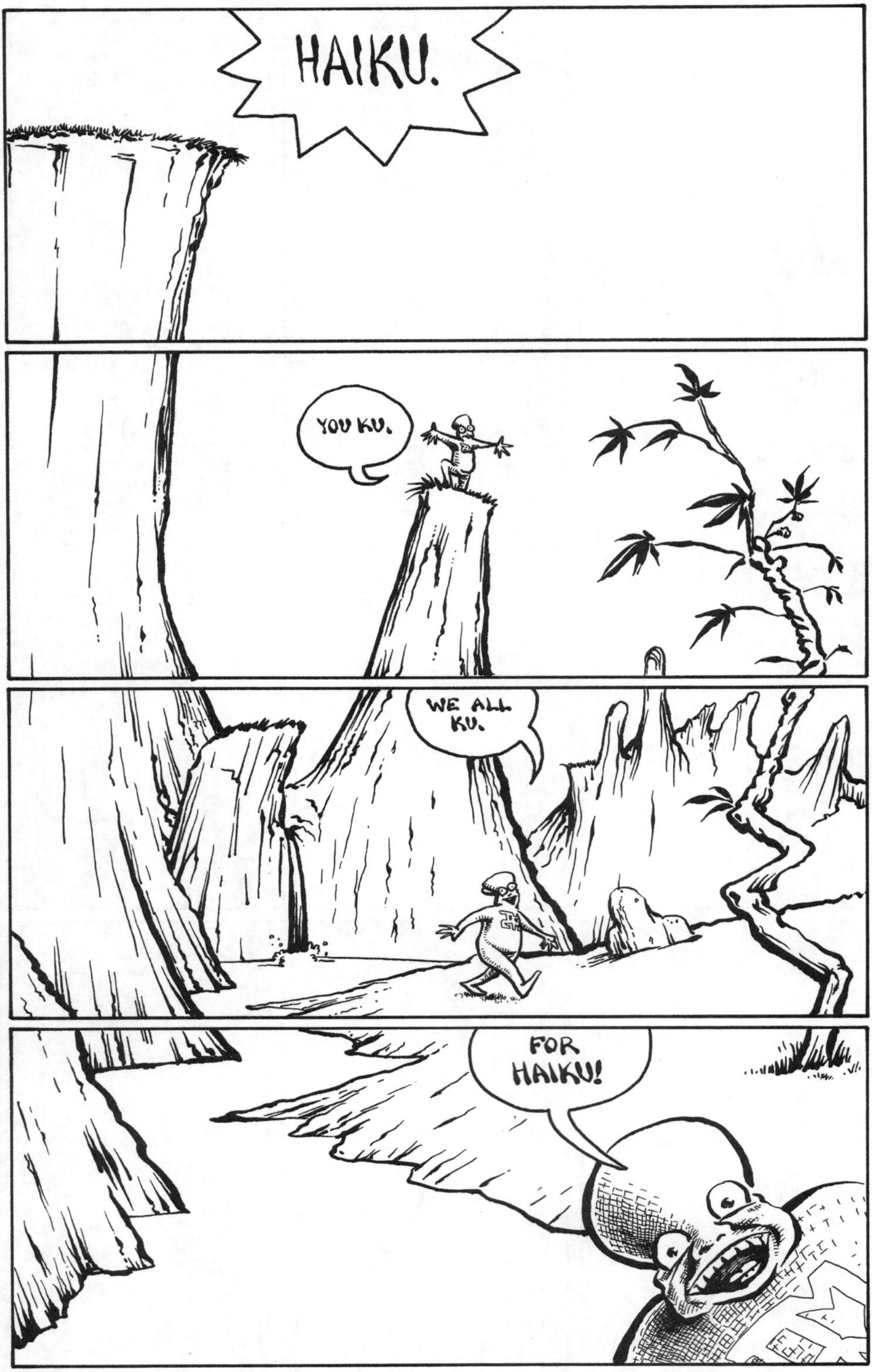
HAIKU.
YOU KU.
WE ALL KU.
FOR HAIKU!

MAYBE BY NOW *ESPRESSO GUY* HAS FOUND SOME *SECRET TO LIFE.*

ACK! WHAT HAPPENED TO YOU? YOU LOOK *TERRIBLE.*

DEBAUCHERY.

I WAS CURIOUS TO SEE JUST HOW *LOW* I COULD SINK.

I DID *EVERYTHING* AND *ANYTHING:* I STARTED A BAND, I POPPED PILLS, I SAW ALL THE HOLLYWOOD SUMMER MOVIES, I SLEPT AROUND, I STAYED UP LATE AND I SLEPT 'TILL NOON, I DATED A WAITRESS, AND I SHOPPED AT THE MALL.

YIKES.

THE WORST PART, WORSE THAN THE HANGOVERS, WORSE THAN THE SOCIAL REPERCUSSIONS...

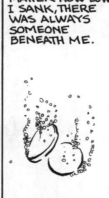

WAS THAT NO MATTER HOW LOW I SANK, THERE WAS ALWAYS SOMEONE BENEATH ME.

IT'S TOTALLY DEPRESSING, BUT I REALIZED THAT I'LL NEVER BE A SUCCESS AT FAILURE.

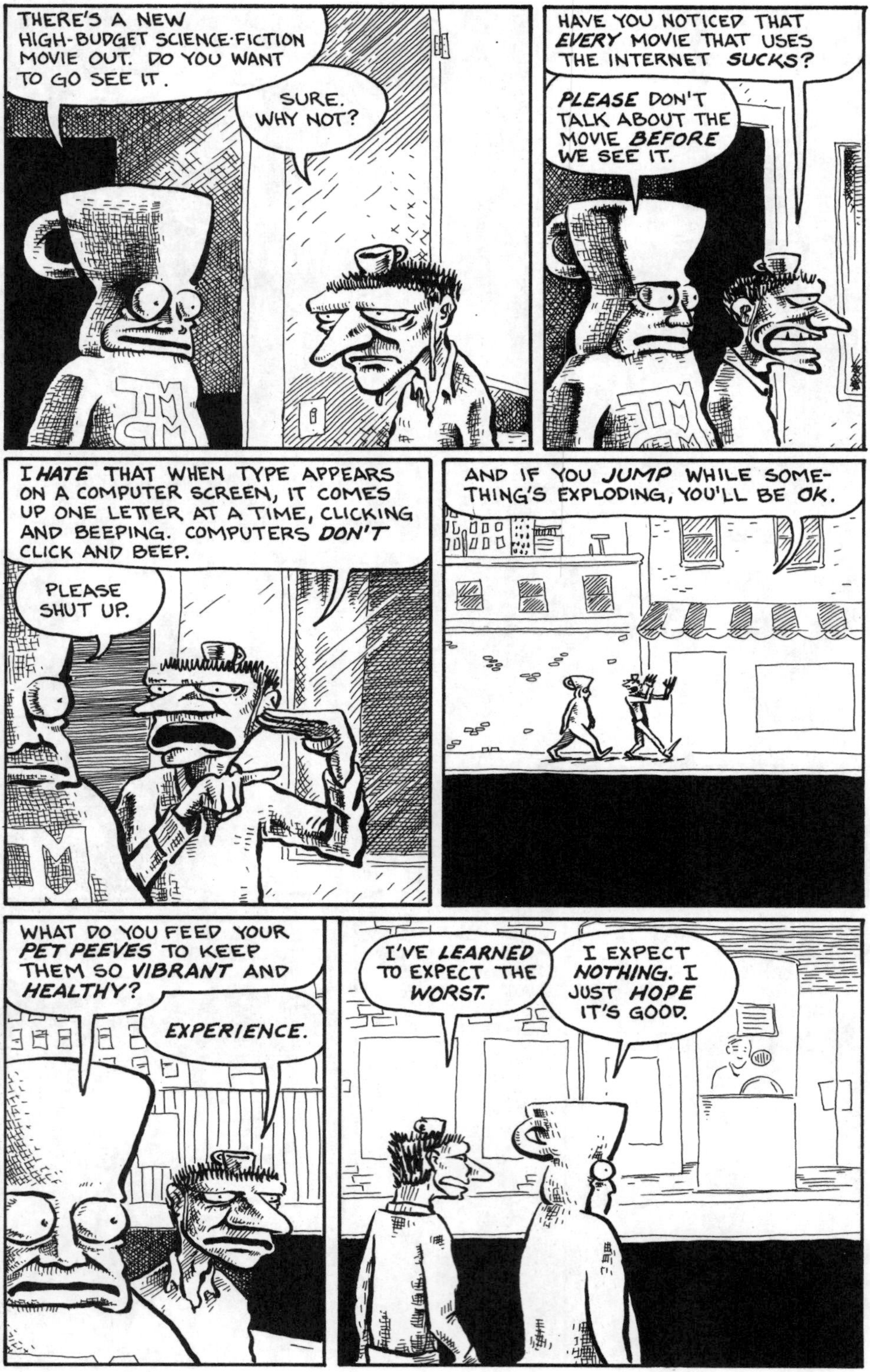
THERE'S A NEW HIGH-BUDGET SCIENCE-FICTION MOVIE OUT. DO YOU WANT TO GO SEE IT.
SURE. WHY NOT?
HAVE YOU NOTICED THAT EVERY MOVIE THAT USES THE INTERNET SUCKS?
PLEASE DON'T TALK ABOUT THE MOVIE BEFORE WE SEE IT.
I HATE THAT WHEN TYPE APPEARS ON A COMPUTER SCREEN, IT COMES UP ONE LETTER AT A TIME, CLICKING AND BEEPING. COMPUTERS DON'T CLICK AND BEEP.
PLEASE SHUT UP.
AND IF YOU JUMP WHILE SOME-THING'S EXPLODING, YOU'LL BE OK.
WHAT DO YOU FEED YOUR PET PEEVES TO KEEP THEM SO VIBRANT AND HEALTHY?
EXPERIENCE.
I'VE LEARNED TO EXPECT THE WORST.
I EXPECT NOTHING. I JUST HOPE IT'S GOOD.

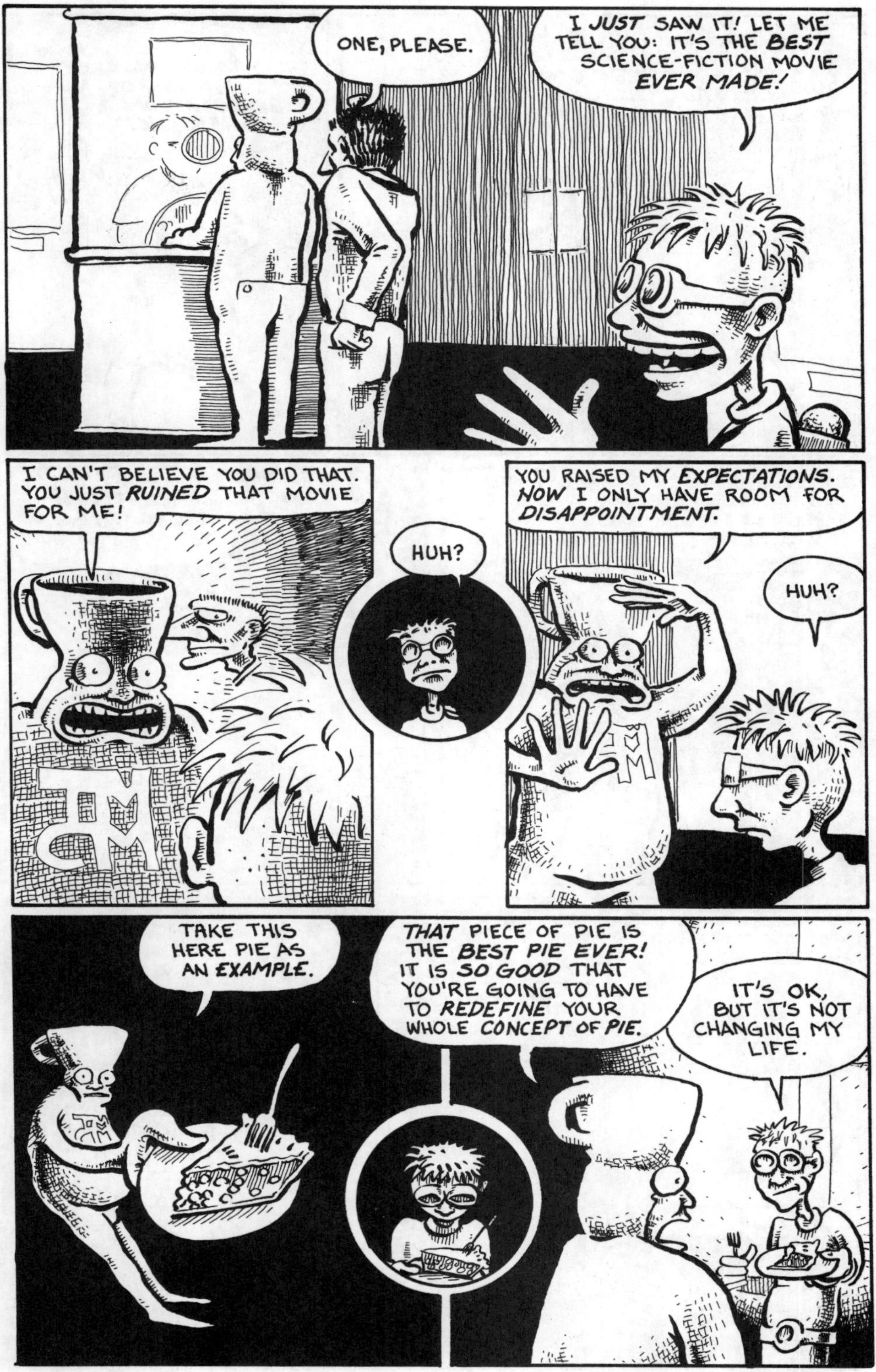
ONE, PLEASE.
I JUST SAW IT! LET ME TELL YOU: IT'S THE BEST SCIENCE-FICTION MOVIE EVER MADE!
I CAN'T BELIEVE YOU DID THAT. YOU JUST RUINED THAT MOVIE FOR ME!
HUH?
YOU RAISED MY EXPECTATIONS. NOW I ONLY HAVE ROOM FOR DISAPPOINTMENT.
HUH?
TAKE THIS HERE PIE AS AN EXAMPLE.
THAT PIECE OF PIE IS THE BEST PIE EVER! IT IS SO GOOD THAT YOU'RE GOING TO HAVE TO REDEFINE YOUR WHOLE CONCEPT OF PIE.
IT'S OK, BUT IT'S NOT CHANGING MY LIFE.

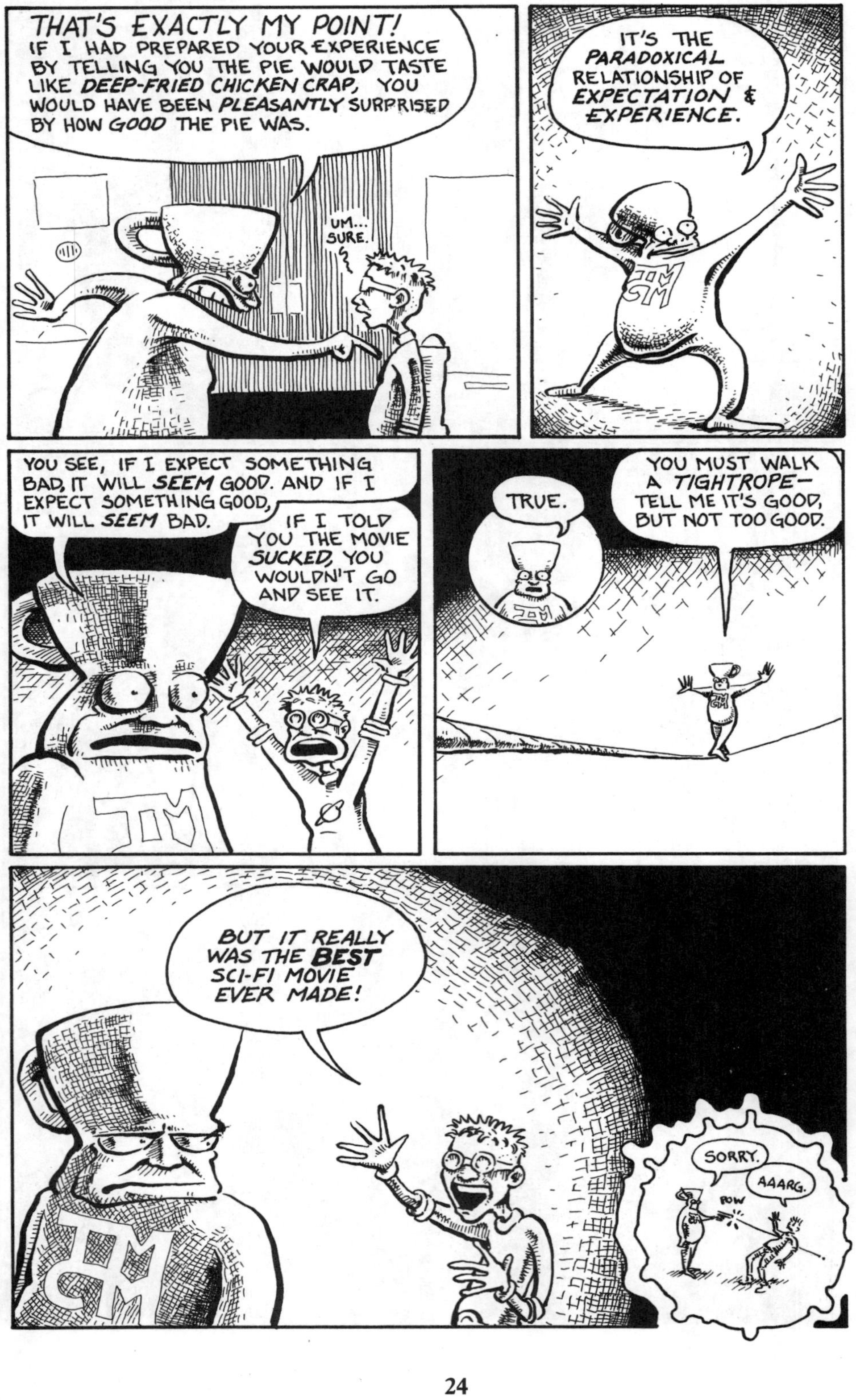
THAT'S EXACTLY MY POINT! IF I HAD PREPARED YOUR EXPERIENCE BY TELLING YOU THE PIE WOULD TASTE LIKE DEEP-FRIED CHICKEN CRAP, YOU WOULD HAVE BEEN PLEASANTLY SURPRISED BY HOW GOOD THE PIE WAS.
UM... SURE.
IT'S THE PARADOXICAL RELATIONSHIP OF EXPECTATION & EXPERIENCE.
YOU SEE, IF I EXPECT SOMETHING BAD, IT WILL SEEM GOOD. AND IF I EXPECT SOMETHING GOOD, IT WILL SEEM BAD.
IF I TOLD YOU THE MOVIE SUCKED, YOU WOULDN'T GO AND SEE IT.
TRUE.
YOU MUST WALK A TIGHTROPE— TELL ME IT'S GOOD, BUT NOT TOO GOOD.
BUT IT REALLY WAS THE BEST SCI-FI MOVIE EVER MADE!
SORRY.
AAARG.
POW

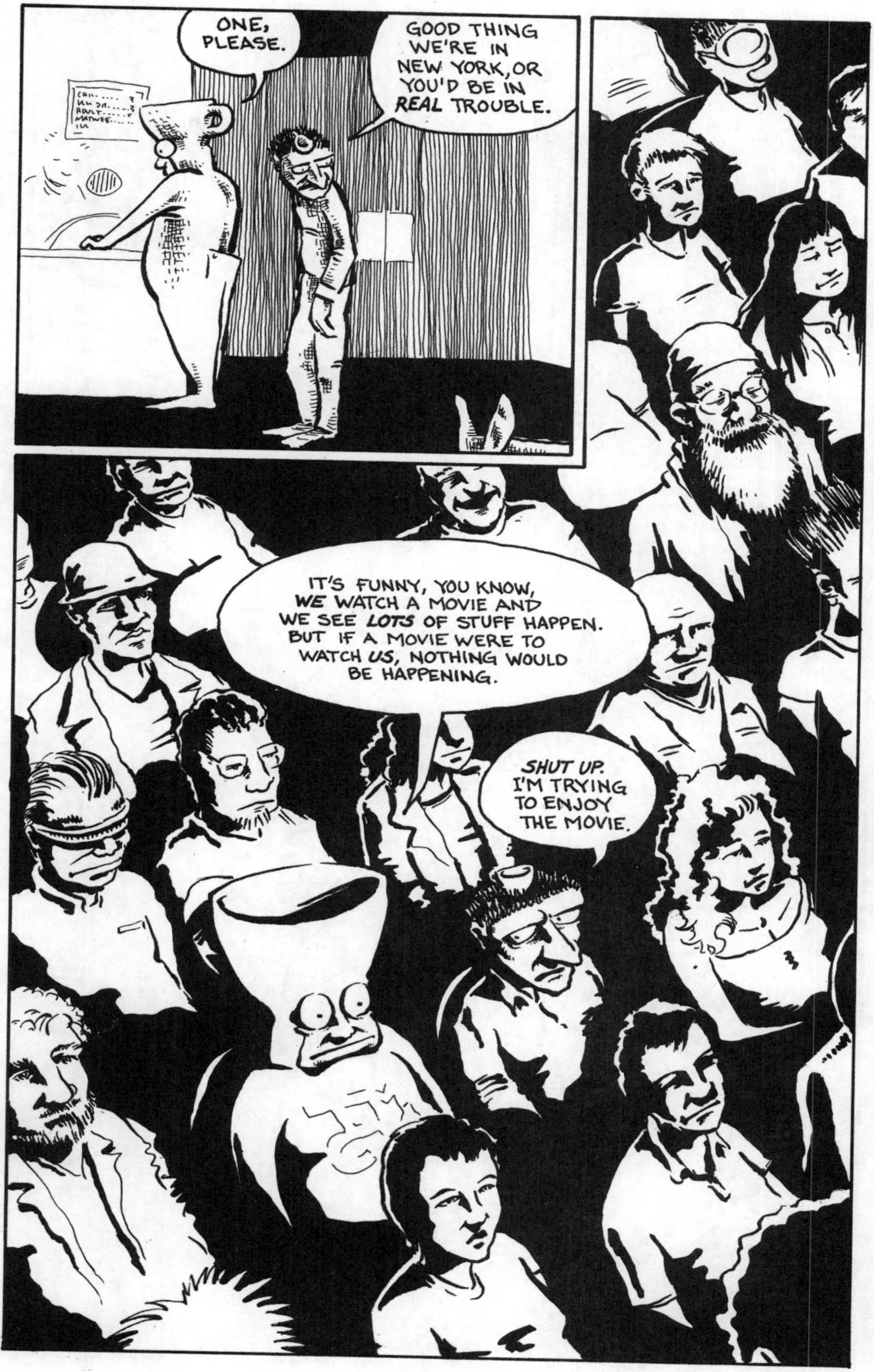
ONE, PLEASE.
GOOD THING WE'RE IN NEW YORK, OR YOU'D BE IN REAL TROUBLE.
IT'S FUNNY, YOU KNOW, WE WATCH A MOVIE AND WE SEE LOTS OF STUFF HAPPEN. BUT IF A MOVIE WERE TO WATCH US, NOTHING WOULD BE HAPPENING.
SHUT UP. I'M TRYING TO ENJOY THE MOVIE.

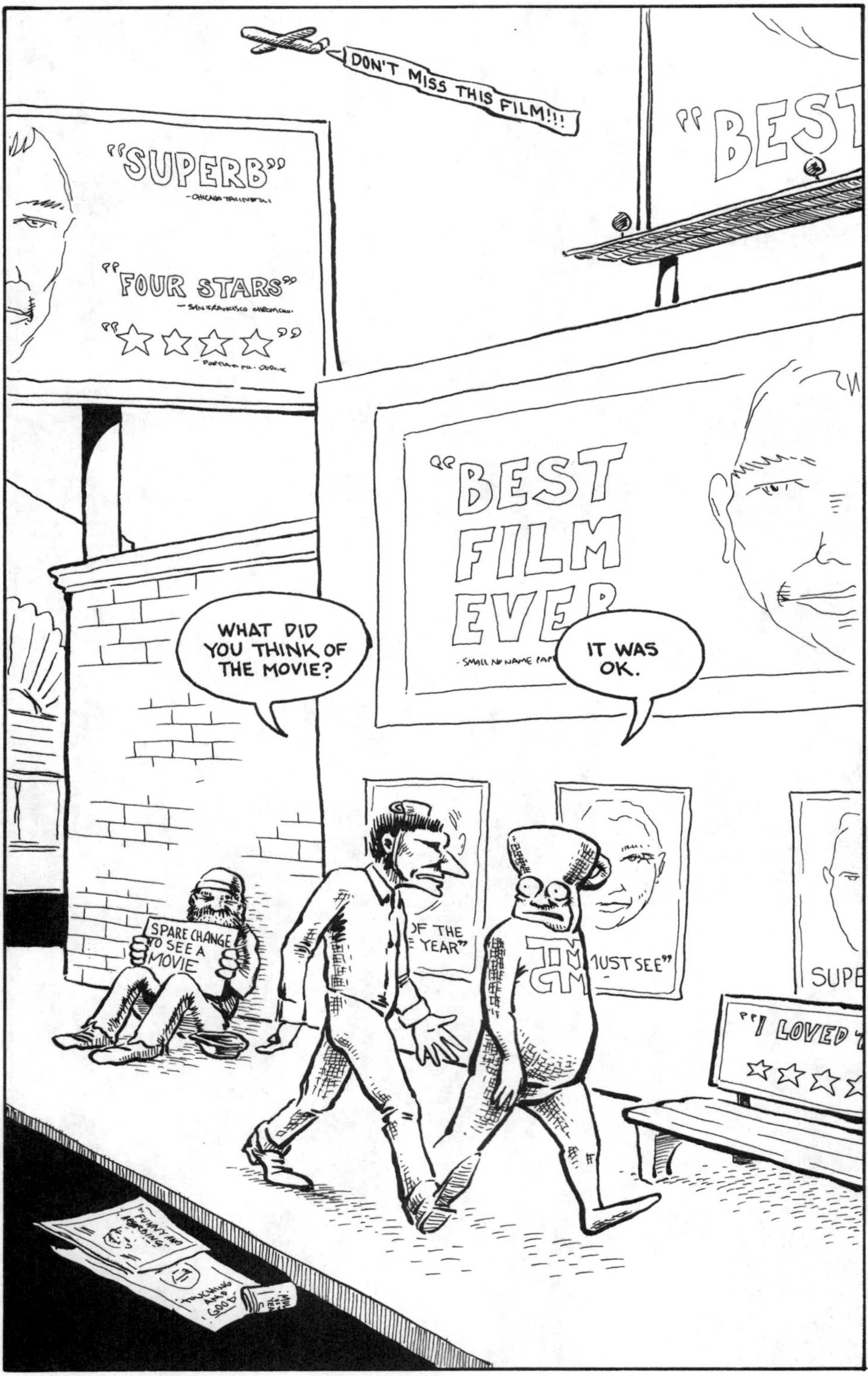
DON'T MISS THIS FILM!!!
"SUPERB"
"FOUR STARS"
"BEST FILM EVER"
WHAT DID YOU THINK OF THE MOVIE?
IT WAS OK.
SPARE CHANGE TO SEE A MOVIE
TOUCHING AND GOOD

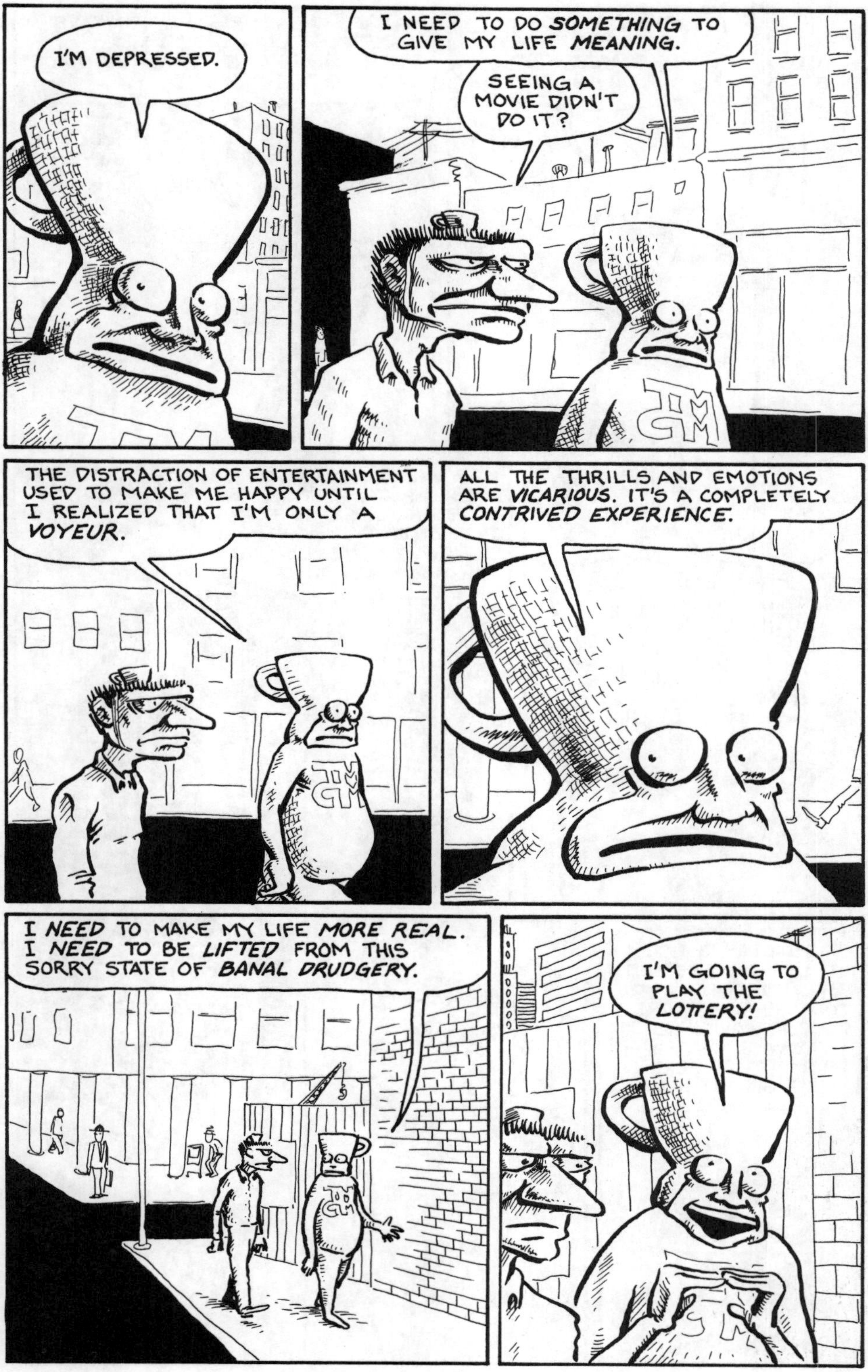
I'M DEPRESSED.
I NEED TO DO SOMETHING TO GIVE MY LIFE MEANING.
SEEING A MOVIE DIDN'T DO IT?
THE DISTRACTION OF ENTERTAINMENT USED TO MAKE ME HAPPY UNTIL I REALIZED THAT I'M ONLY A VOYEUR.
ALL THE THRILLS AND EMOTIONS ARE VICARIOUS. IT'S A COMPLETELY CONTRIVED EXPERIENCE.
I NEED TO MAKE MY LIFE MORE REAL. I NEED TO BE LIFTED FROM THIS SORRY STATE OF BANAL DRUDGERY.
I'M GOING TO PLAY THE LOTTERY!

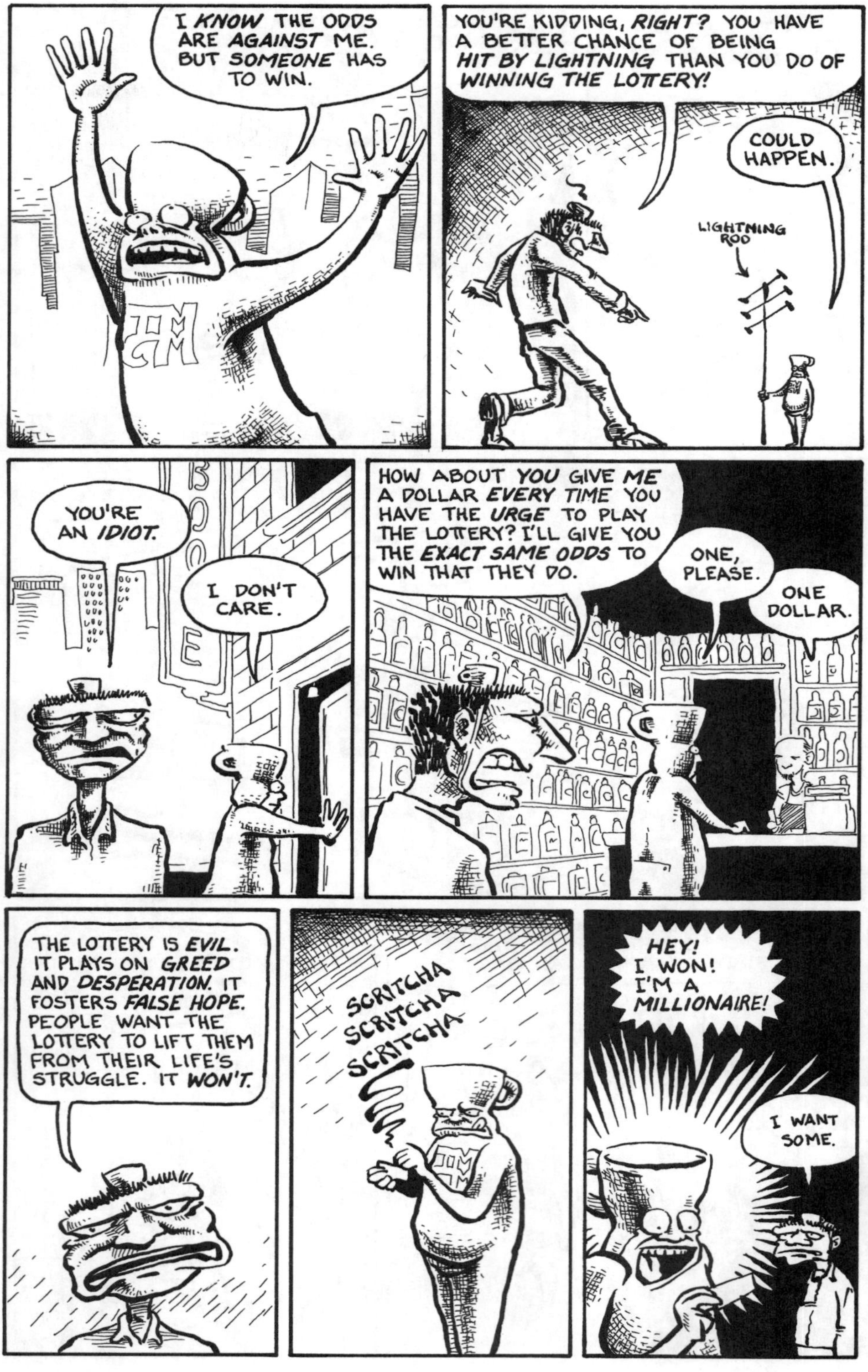

I KNOW THE ODDS ARE AGAINST ME. BUT SOMEONE HAS TO WIN.
YOU'RE KIDDING, RIGHT? YOU HAVE A BETTER CHANCE OF BEING HIT BY LIGHTNING THAN YOU DO OF WINNING THE LOTTERY!
COULD HAPPEN.
LIGHTNING ROD
YOU'RE AN IDIOT.
I DON'T CARE.
HOW ABOUT YOU GIVE ME A DOLLAR EVERY TIME YOU HAVE THE URGE TO PLAY THE LOTTERY? I'LL GIVE YOU THE EXACT SAME ODDS TO WIN THAT THEY DO.
ONE, PLEASE.
ONE DOLLAR.
THE LOTTERY IS EVIL. IT PLAYS ON GREED AND DESPERATION. IT FOSTERS FALSE HOPE. PEOPLE WANT THE LOTTERY TO LIFT THEM FROM THEIR LIFE'S STRUGGLE. IT WON'T.
SCRITCHA SCRITCHA SCRITCHA
HEY! I WON! I'M A MILLIONAIRE!
I WANT SOME.

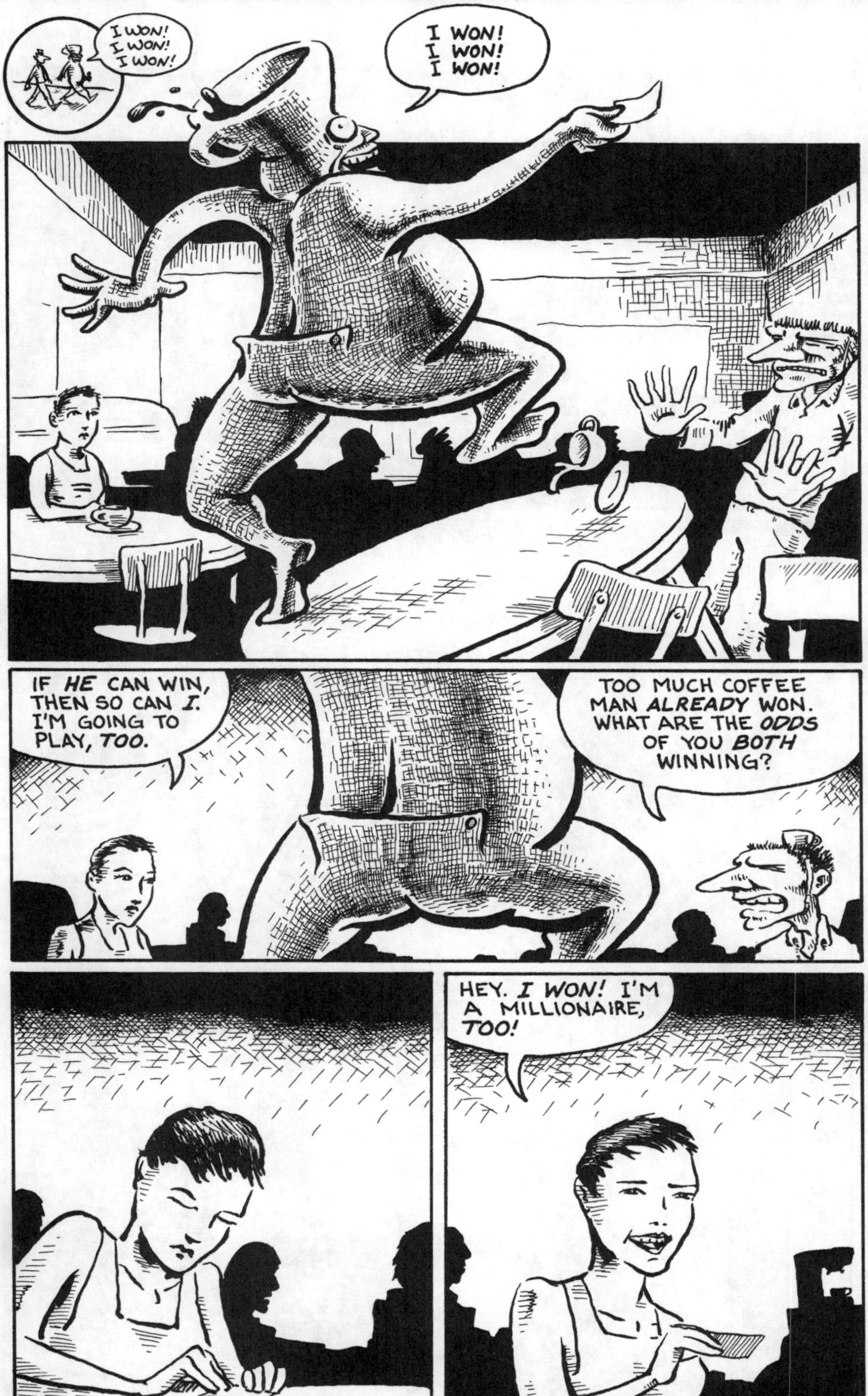
I WON! I WON! I WON!
I WON! I WON! I WON!
IF HE CAN WIN, THEN SO CAN I. I'M GOING TO PLAY, TOO.
TOO MUCH COFFEE MAN ALREADY WON. WHAT ARE THE ODDS OF YOU BOTH WINNING?
HEY. I WON! I'M A MILLIONAIRE, TOO!

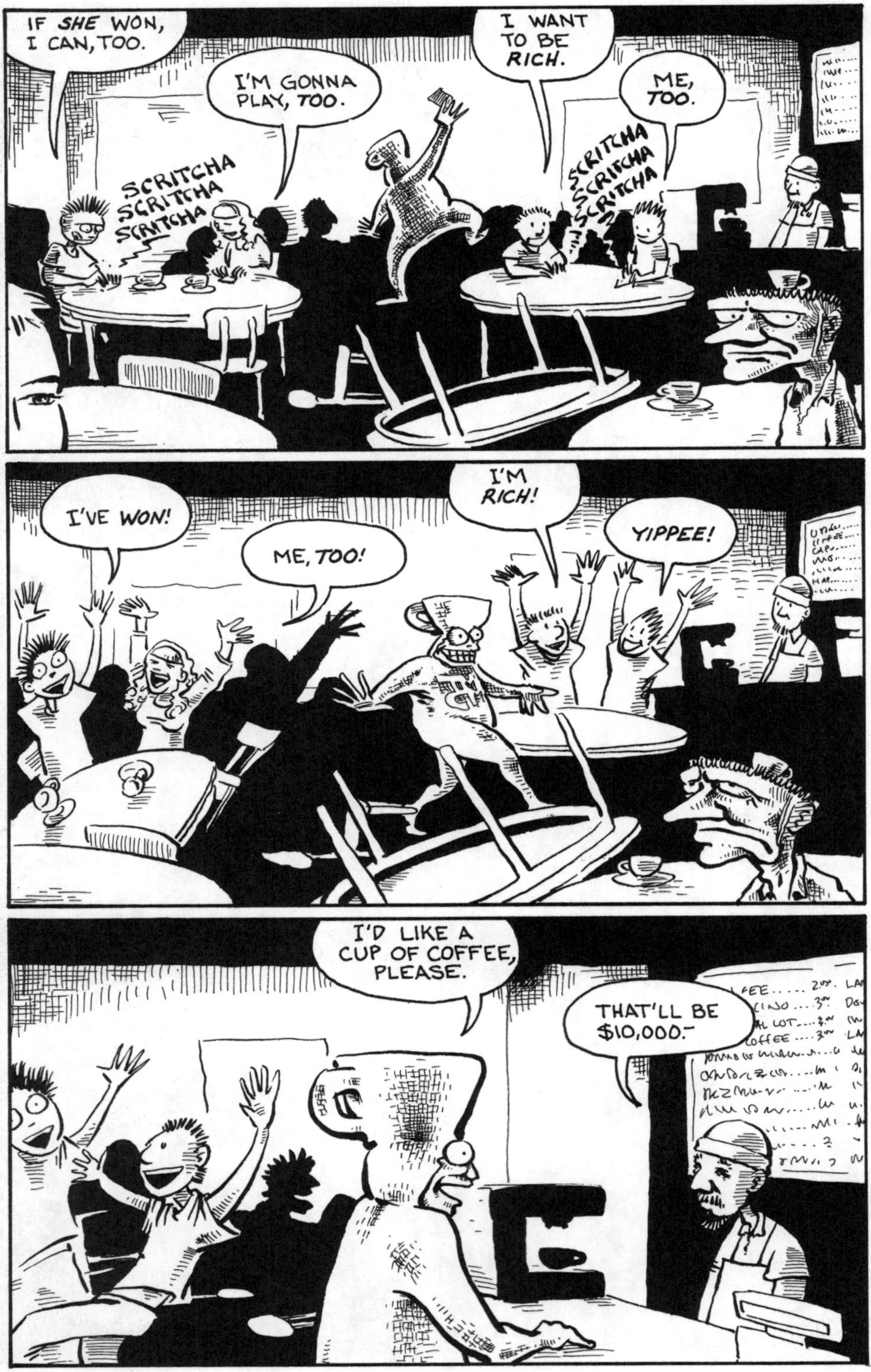

IF SHE WON, I CAN, TOO.
I'M GONNA PLAY, TOO.
SCRITCHA SCRITCHA SCRITCHA
I WANT TO BE RICH.
ME, TOO.
SCRITCHA SCRITCHA SCRITCHA
I'VE WON!
ME, TOO!
I'M RICH!
YIPPEE!
I'D LIKE A CUP OF COFFEE, PLEASE.
THAT'LL BE $10,000.–

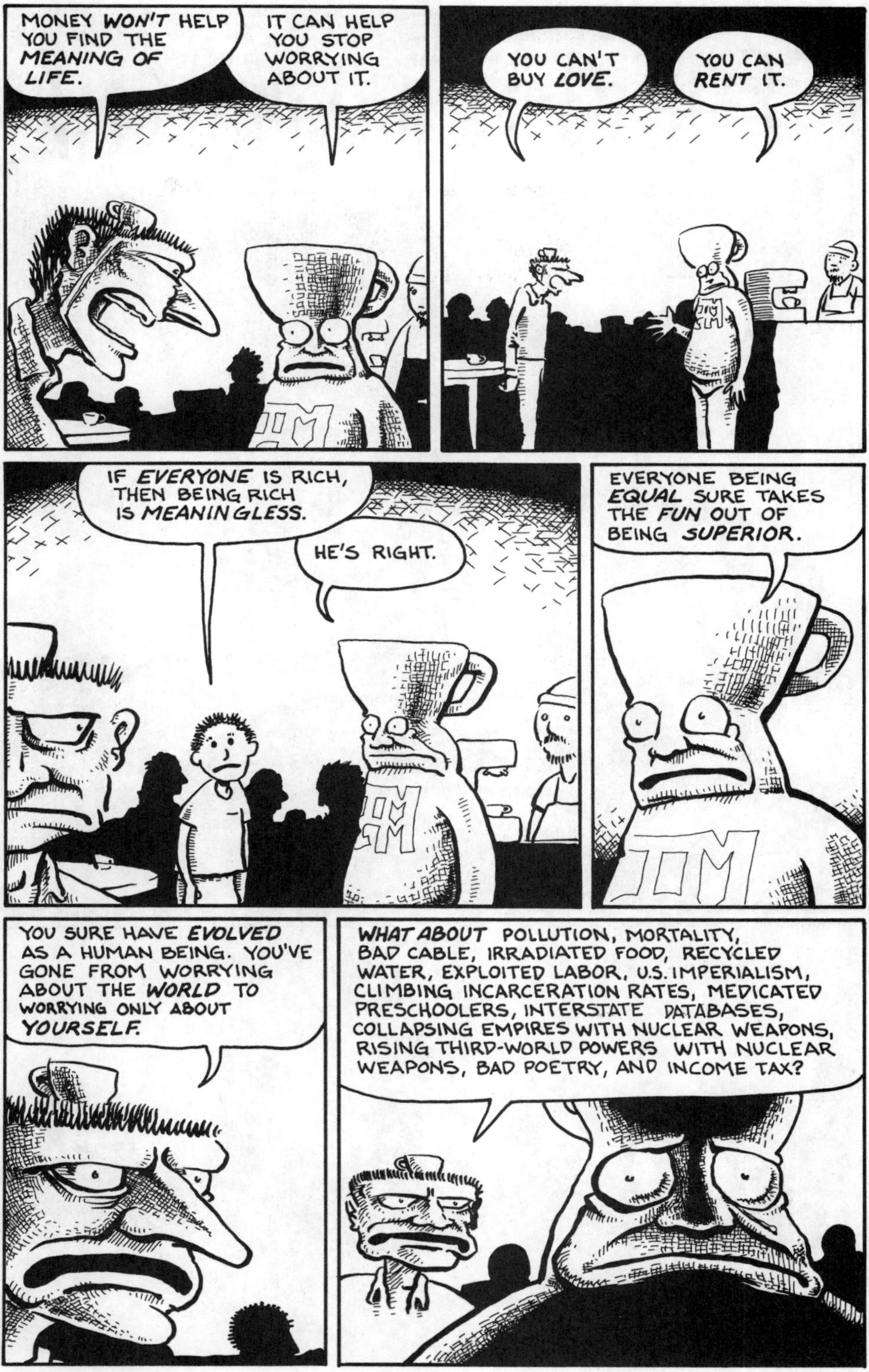
MONEY WON'T HELP YOU FIND THE MEANING OF LIFE.
IT CAN HELP YOU STOP WORRYING ABOUT IT.
YOU CAN'T BUY LOVE.
YOU CAN RENT IT.
IF EVERYONE IS RICH, THEN BEING RICH IS MEANINGLESS.
HE'S RIGHT.
EVERYONE BEING EQUAL SURE TAKES THE FUN OUT OF BEING SUPERIOR.
YOU SURE HAVE EVOLVED AS A HUMAN BEING. YOU'VE GONE FROM WORRYING ABOUT THE WORLD TO WORRYING ONLY ABOUT YOURSELF.
WHAT ABOUT POLLUTION, MORTALITY, BAD CABLE, IRRADIATED FOOD, RECYCLED WATER, EXPLOITED LABOR, U.S. IMPERIALISM, CLIMBING INCARCERATION RATES, MEDICATED PRESCHOOLERS, INTERSTATE DATABASES, COLLAPSING EMPIRES WITH NUCLEAR WEAPONS, RISING THIRD-WORLD POWERS WITH NUCLEAR WEAPONS, BAD POETRY, AND INCOME TAX?

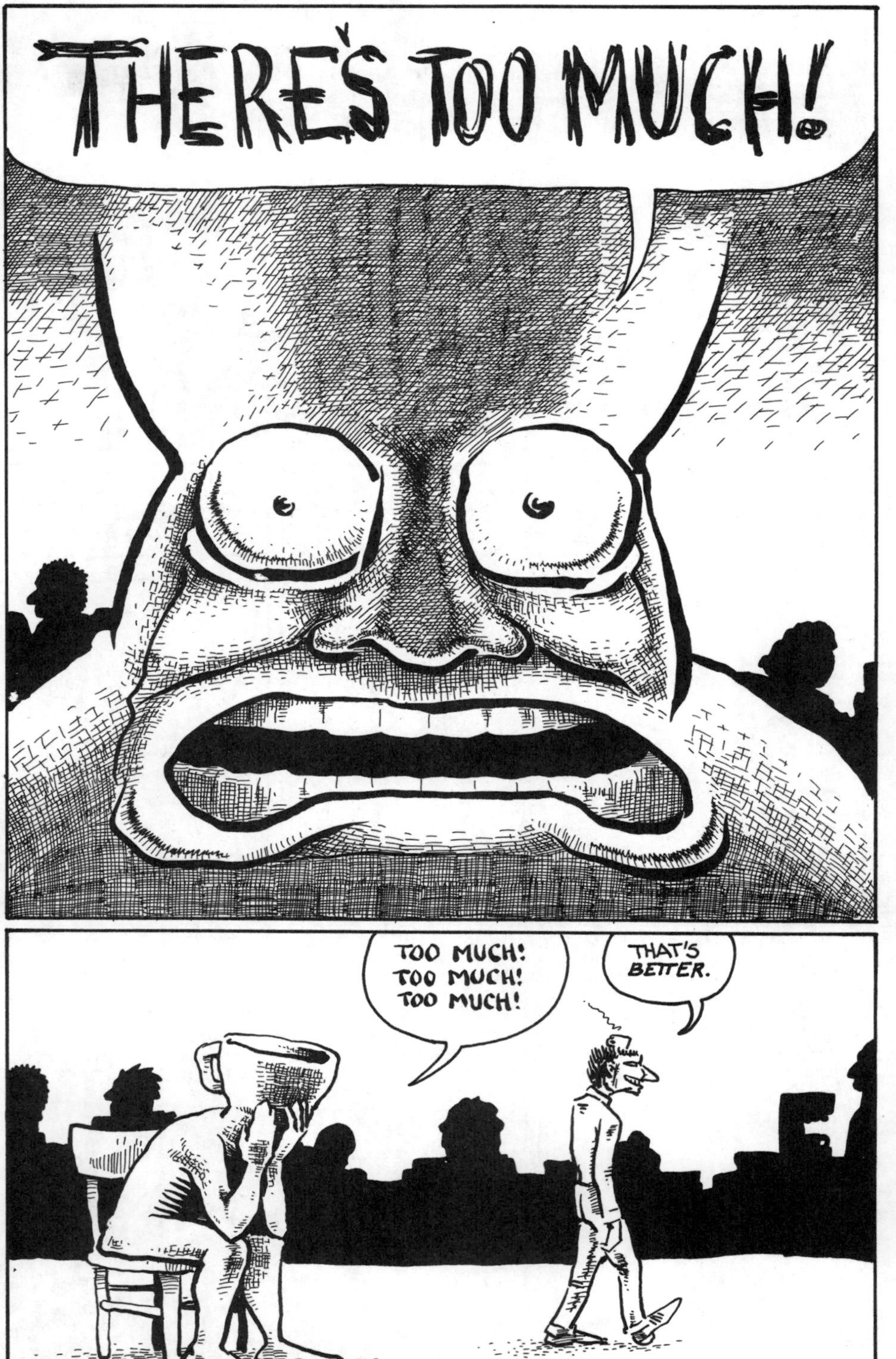
THERE'S TOO MUCH!
TOO MUCH! TOO MUCH! TOO MUCH!
THAT'S BETTER.

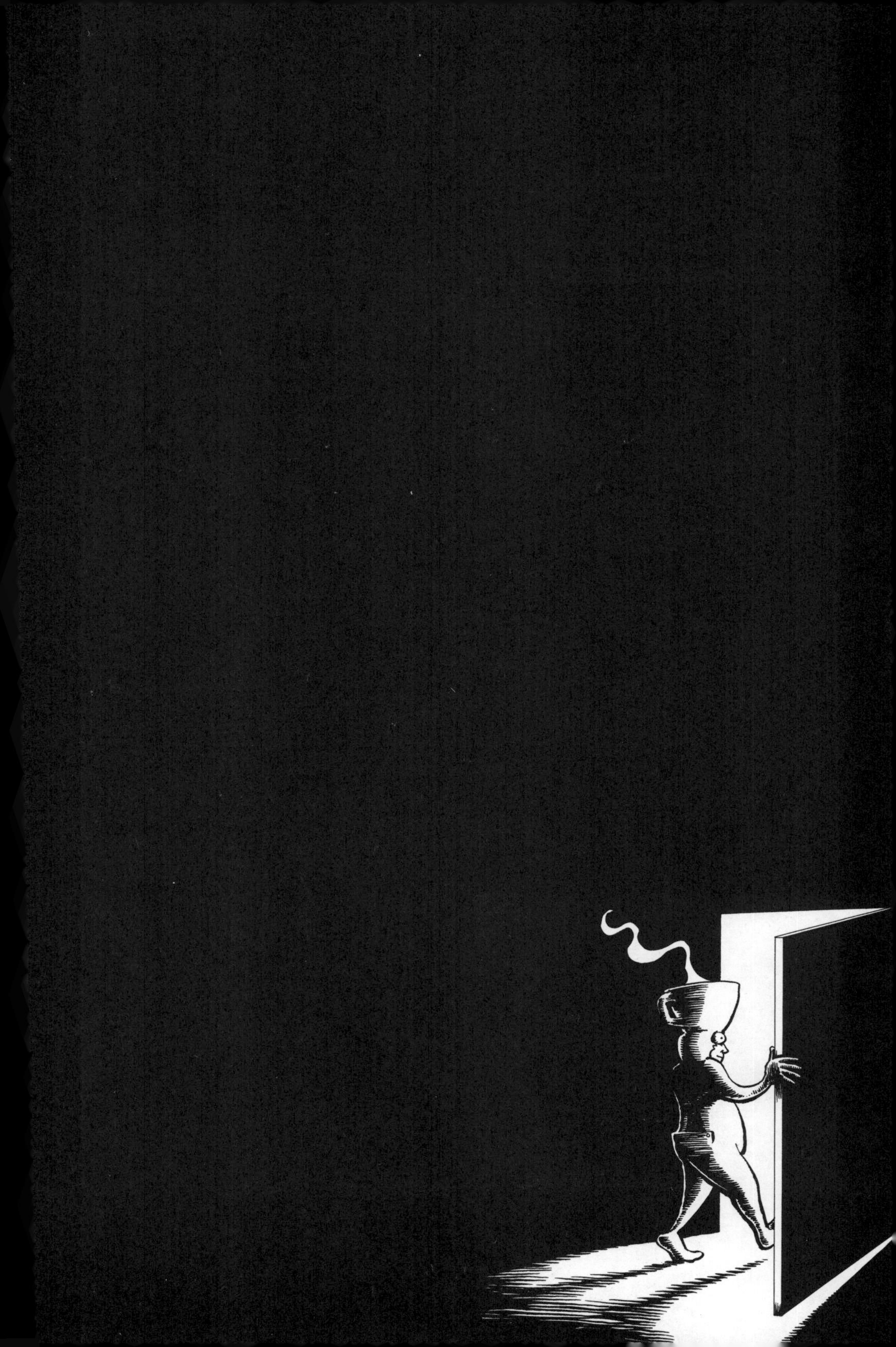

chapter 2

TELEVISION, ADVERTISING, AND INFOTAINMENT

How to feel better about yourself, and other insights

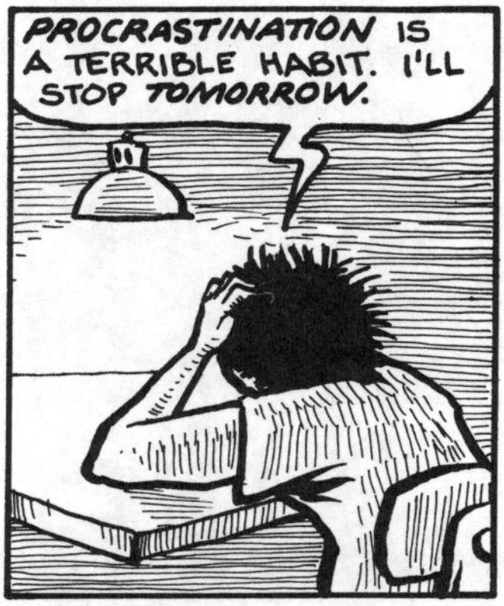
PROCRASTINATION IS A TERRIBLE HABIT. I'LL STOP TOMORROW.

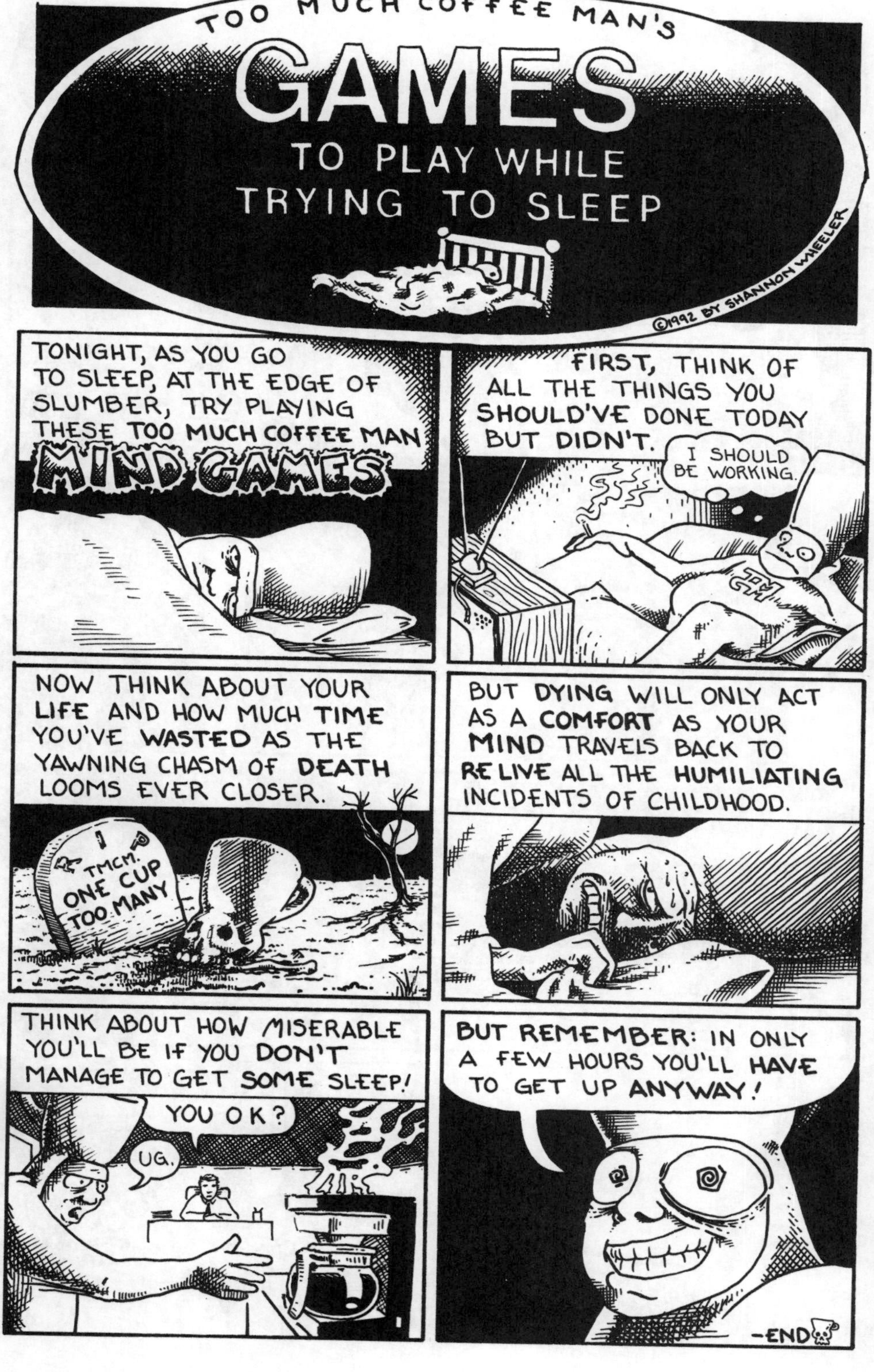
TOO MUCH COFFEE MAN'S
GAMES
TO PLAY WHILE
TRYING TO SLEEP
©1992 BY SHANNON WHEELER
TONIGHT, AS YOU GO TO SLEEP, AT THE EDGE OF SLUMBER, TRY PLAYING THESE TOO MUCH COFFEE MAN
MIND GAMES
FIRST, THINK OF ALL THE THINGS YOU SHOULD'VE DONE TODAY BUT DIDN'T.
I SHOULD BE WORKING.
NOW THINK ABOUT YOUR LIFE AND HOW MUCH TIME YOU'VE WASTED AS THE YAWNING CHASM OF DEATH LOOMS EVER CLOSER.
R I P
TMCM.
ONE CUP TOO MANY
BUT DYING WILL ONLY ACT AS A COMFORT AS YOUR MIND TRAVELS BACK TO RELIVE ALL THE HUMILIATING INCIDENTS OF CHILDHOOD.
THINK ABOUT HOW MISERABLE YOU'LL BE IF YOU DON'T MANAGE TO GET SOME SLEEP!
YOU OK?
UG.
BUT REMEMBER: IN ONLY A FEW HOURS YOU'LL HAVE TO GET UP ANYWAY!
-END

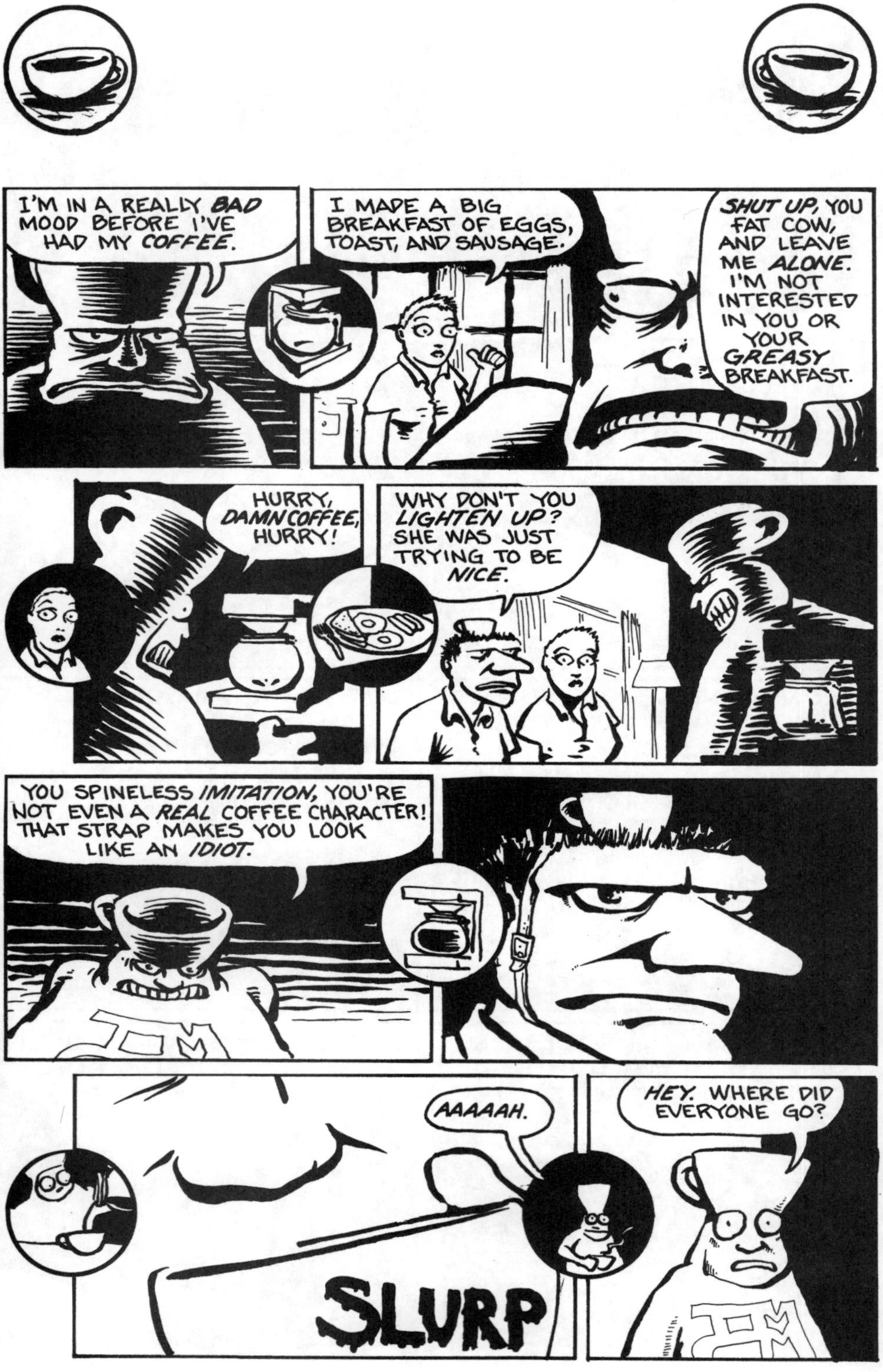

I'M IN A REALLY *BAD* MOOD BEFORE I'VE HAD MY *COFFEE*.
I MADE A BIG BREAKFAST OF EGGS, TOAST, AND SAUSAGE.
SHUT UP, YOU FAT COW, AND LEAVE ME *ALONE*. I'M NOT INTERESTED IN YOU OR YOUR *GREASY* BREAKFAST.
HURRY, *DAMN COFFEE*, HURRY!
WHY DON'T YOU *LIGHTEN UP*? SHE WAS JUST TRYING TO BE *NICE*.
YOU SPINELESS *IMITATION*, YOU'RE NOT EVEN A *REAL* COFFEE CHARACTER! THAT STRAP MAKES YOU LOOK LIKE AN *IDIOT*.
AAAAAH.
SLURP
HEY. WHERE DID EVERYONE GO?

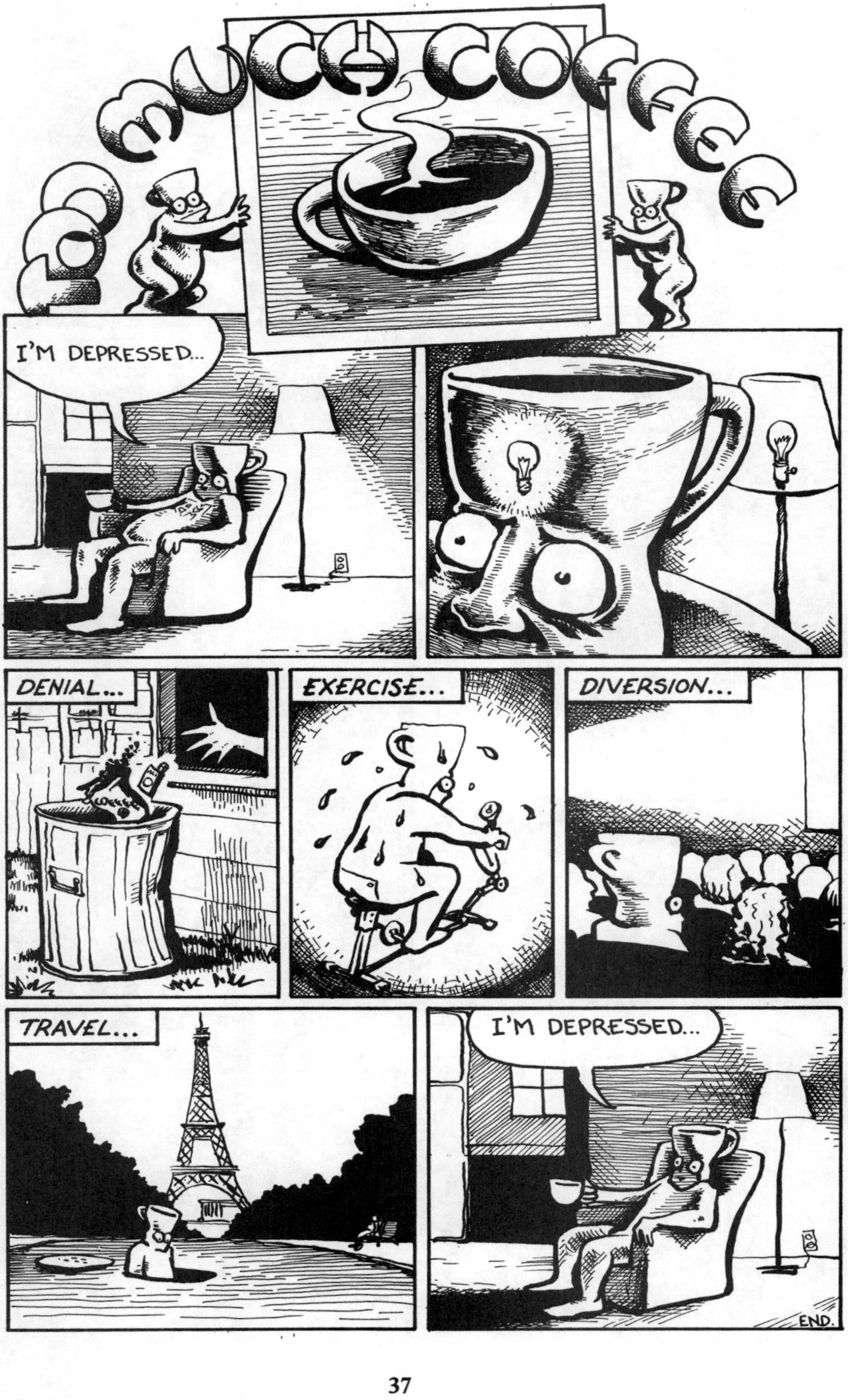
TOO MUCH COFFEE
I'M DEPRESSED...
DENIAL...
EXERCISE...
DIVERSION...
TRAVEL...
I'M DEPRESSED...
END.

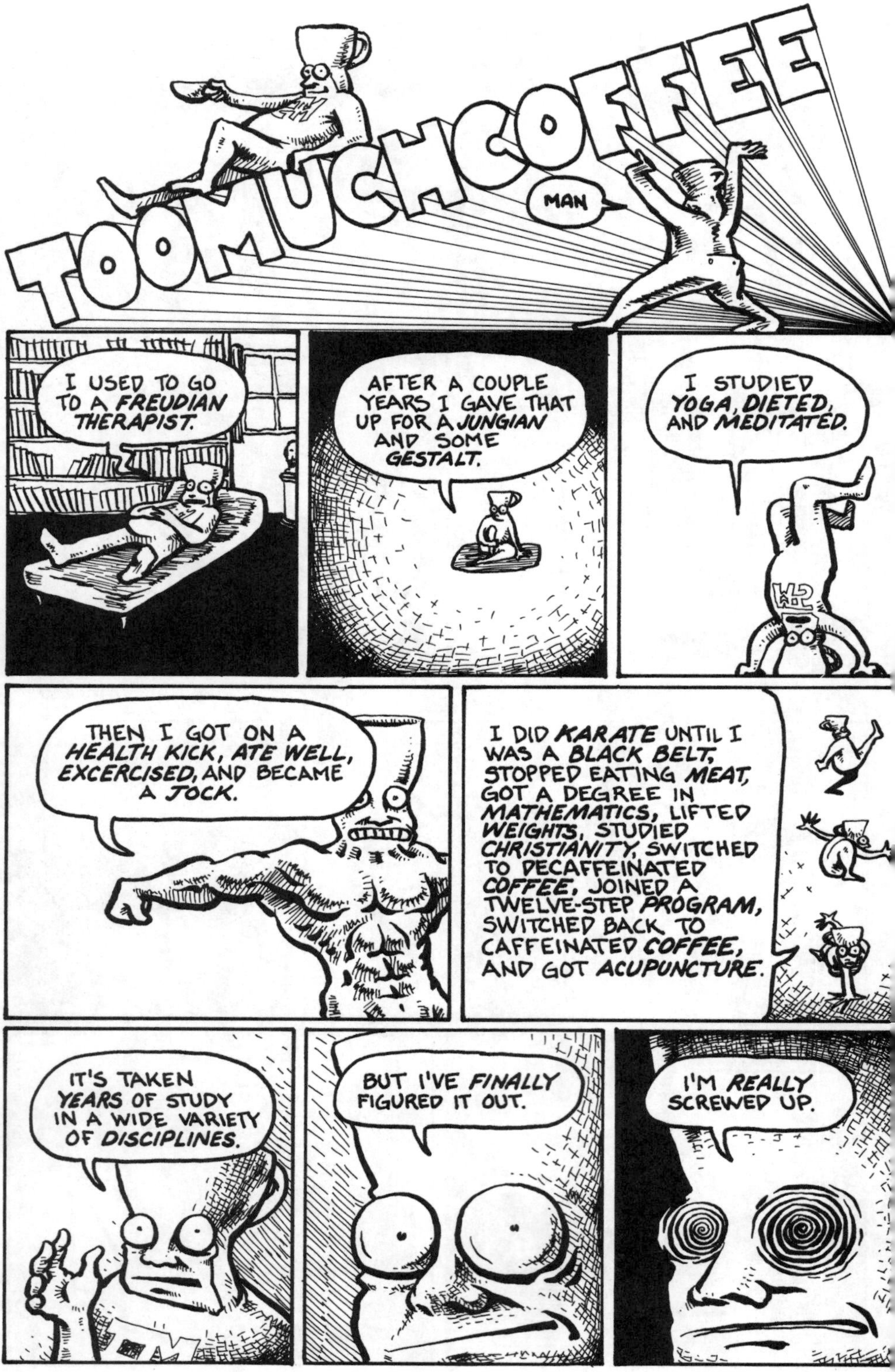
TOO MUCH COFFEE
MAN
I USED TO GO TO A FREUDIAN THERAPIST.
AFTER A COUPLE YEARS I GAVE THAT UP FOR A JUNGIAN AND SOME GESTALT.
I STUDIED YOGA, DIETED, AND MEDITATED.
THEN I GOT ON A HEALTH KICK, ATE WELL, EXCERCISED, AND BECAME A JOCK.
I DID KARATE UNTIL I WAS A BLACK BELT, STOPPED EATING MEAT, GOT A DEGREE IN MATHEMATICS, LIFTED WEIGHTS, STUDIED CHRISTIANITY, SWITCHED TO DECAFFEINATED COFFEE, JOINED A TWELVE-STEP PROGRAM, SWITCHED BACK TO CAFFEINATED COFFEE, AND GOT ACUPUNCTURE.
IT'S TAKEN YEARS OF STUDY IN A WIDE VARIETY OF DISCIPLINES.
BUT I'VE FINALLY FIGURED IT OUT.
I'M REALLY SCREWED UP.

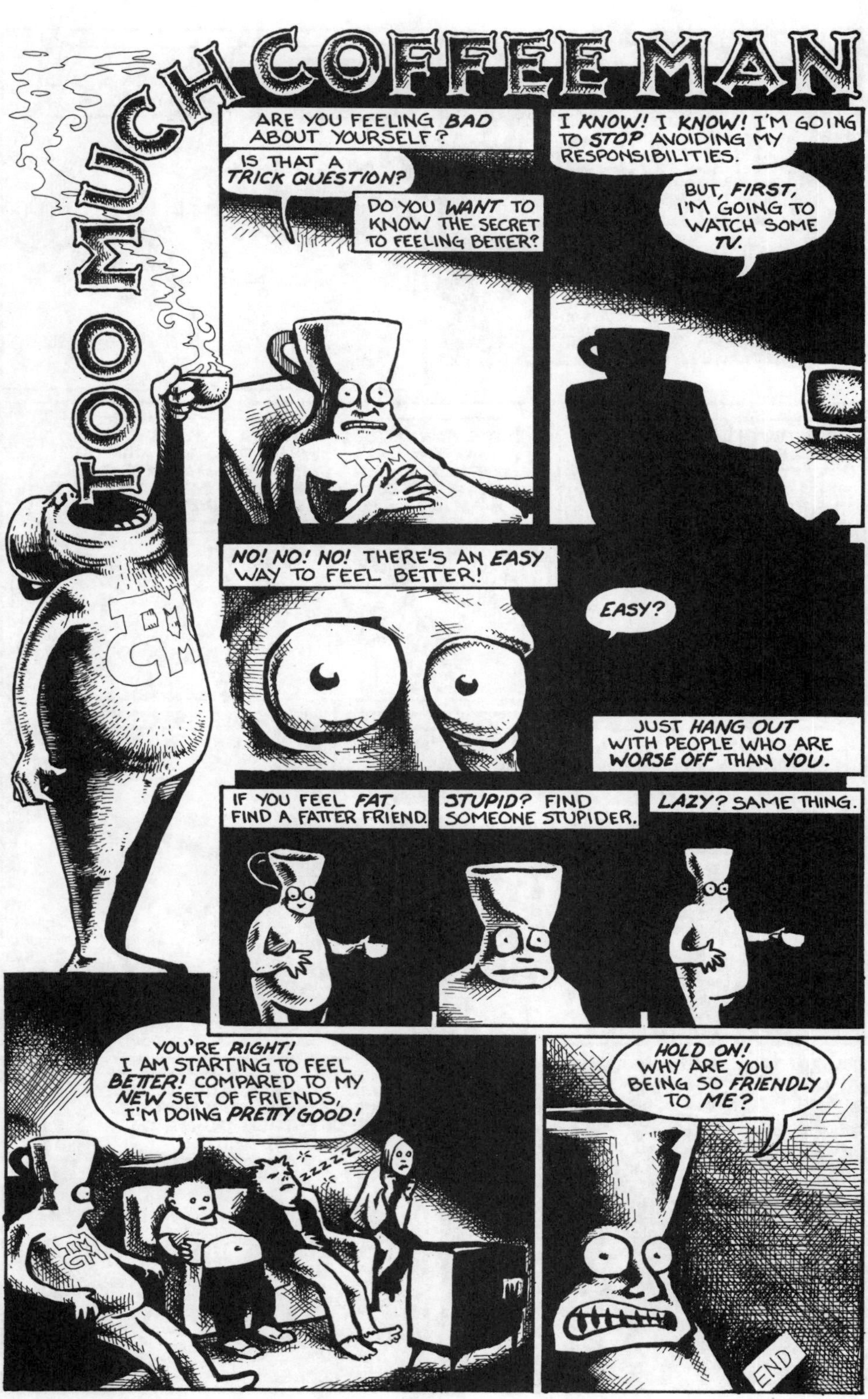
TOO MUCH COFFEE MAN
ARE YOU FEELING BAD ABOUT YOURSELF?
IS THAT A TRICK QUESTION?
DO YOU WANT TO KNOW THE SECRET TO FEELING BETTER?
I KNOW! I KNOW! I'M GOING TO STOP AVOIDING MY RESPONSIBILITIES.
BUT, FIRST, I'M GOING TO WATCH SOME TV.
NO! NO! NO! THERE'S AN EASY WAY TO FEEL BETTER!
EASY?
JUST HANG OUT WITH PEOPLE WHO ARE WORSE OFF THAN YOU.
IF YOU FEEL FAT, FIND A FATTER FRIEND.
STUPID? FIND SOMEONE STUPIDER.
LAZY? SAME THING.
YOU'RE RIGHT! I AM STARTING TO FEEL BETTER! COMPARED TO MY NEW SET OF FRIENDS, I'M DOING PRETTY GOOD!
ZZZZZ
HOLD ON! WHY ARE YOU BEING SO FRIENDLY TO ME?
END

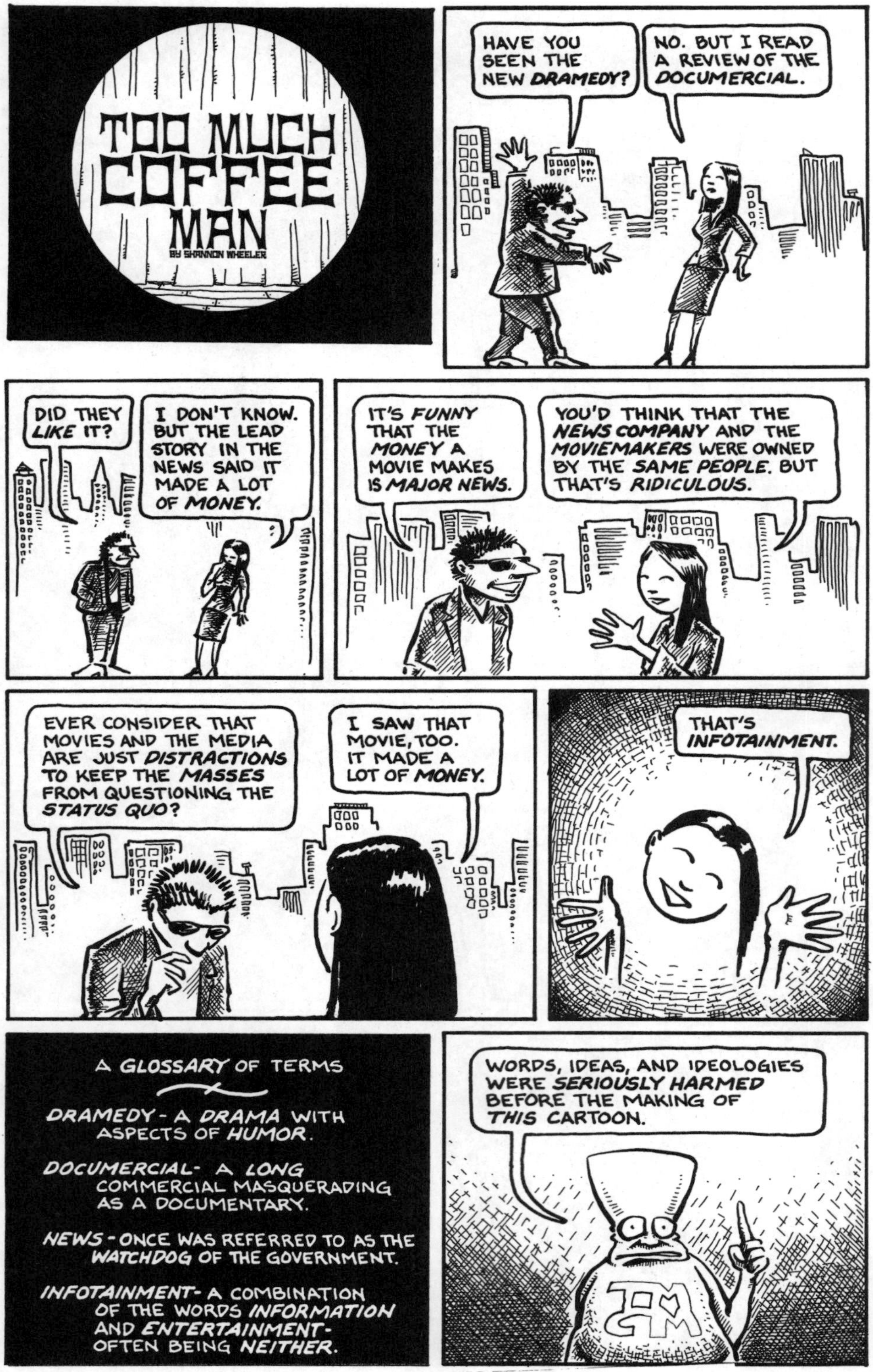
TOO MUCH COFFEE MAN
BY SHANNON WHEELER
HAVE YOU SEEN THE NEW DRAMEDY?
NO. BUT I READ A REVIEW OF THE DOCUMERCIAL.
DID THEY LIKE IT?
I DON'T KNOW. BUT THE LEAD STORY IN THE NEWS SAID IT MADE A LOT OF MONEY.
IT'S FUNNY THAT THE MONEY A MOVIE MAKES IS MAJOR NEWS.
YOU'D THINK THAT THE NEWS COMPANY AND THE MOVIEMAKERS WERE OWNED BY THE SAME PEOPLE. BUT THAT'S RIDICULOUS.
EVER CONSIDER THAT MOVIES AND THE MEDIA ARE JUST DISTRACTIONS TO KEEP THE MASSES FROM QUESTIONING THE STATUS QUO?
I SAW THAT MOVIE, TOO. IT MADE A LOT OF MONEY.
THAT'S INFOTAINMENT.
A GLOSSARY OF TERMS
DRAMEDY - A DRAMA WITH ASPECTS OF HUMOR.
DOCUMERCIAL- A LONG COMMERCIAL MASQUERADING AS A DOCUMENTARY.
NEWS - ONCE WAS REFERRED TO AS THE WATCHDOG OF THE GOVERNMENT.
INFOTAINMENT- A COMBINATION OF THE WORDS INFORMATION AND ENTERTAINMENT- OFTEN BEING NEITHER.
WORDS, IDEAS, AND IDEOLOGIES WERE SERIOUSLY HARMED BEFORE THE MAKING OF THIS CARTOON.
TCM

TELEVISION IS *STUPID!*

NO, IT'S NOT. IT'S *BRILLIANT.*

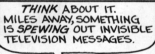

THINK ABOUT IT. MILES AWAY, SOMETHING IS *SPEWING* OUT INVISIBLE TELEVISION MESSAGES.

THEY TRAVEL THROUGH THE *AIR* ALONG WITH THOUSANDS OF OTHER TELEVISION, RADIO, AND *WEIRD* SIGNALS.

THEY *FILL* THE AIR AND CONSTANTLY *HIT* YOU. SOME BOUNCE OFF, AND SOME SHOOT THROUGH YOUR BODY. BUT YOU *DON'T* EVER SEE, HEAR, OR FEEL THEM.

THEN *OUR* LITTLE TV MANAGES TO PLUCK A *SINGLE SIGNAL* FROM THIS *MESS* AND CONVERT IT TO LIGHT AND SOUND THAT WE SIT AND *STARE* AT.

IT'S *AMAZING* HOW SOMETHING SO *INGENIOUS* COULD BE SO *STUPID.*

WE *NEED* CABLE.

I THOUGHT WE WERE GOING TO *RENT* A MOVIE.

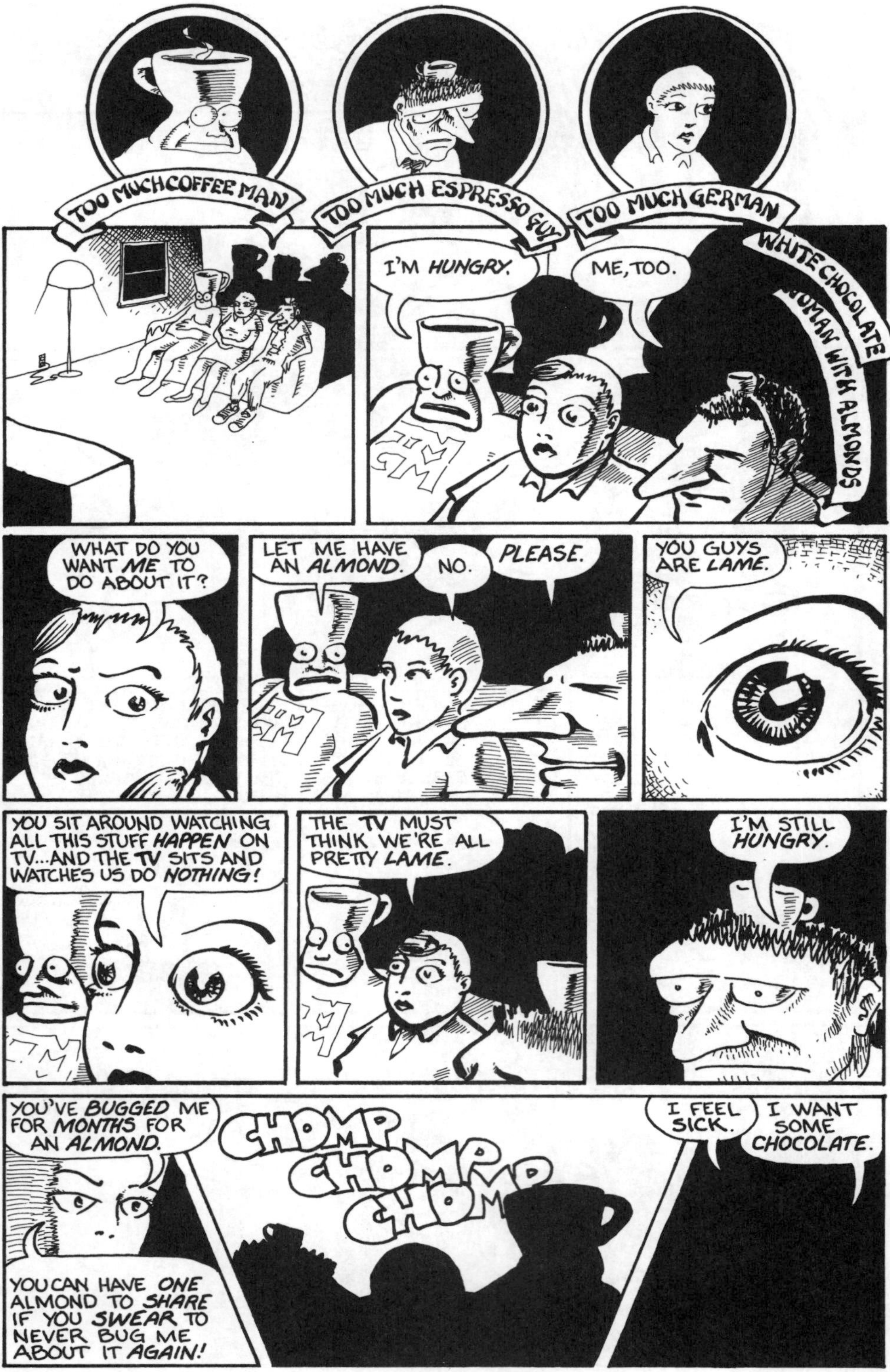
TOO MUCH COFFEE MAN
TOO MUCH ESPRESSO GUY
TOO MUCH GERMAN
I'M HUNGRY.
ME, TOO.
WHITE CHOCOLATE WOMAN WITH ALMONDS
WHAT DO YOU WANT ME TO DO ABOUT IT?
LET ME HAVE AN ALMOND.
NO.
PLEASE.
YOU GUYS ARE LAME.
YOU SIT AROUND WATCHING ALL THIS STUFF HAPPEN ON TV...AND THE TV SITS AND WATCHES US DO NOTHING!
THE TV MUST THINK WE'RE ALL PRETTY LAME.
I'M STILL HUNGRY.
YOU'VE BUGGED ME FOR MONTHS FOR AN ALMOND.
YOU CAN HAVE ONE ALMOND TO SHARE IF YOU SWEAR TO NEVER BUG ME ABOUT IT AGAIN!
CHOMP CHOMP CHOMP
I FEEL SICK.
I WANT SOME CHOCOLATE.

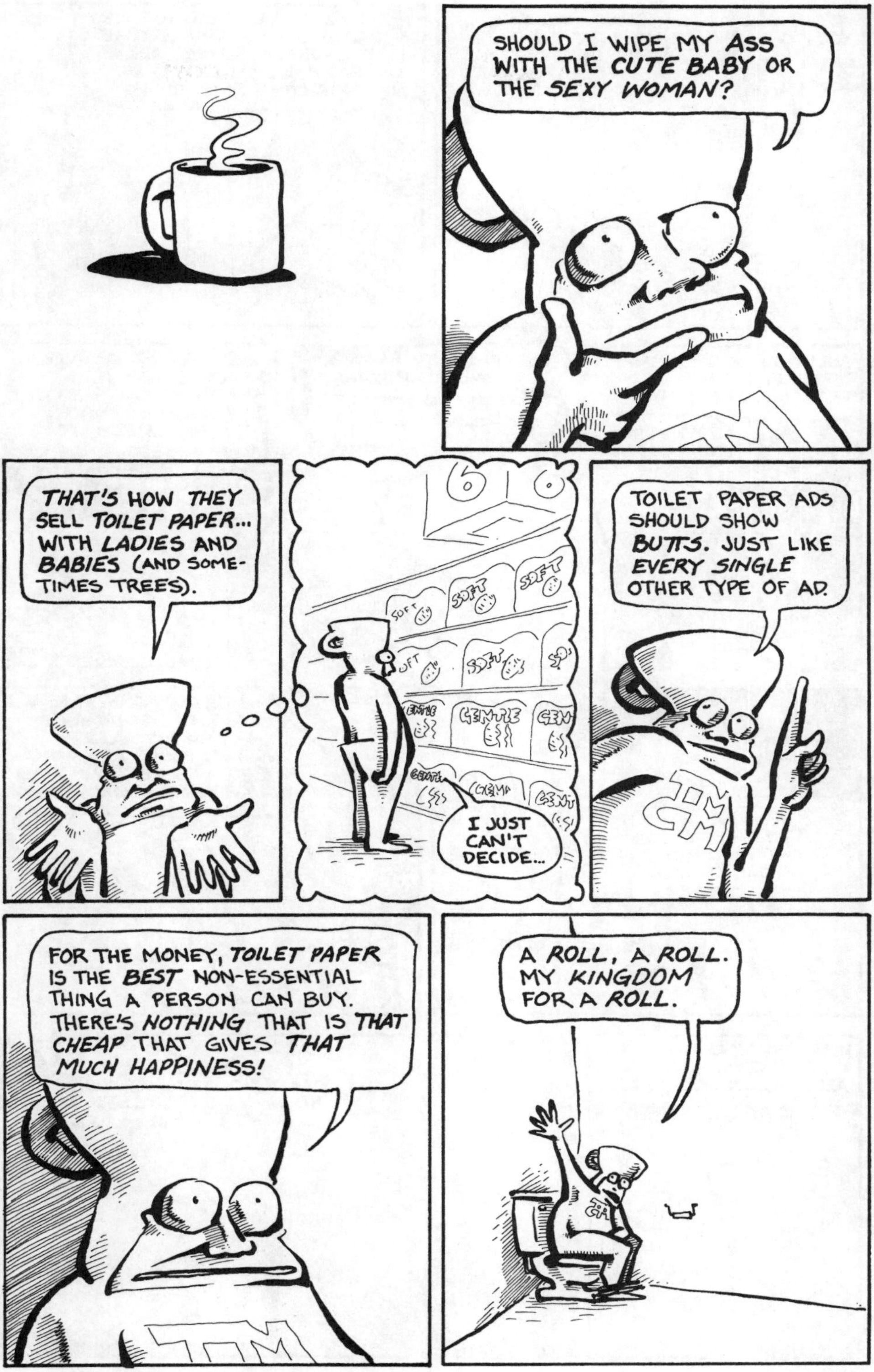
SHOULD I WIPE MY ASS WITH THE CUTE BABY OR THE SEXY WOMAN?
THAT'S HOW THEY SELL TOILET PAPER... WITH LADIES AND BABIES (AND SOME-TIMES TREES).
SOFT
GENTLE
I JUST CAN'T DECIDE...
TOILET PAPER ADS SHOULD SHOW BUTTS. JUST LIKE EVERY SINGLE OTHER TYPE OF AD.
FOR THE MONEY, TOILET PAPER IS THE BEST NON-ESSENTIAL THING A PERSON CAN BUY. THERE'S NOTHING THAT IS THAT CHEAP THAT GIVES THAT MUCH HAPPINESS!
A ROLL, A ROLL. MY KINGDOM FOR A ROLL.

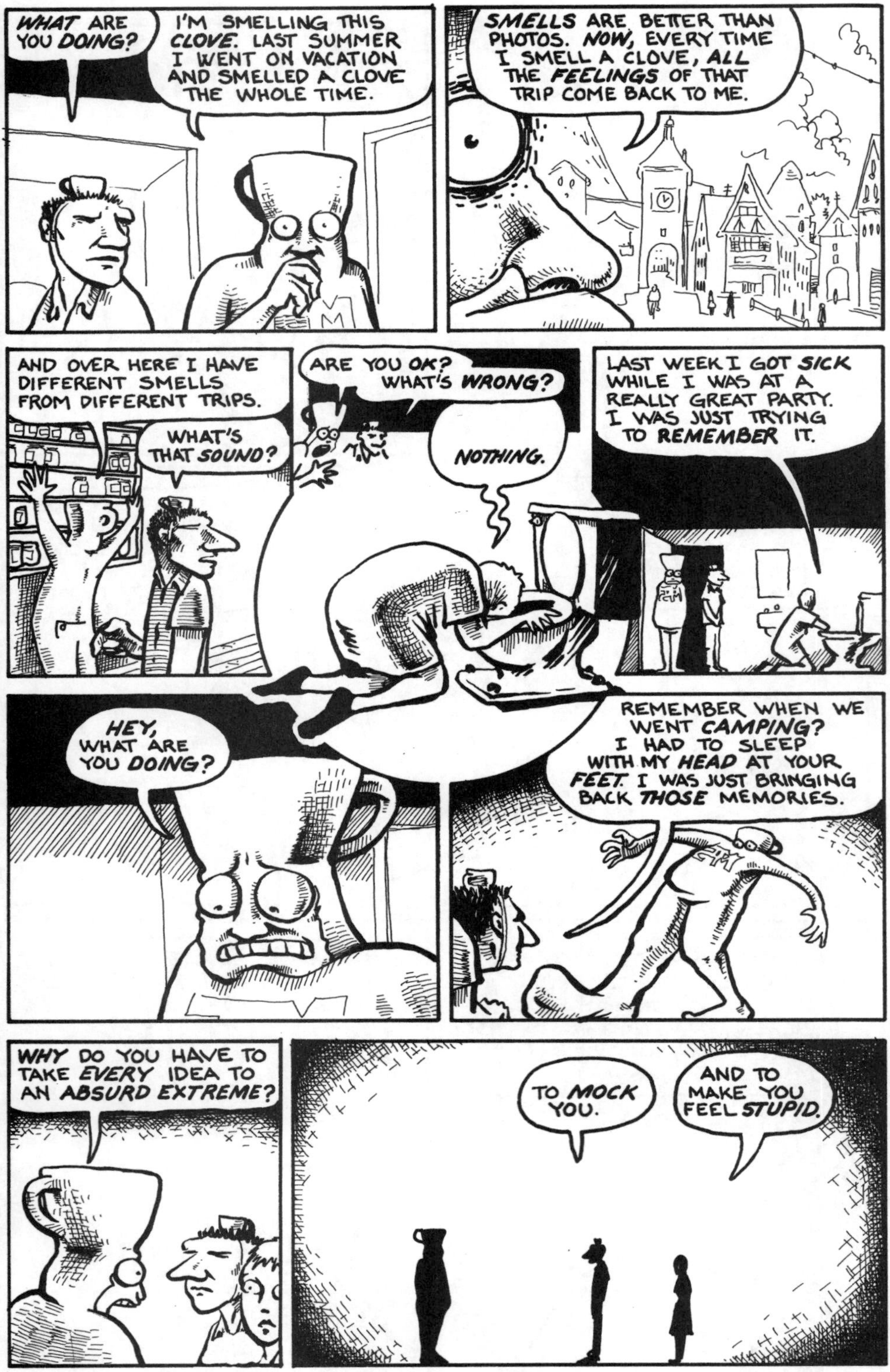
WHAT ARE YOU DOING?
I'M SMELLING THIS CLOVE. LAST SUMMER I WENT ON VACATION AND SMELLED A CLOVE THE WHOLE TIME.
SMELLS ARE BETTER THAN PHOTOS. NOW, EVERY TIME I SMELL A CLOVE, ALL THE FEELINGS OF THAT TRIP COME BACK TO ME.
AND OVER HERE I HAVE DIFFERENT SMELLS FROM DIFFERENT TRIPS.
WHAT'S THAT SOUND?
ARE YOU OK? WHAT'S WRONG?
NOTHING.
LAST WEEK I GOT SICK WHILE I WAS AT A REALLY GREAT PARTY. I WAS JUST TRYING TO REMEMBER IT.
HEY, WHAT ARE YOU DOING?
REMEMBER WHEN WE WENT CAMPING? I HAD TO SLEEP WITH MY HEAD AT YOUR FEET. I WAS JUST BRINGING BACK THOSE MEMORIES.
WHY DO YOU HAVE TO TAKE EVERY IDEA TO AN ABSURD EXTREME?
TO MOCK YOU.
AND TO MAKE YOU FEEL STUPID.

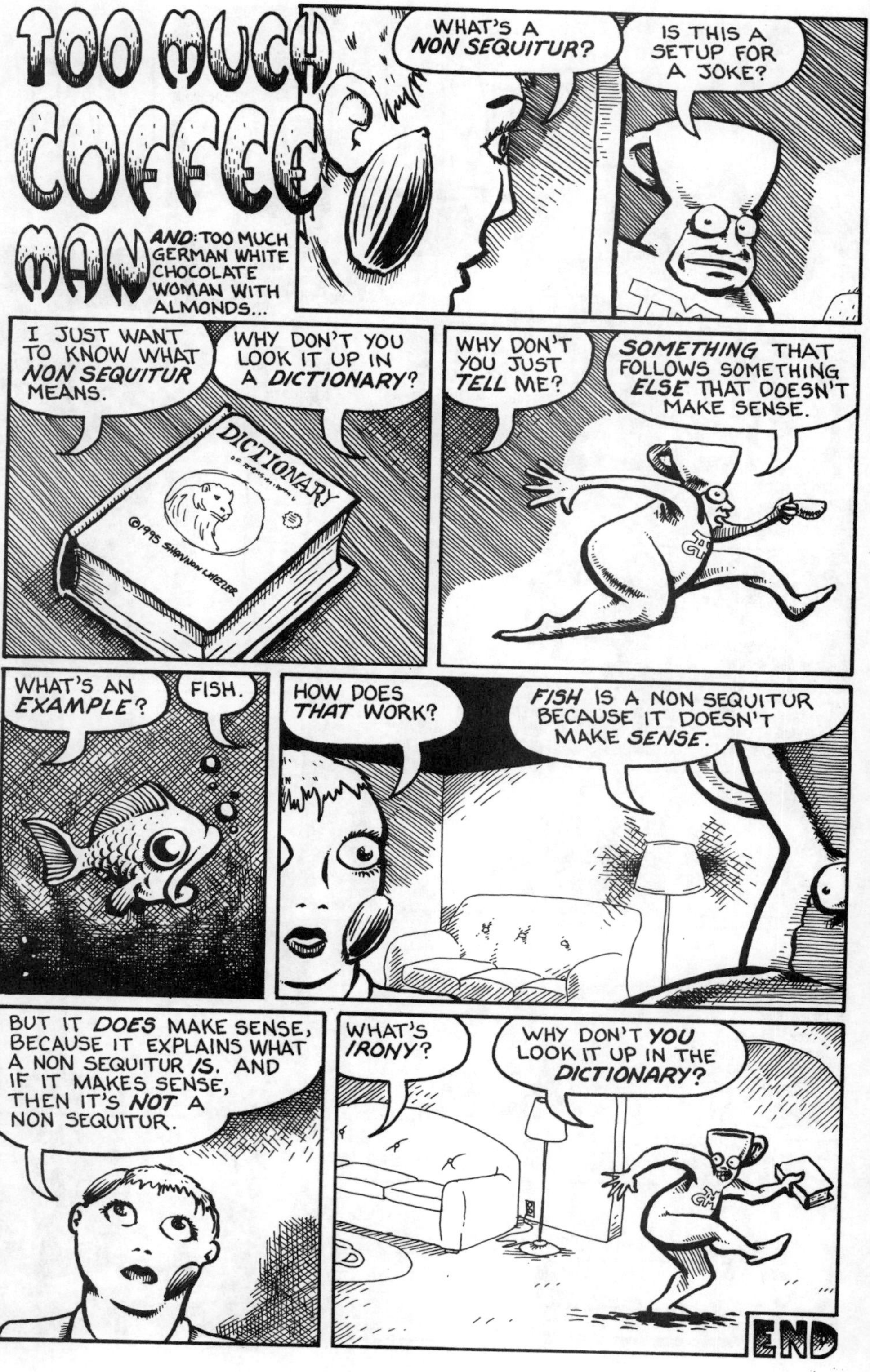
TOO MUCH COFFEE MAN
AND: TOO MUCH GERMAN WHITE CHOCOLATE WOMAN WITH ALMONDS...
WHAT'S A NON SEQUITUR?
IS THIS A SETUP FOR A JOKE?
I JUST WANT TO KNOW WHAT NON SEQUITUR MEANS.
WHY DON'T YOU LOOK IT UP IN A DICTIONARY?
DICTIONARY
©1995 SHANNON WHEELER
WHY DON'T YOU JUST TELL ME?
SOMETHING THAT FOLLOWS SOMETHING ELSE THAT DOESN'T MAKE SENSE.
WHAT'S AN EXAMPLE?
FISH.
HOW DOES THAT WORK?
FISH IS A NON SEQUITUR BECAUSE IT DOESN'T MAKE SENSE.
BUT IT DOES MAKE SENSE, BECAUSE IT EXPLAINS WHAT A NON SEQUITUR IS. AND IF IT MAKES SENSE, THEN IT'S NOT A NON SEQUITUR.
WHAT'S IRONY?
WHY DON'T YOU LOOK IT UP IN THE DICTIONARY?
END

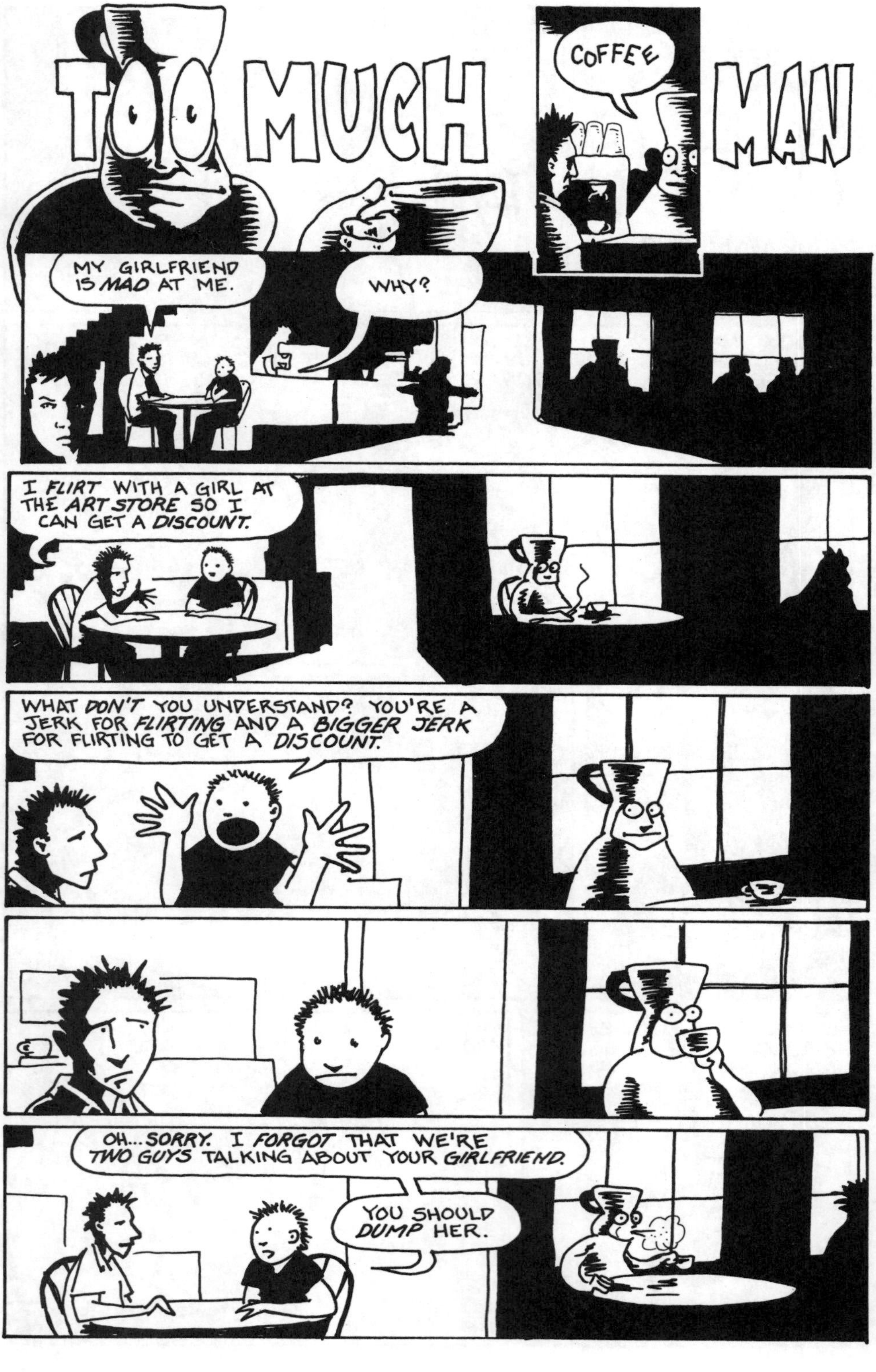
TOO MUCH COFFEE MAN
COFFEE
MY GIRLFRIEND IS MAD AT ME.
WHY?
I FLIRT WITH A GIRL AT THE ART STORE SO I CAN GET A DISCOUNT.
WHAT DON'T YOU UNDERSTAND? YOU'RE A JERK FOR FLIRTING AND A BIGGER JERK FOR FLIRTING TO GET A DISCOUNT.
OH...SORRY. I FORGOT THAT WE'RE TWO GUYS TALKING ABOUT YOUR GIRLFRIEND.
YOU SHOULD DUMP HER.

chapter 3

A BRINE SHRIMP ADVENTURE

If I had a time machine,
I'd give it to myself, and other ideas

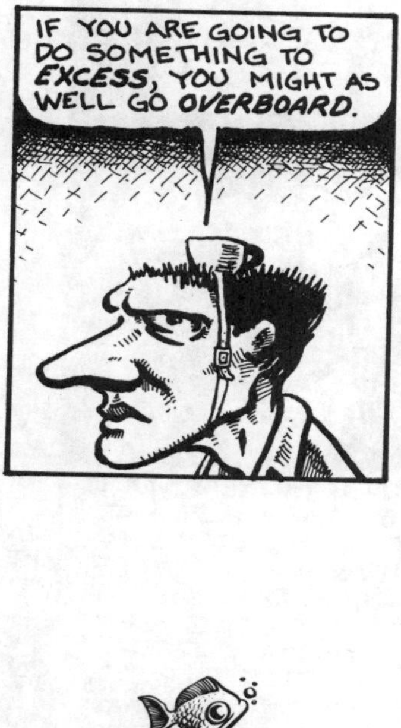
IF YOU ARE GOING TO DO SOMETHING TO EXCESS, YOU MIGHT AS WELL GO OVERBOARD.

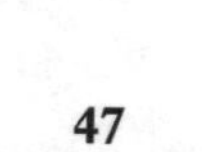

TOO MUCH COFFEE
HEY, KID, HOW WOULD YOU LIKE A CRAPPY JOB?
I GUESS. I NEED A JOB.
OF COURSE, YOUR HAIR IS TOO LONG AND YOU'LL HAVE TO SHAVE YOUR GOATEE.
OH... UM... OK...
HEY, GIRL OVER THERE, I HAVE A CRAPPY JOB FOR YOU, TOO.
BUT YOUR HAIR IS TOO SHORT. YOU'LL HAVE TO WEAR A HAT UNTIL IT GROWS OUT.
BOTH OF YOU NEED TO DRESS TO HIDE YOUR TATTOOS AND PIERCINGS.
WHAT'S THE JOB?
YOU SERVE FAT AND DRUNK PEOPLE LIQUOR AND FOOD... AND DON'T FORGET TO PUSH THE EXPENSIVE STUFF.
I PAY LESS THAN THE MINIMUM WAGE—MOST OF YOUR MONEY WILL COME FROM TIPS, SO YOU'LL NEED TO BE FRIENDLY AND POLITE EVEN WHEN THE CUSTOMERS ARE JERKS.
OVER THE YEARS YOU'LL BECOME BITTER AND DISILLUSIONED, YOUR HEALTH WILL SUFFER, AND THERE WON'T BE MUCH CHANCE FOR JOB IMPROVEMENT.
SOUNDS GREAT.
WHAT A TERRIBLE DREAM. I KNEW I SHOULDN'T HAVE EATEN THAT BURRITO BEFORE GOING TO BED.
APOLOGIES TO WINSOR McCAY

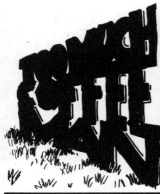

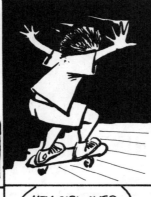

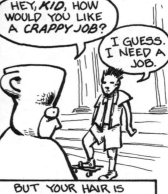

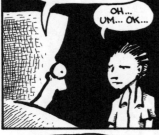

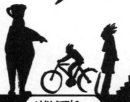

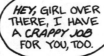

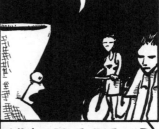

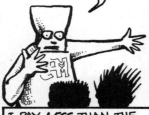

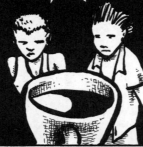

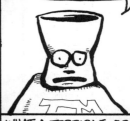

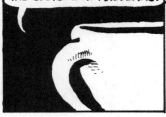

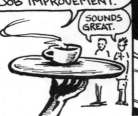

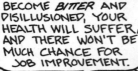

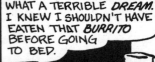

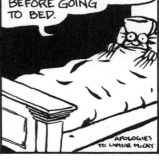

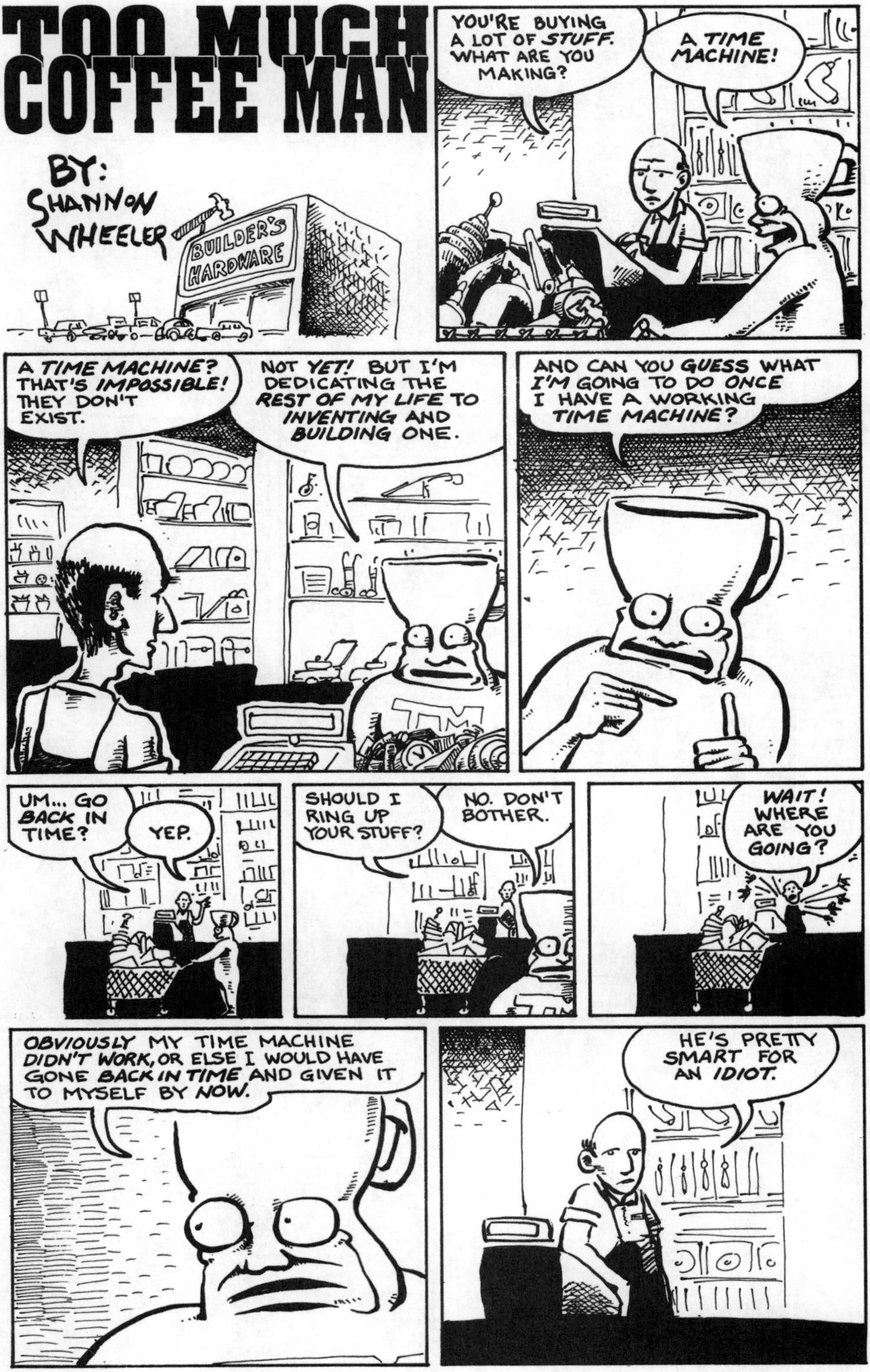
TOO MUCH COFFEE MAN
BY: SHANNON WHEELER
BUILDER'S HARDWARE
YOU'RE BUYING A LOT OF STUFF. WHAT ARE YOU MAKING?
A TIME MACHINE!
A TIME MACHINE? THAT'S IMPOSSIBLE! THEY DON'T EXIST.
NOT YET! BUT I'M DEDICATING THE REST OF MY LIFE TO INVENTING AND BUILDING ONE.
AND CAN YOU GUESS WHAT I'M GOING TO DO ONCE I HAVE A WORKING TIME MACHINE?
UM... GO BACK IN TIME?
YEP.
SHOULD I RING UP YOUR STUFF?
NO. DON'T BOTHER.
WAIT! WHERE ARE YOU GOING?
OBVIOUSLY MY TIME MACHINE DIDN'T WORK, OR ELSE I WOULD HAVE GONE BACK IN TIME AND GIVEN IT TO MYSELF BY NOW.
HE'S PRETTY SMART FOR AN IDIOT.

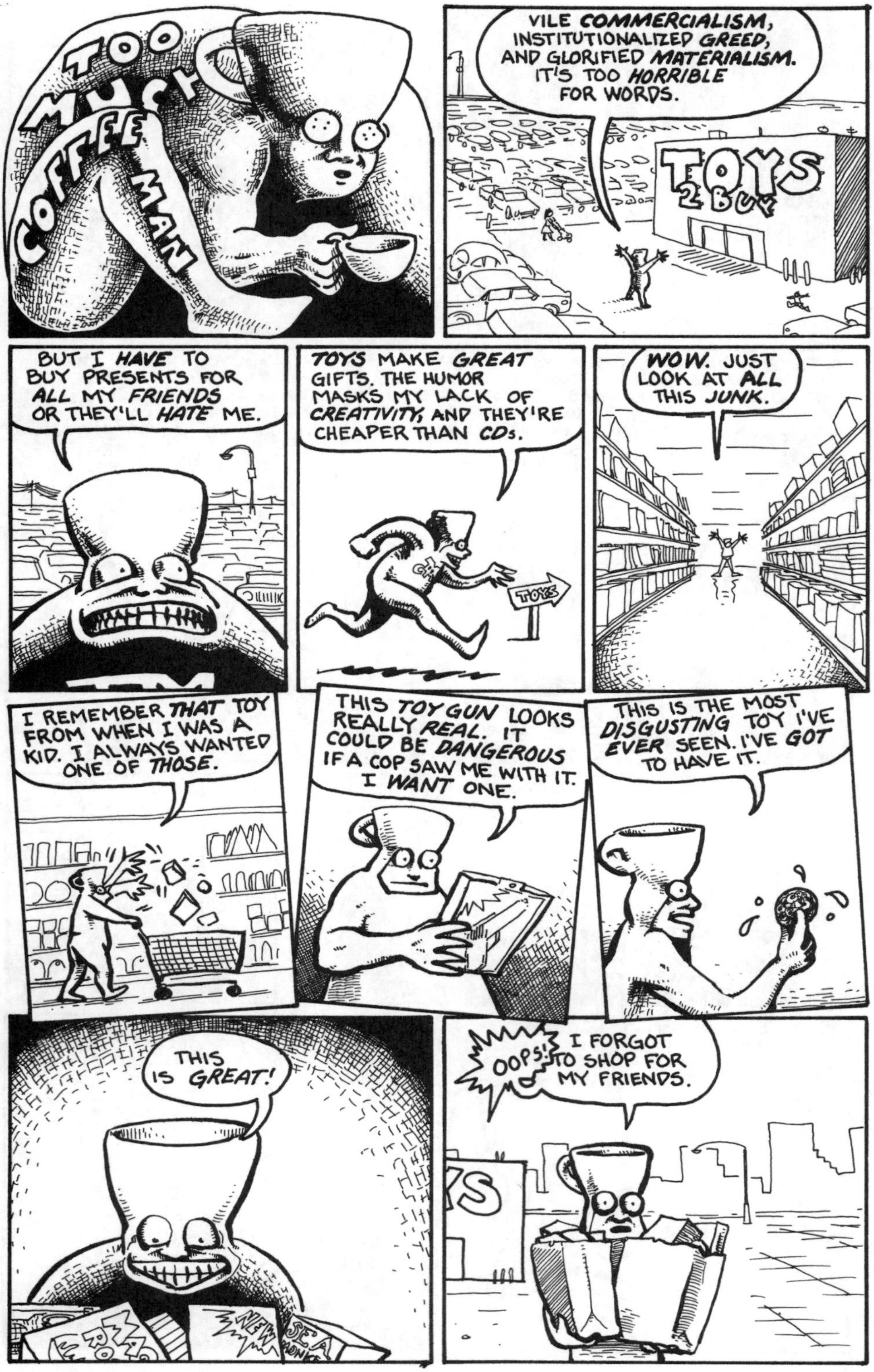
TOO MUCH COFFEE MAN
VILE COMMERCIALISM, INSTITUTIONALIZED GREED, AND GLORIFIED MATERIALISM. IT'S TOO HORRIBLE FOR WORDS.
TOYS 2 BUY
BUT I HAVE TO BUY PRESENTS FOR ALL MY FRIENDS OR THEY'LL HATE ME.
TOYS MAKE GREAT GIFTS. THE HUMOR MASKS MY LACK OF CREATIVITY, AND THEY'RE CHEAPER THAN CDs.
TOYS
WOW. JUST LOOK AT ALL THIS JUNK.
I REMEMBER THAT TOY FROM WHEN I WAS A KID. I ALWAYS WANTED ONE OF THOSE.
THIS TOY GUN LOOKS REALLY REAL. IT COULD BE DANGEROUS IF A COP SAW ME WITH IT. I WANT ONE.
THIS IS THE MOST DISGUSTING TOY I'VE EVER SEEN. I'VE GOT TO HAVE IT.
THIS IS GREAT!
OOPS!
I FORGOT TO SHOP FOR MY FRIENDS.

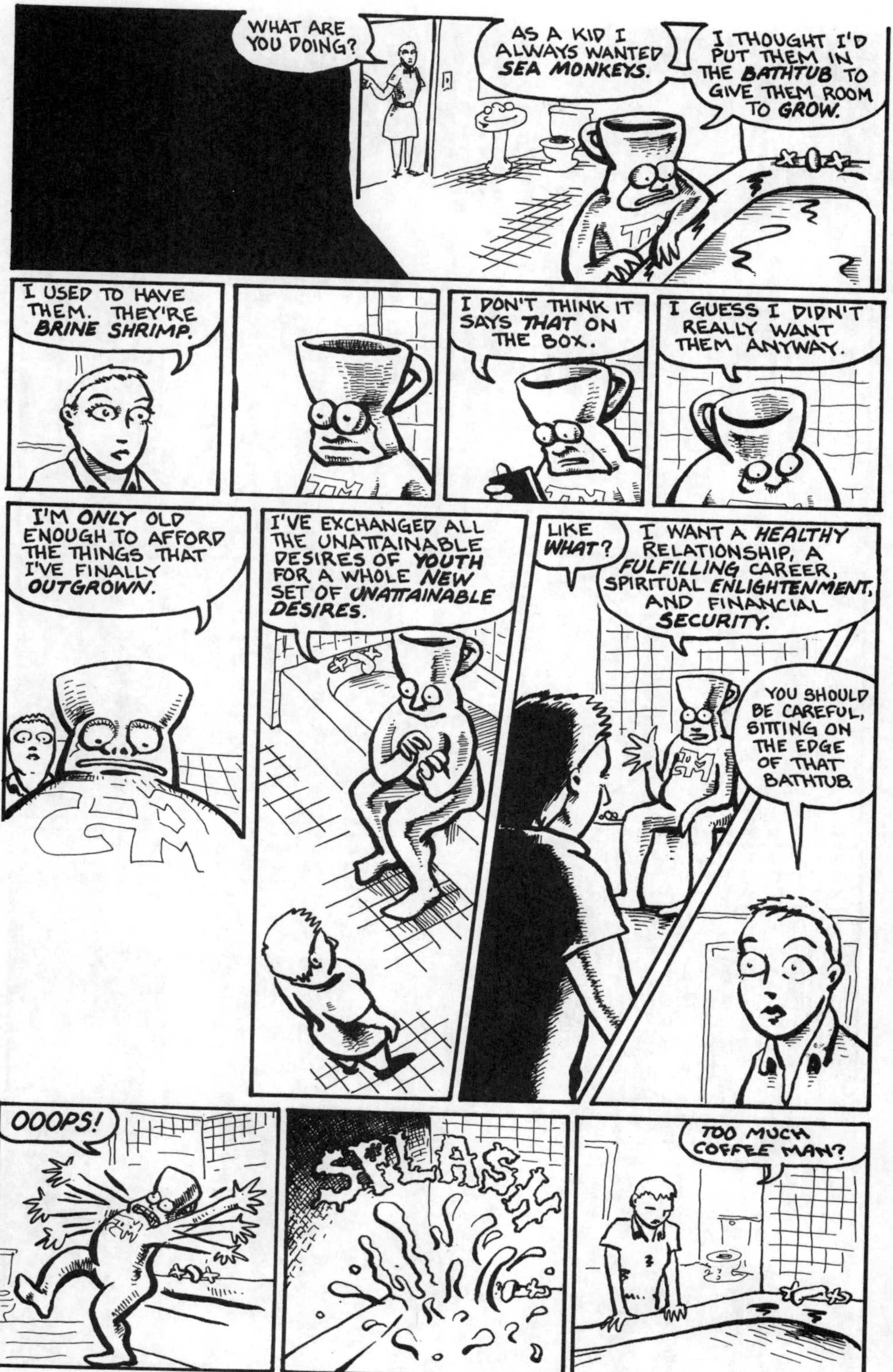
WHAT ARE YOU DOING?
AS A KID I ALWAYS WANTED SEA MONKEYS.
I THOUGHT I'D PUT THEM IN THE BATHTUB TO GIVE THEM ROOM TO GROW.
I USED TO HAVE THEM. THEY'RE BRINE SHRIMP.
I DON'T THINK IT SAYS THAT ON THE BOX.
I GUESS I DIDN'T REALLY WANT THEM ANYWAY.
I'M ONLY OLD ENOUGH TO AFFORD THE THINGS THAT I'VE FINALLY OUTGROWN.
I'VE EXCHANGED ALL THE UNATTAINABLE DESIRES OF YOUTH FOR A WHOLE NEW SET OF UNATTAINABLE DESIRES.
LIKE WHAT?
I WANT A HEALTHY RELATIONSHIP, A FULFILLING CAREER, SPIRITUAL ENLIGHTENMENT, AND FINANCIAL SECURITY.
YOU SHOULD BE CAREFUL, SITTING ON THE EDGE OF THAT BATHTUB.
OOOPS!
SPLASH
TOO MUCH COFFEE MAN?

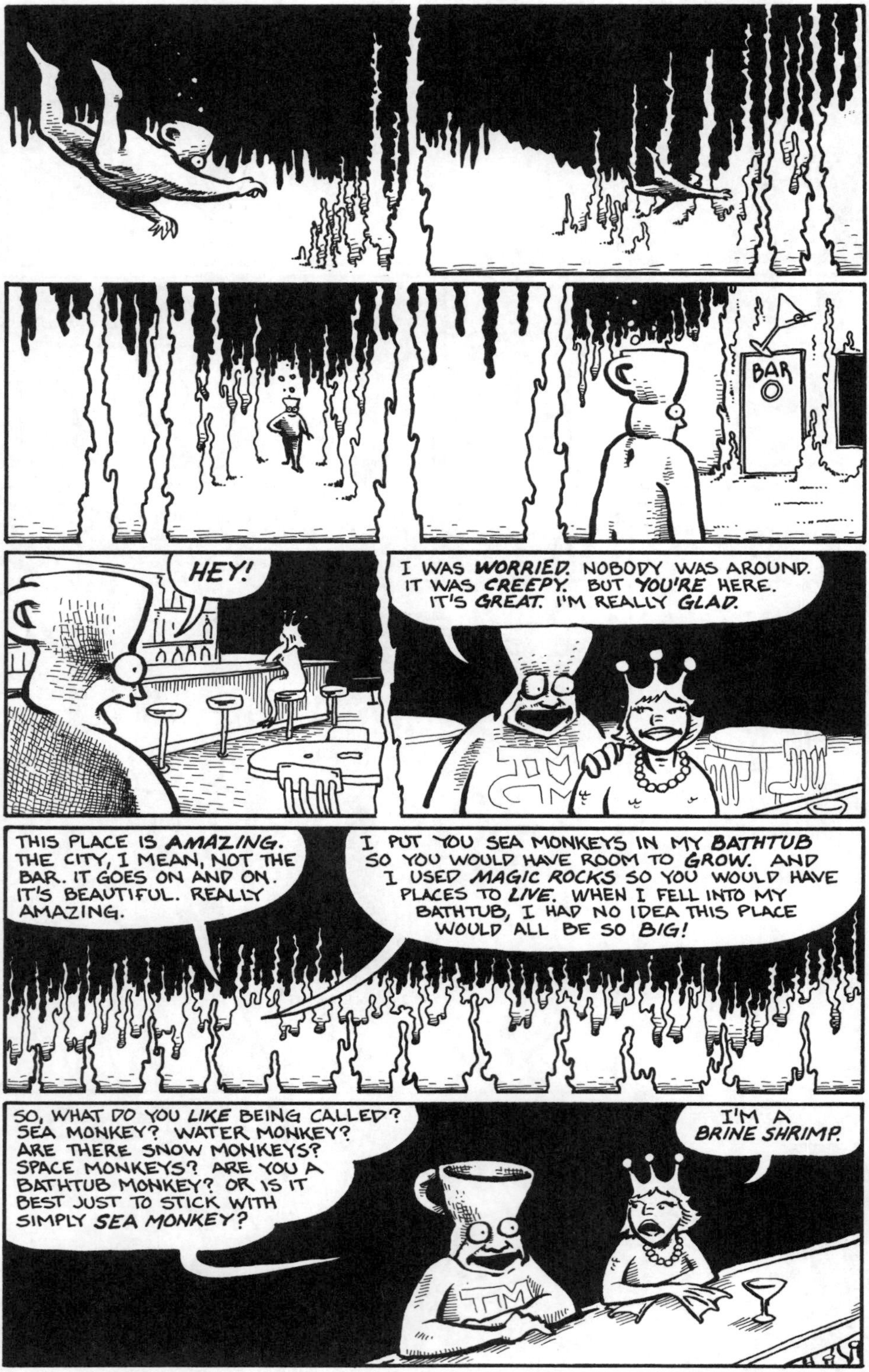
BAR
HEY!
I WAS WORRIED. NOBODY WAS AROUND. IT WAS CREEPY. BUT YOU'RE HERE. IT'S GREAT. I'M REALLY GLAD.
THIS PLACE IS AMAZING. THE CITY, I MEAN, NOT THE BAR. IT GOES ON AND ON. IT'S BEAUTIFUL. REALLY AMAZING.
I PUT YOU SEA MONKEYS IN MY BATHTUB SO YOU WOULD HAVE ROOM TO GROW. AND I USED MAGIC ROCKS SO YOU WOULD HAVE PLACES TO LIVE. WHEN I FELL INTO MY BATHTUB, I HAD NO IDEA THIS PLACE WOULD ALL BE SO BIG!
SO, WHAT DO YOU LIKE BEING CALLED? SEA MONKEY? WATER MONKEY? ARE THERE SNOW MONKEYS? SPACE MONKEYS? ARE YOU A BATHTUB MONKEY? OR IS IT BEST JUST TO STICK WITH SIMPLY SEA MONKEY?
I'M A BRINE SHRIMP.

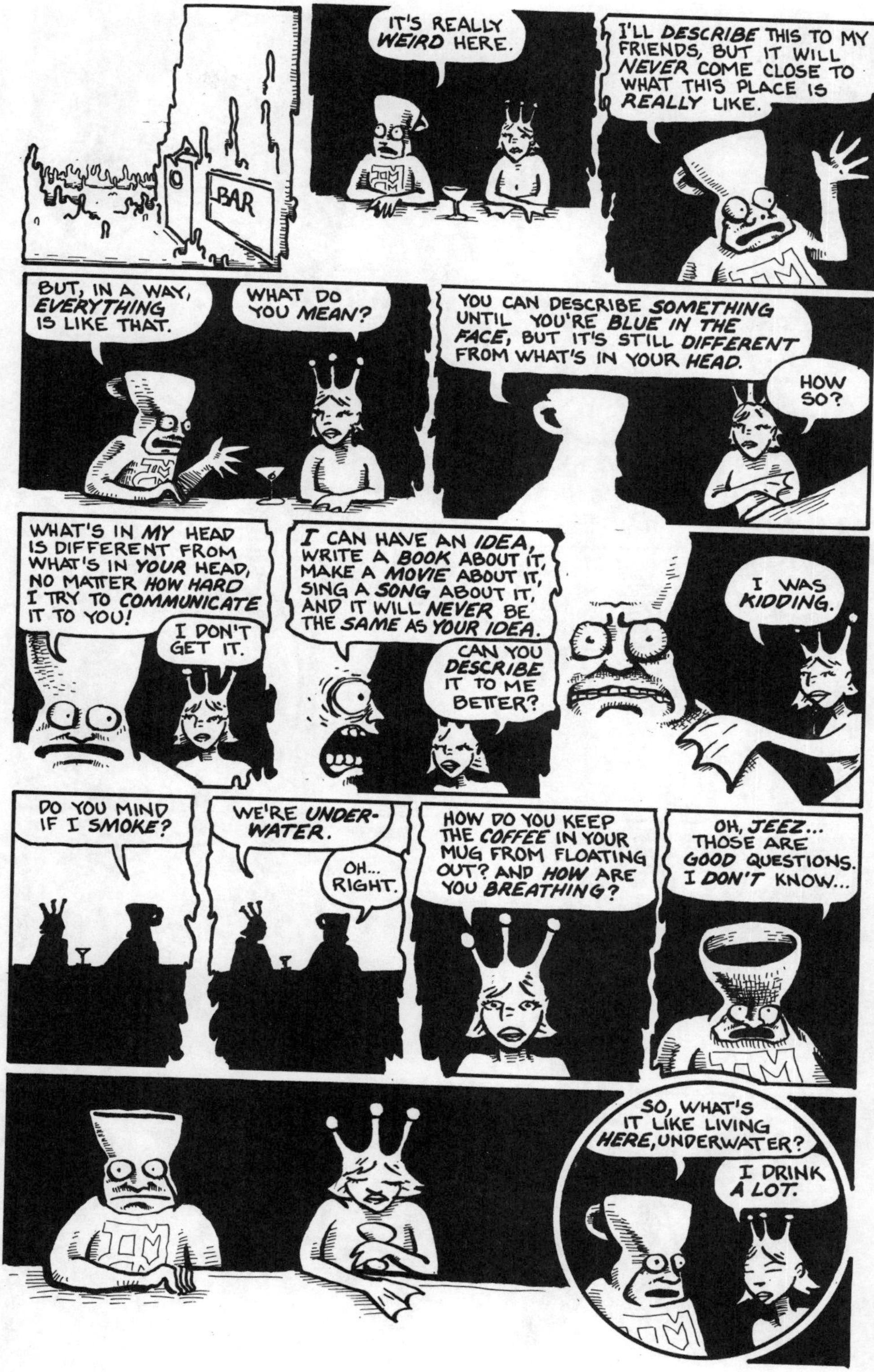
BAR
IT'S REALLY WEIRD HERE.
I'LL DESCRIBE THIS TO MY FRIENDS, BUT IT WILL NEVER COME CLOSE TO WHAT THIS PLACE IS REALLY LIKE.
BUT, IN A WAY, EVERYTHING IS LIKE THAT.
WHAT DO YOU MEAN?
YOU CAN DESCRIBE SOMETHING UNTIL YOU'RE BLUE IN THE FACE, BUT IT'S STILL DIFFERENT FROM WHAT'S IN YOUR HEAD.
HOW SO?
WHAT'S IN MY HEAD IS DIFFERENT FROM WHAT'S IN YOUR HEAD, NO MATTER HOW HARD I TRY TO COMMUNICATE IT TO YOU!
I DON'T GET IT.
I CAN HAVE AN IDEA, WRITE A BOOK ABOUT IT, MAKE A MOVIE ABOUT IT, SING A SONG ABOUT IT, AND IT WILL NEVER BE THE SAME AS YOUR IDEA.
CAN YOU DESCRIBE IT TO ME BETTER?
I WAS KIDDING.
DO YOU MIND IF I SMOKE?
WE'RE UNDER-WATER.
OH... RIGHT.
HOW DO YOU KEEP THE COFFEE IN YOUR MUG FROM FLOATING OUT? AND HOW ARE YOU BREATHING?
OH, JEEZ... THOSE ARE GOOD QUESTIONS. I DON'T KNOW...
SO, WHAT'S IT LIKE LIVING HERE, UNDERWATER?
I DRINK A LOT.

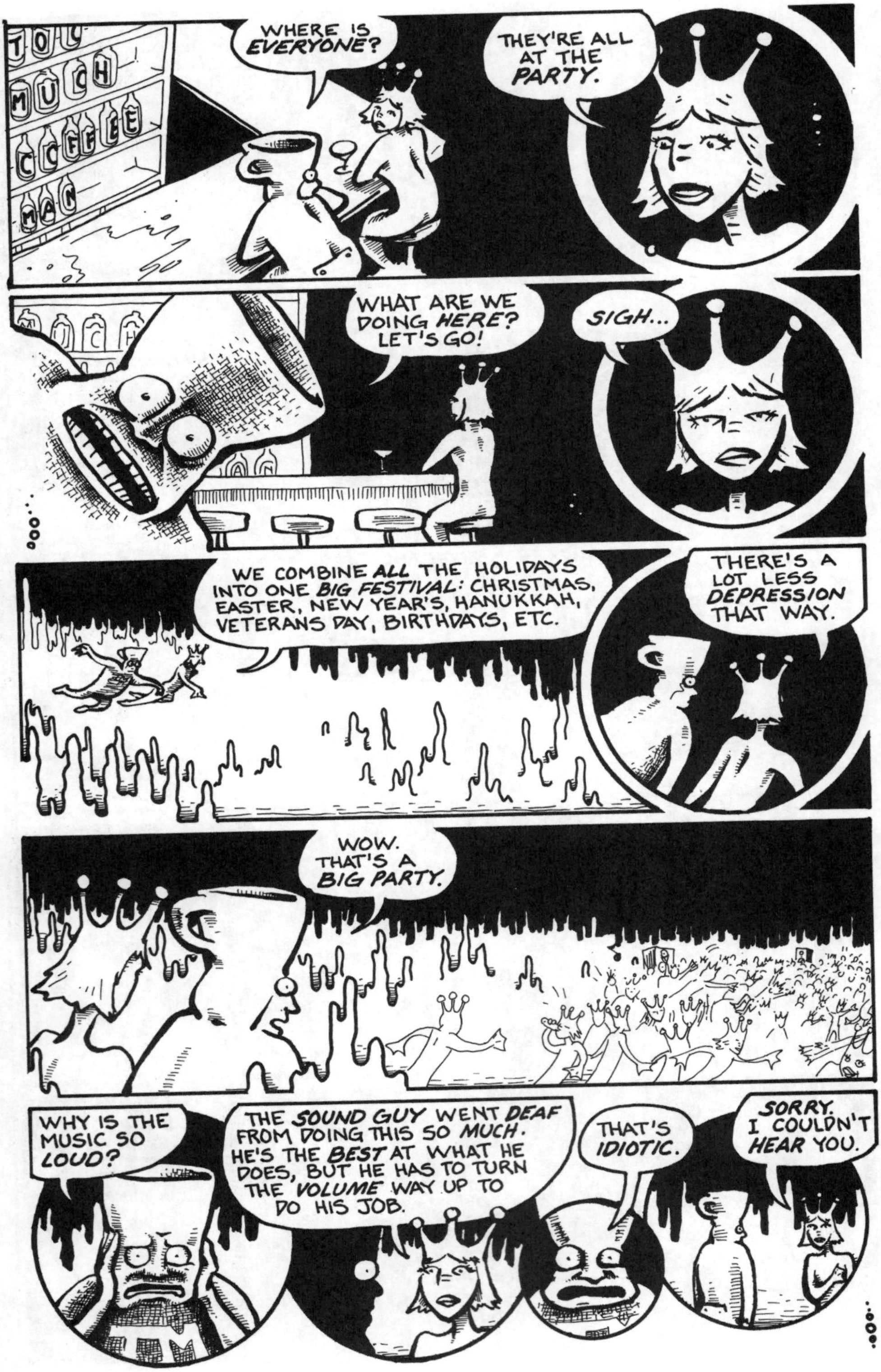
TOO MUCH COFFEE MAN
WHERE IS EVERYONE?
THEY'RE ALL AT THE PARTY.
WHAT ARE WE DOING HERE? LET'S GO!
SIGH...
WE COMBINE ALL THE HOLIDAYS INTO ONE BIG FESTIVAL: CHRISTMAS, EASTER, NEW YEAR'S, HANUKKAH, VETERANS DAY, BIRTHDAYS, ETC.
THERE'S A LOT LESS DEPRESSION THAT WAY.
WOW. THAT'S A BIG PARTY.
WHY IS THE MUSIC SO LOUD?
THE SOUND GUY WENT DEAF FROM DOING THIS SO MUCH. HE'S THE BEST AT WHAT HE DOES, BUT HE HAS TO TURN THE VOLUME WAY UP TO DO HIS JOB.
THAT'S IDIOTIC.
SORRY. I COULDN'T HEAR YOU.

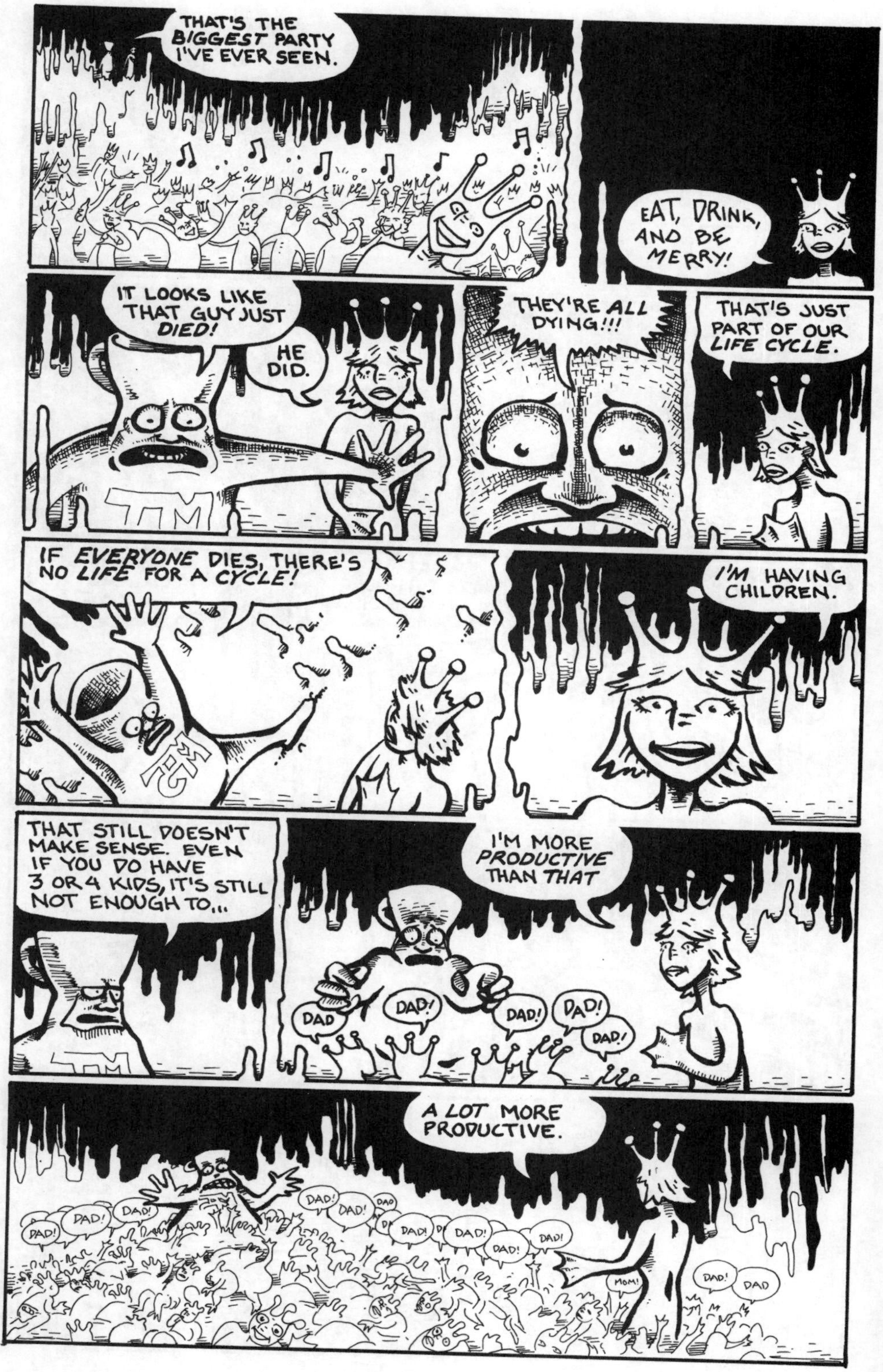
THAT'S THE BIGGEST PARTY I'VE EVER SEEN.
EAT, DRINK, AND BE MERRY!
IT LOOKS LIKE THAT GUY JUST DIED!
HE DID.
THEY'RE ALL DYING!!!
THAT'S JUST PART OF OUR LIFE CYCLE.
IF EVERYONE DIES, THERE'S NO LIFE FOR A CYCLE!
I'M HAVING CHILDREN.
THAT STILL DOESN'T MAKE SENSE. EVEN IF YOU DO HAVE 3 OR 4 KIDS, IT'S STILL NOT ENOUGH TO...
I'M MORE PRODUCTIVE THAN THAT
DAD
DAD!
DAD!
DAD!
DAD!
A LOT MORE PRODUCTIVE.
DAD!
DAD!
DAD!
DAD!
DAD!
DAD
DAD!
DAD!
DAD!
DAD!
MOM!
DAD!
DAD

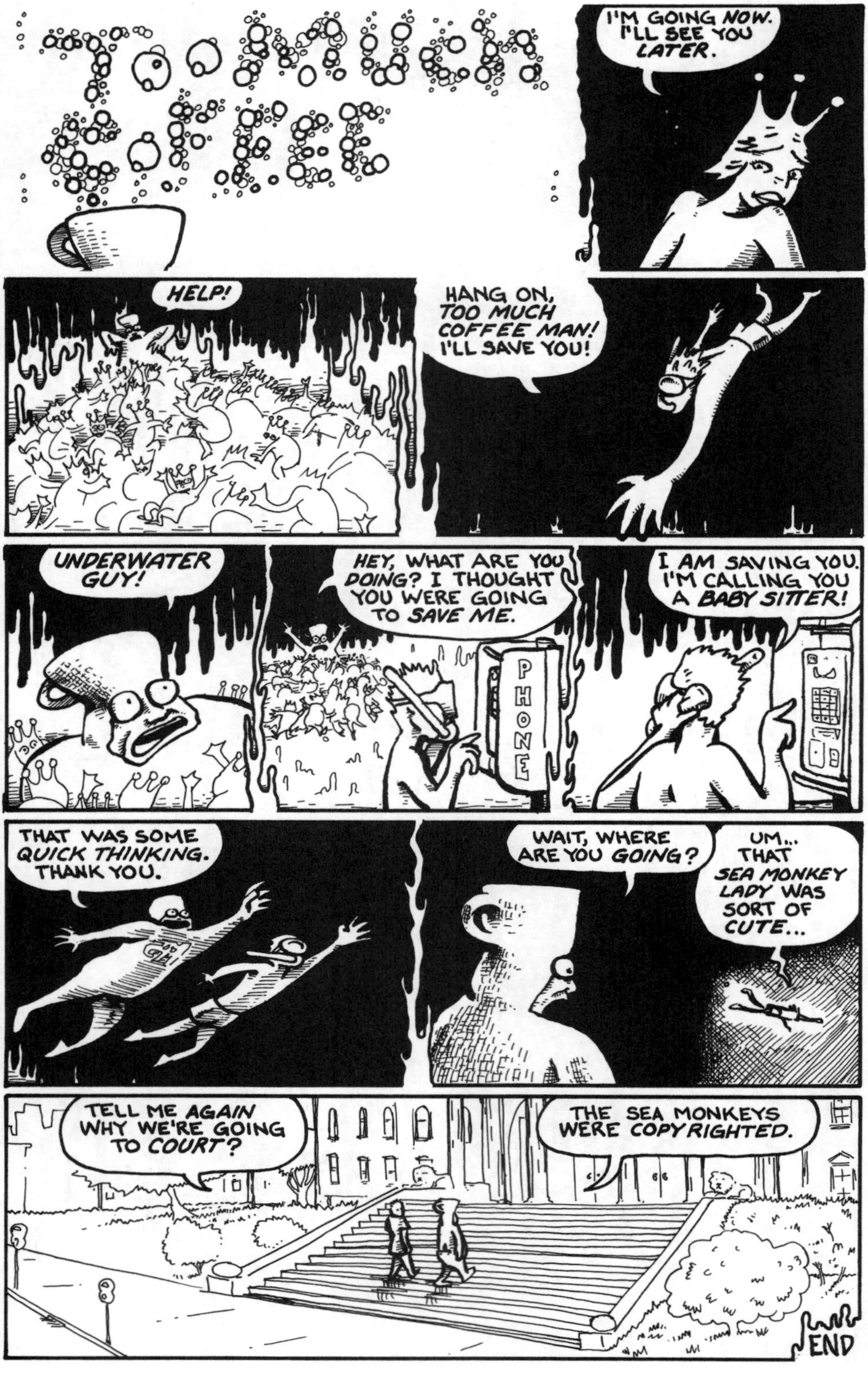
TOO MUCH COFFEE
I'M GOING NOW. I'LL SEE YOU LATER.
HELP!
HANG ON, TOO MUCH COFFEE MAN! I'LL SAVE YOU!
UNDERWATER GUY!
HEY, WHAT ARE YOU DOING? I THOUGHT YOU WERE GOING TO SAVE ME.
PHONE
I AM SAVING YOU. I'M CALLING YOU A BABY SITTER!
THAT WAS SOME QUICK THINKING. THANK YOU.
WAIT, WHERE ARE YOU GOING?
UM... THAT SEA MONKEY LADY WAS SORT OF CUTE...
TELL ME AGAIN WHY WE'RE GOING TO COURT?
THE SEA MONKEYS WERE COPYRIGHTED.
END

chapter 4

THE McDONALD'S COFFEE LAWSUIT

*Misinformation in the information age
and other theories of conspiracy*

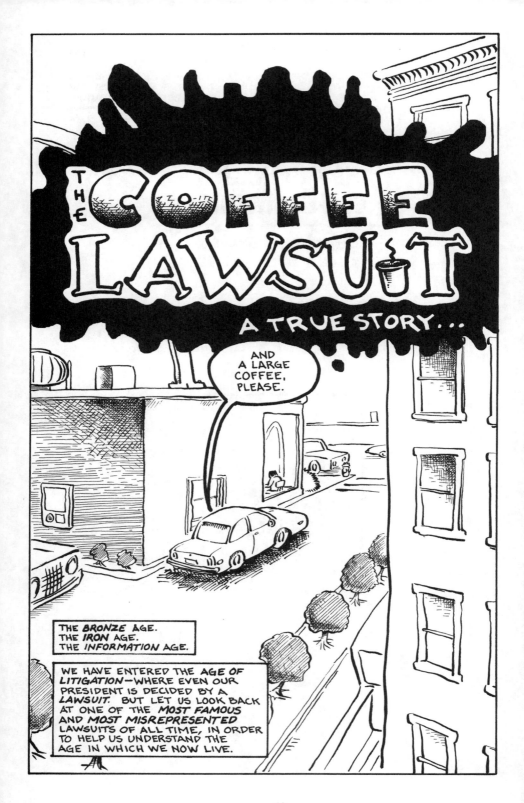

THE **COFFEE** LAWSUIT

A TRUE STORY....

AND A LARGE COFFEE, PLEASE.

THE *BRONZE* AGE.
THE *IRON* AGE.
THE *INFORMATION* AGE.

WE HAVE ENTERED THE *AGE OF LITIGATION*—WHERE EVEN OUR PRESIDENT IS DECIDED BY A *LAWSUIT.* BUT LET US LOOK BACK AT ONE OF THE *MOST FAMOUS* AND *MOST MISREPRESENTED* LAWSUITS OF ALL TIME, IN ORDER TO HELP US UNDERSTAND THE AGE IN WHICH WE NOW LIVE.

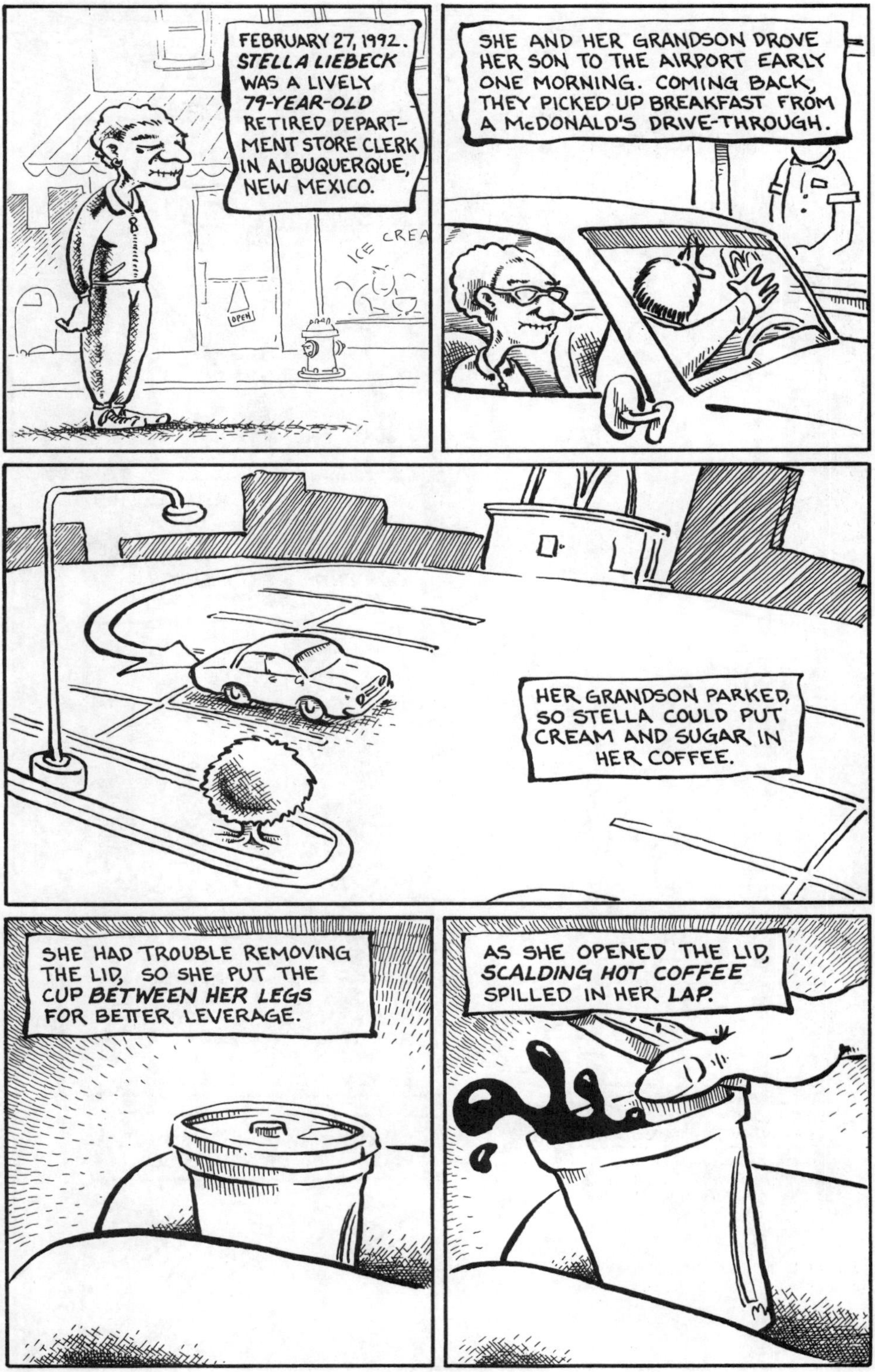
FEBRUARY 27, 1992. STELLA LIEBECK WAS A LIVELY 79-YEAR-OLD RETIRED DEPARTMENT STORE CLERK IN ALBUQUERQUE, NEW MEXICO.
ICE CREA
OPEN
SHE AND HER GRANDSON DROVE HER SON TO THE AIRPORT EARLY ONE MORNING. COMING BACK, THEY PICKED UP BREAKFAST FROM A McDONALD'S DRIVE-THROUGH.
HER GRANDSON PARKED, SO STELLA COULD PUT CREAM AND SUGAR IN HER COFFEE.
SHE HAD TROUBLE REMOVING THE LID, SO SHE PUT THE CUP BETWEEN HER LEGS FOR BETTER LEVERAGE.
AS SHE OPENED THE LID, SCALDING HOT COFFEE SPILLED IN HER LAP.

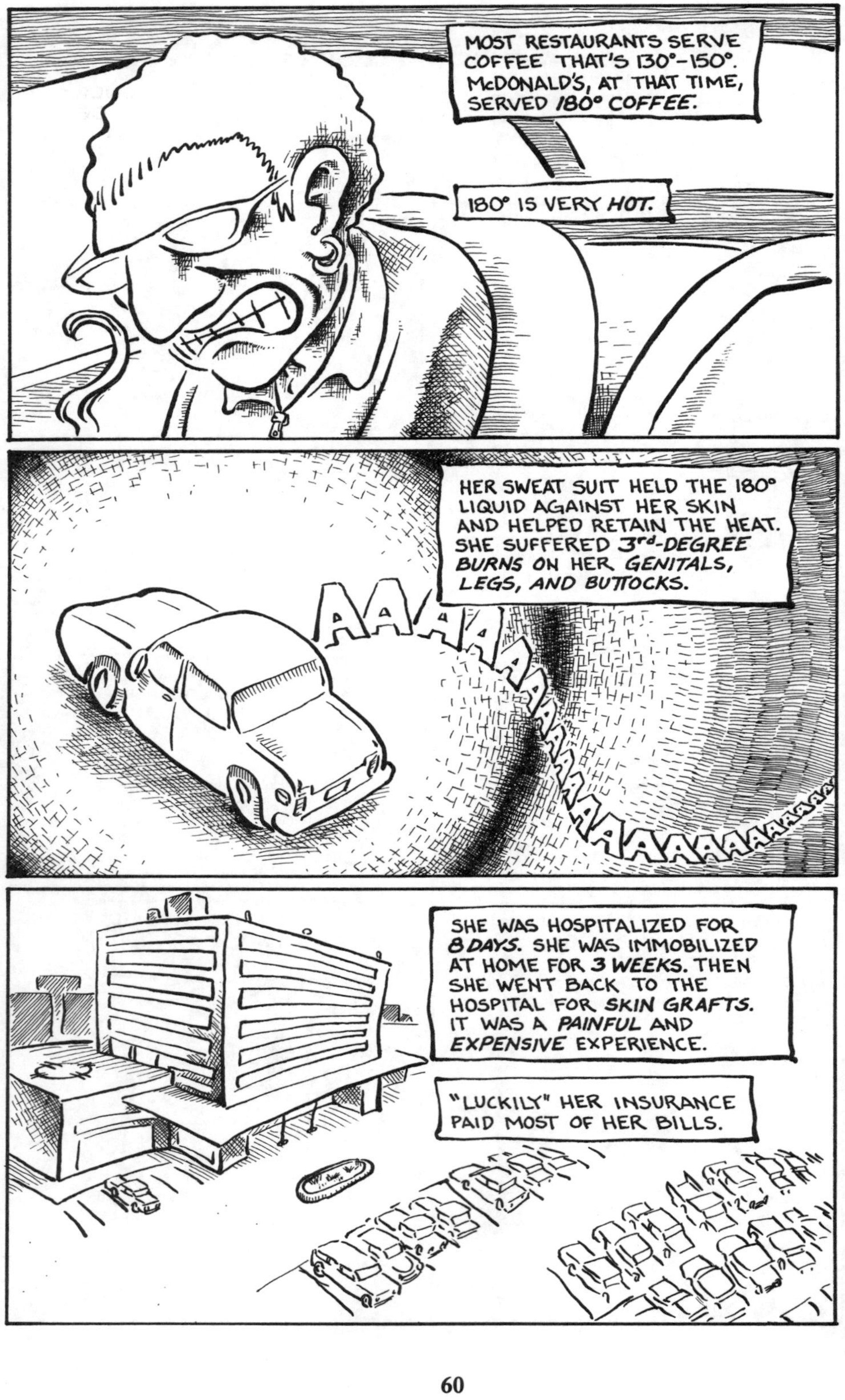
MOST RESTAURANTS SERVE COFFEE THAT'S 130°–150°. McDONALD'S, AT THAT TIME, SERVED 180° COFFEE.
180° IS VERY HOT.
HER SWEAT SUIT HELD THE 180° LIQUID AGAINST HER SKIN AND HELPED RETAIN THE HEAT. SHE SUFFERED 3rd-DEGREE BURNS ON HER GENITALS, LEGS, AND BUTTOCKS.
SHE WAS HOSPITALIZED FOR 8 DAYS. SHE WAS IMMOBILIZED AT HOME FOR 3 WEEKS. THEN SHE WENT BACK TO THE HOSPITAL FOR SKIN GRAFTS. IT WAS A PAINFUL AND EXPENSIVE EXPERIENCE.
"LUCKILY" HER INSURANCE PAID MOST OF HER BILLS.

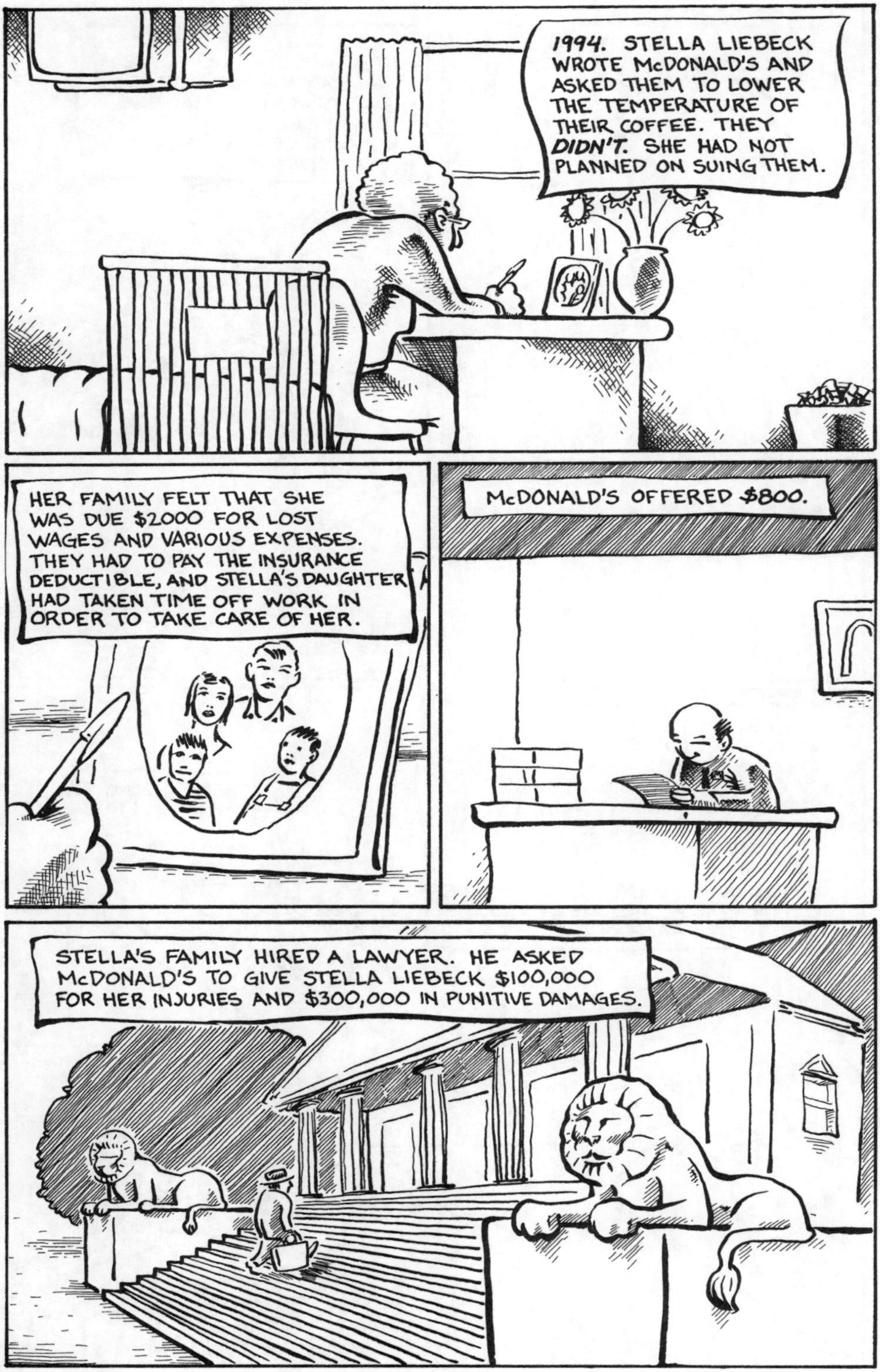
1994. STELLA LIEBECK WROTE McDONALD'S AND ASKED THEM TO LOWER THE TEMPERATURE OF THEIR COFFEE. THEY DIDN'T. SHE HAD NOT PLANNED ON SUING THEM.
HER FAMILY FELT THAT SHE WAS DUE $2000 FOR LOST WAGES AND VARIOUS EXPENSES. THEY HAD TO PAY THE INSURANCE DEDUCTIBLE, AND STELLA'S DAUGHTER HAD TAKEN TIME OFF WORK IN ORDER TO TAKE CARE OF HER.
McDONALD'S OFFERED $800.
STELLA'S FAMILY HIRED A LAWYER. HE ASKED McDONALD'S TO GIVE STELLA LIEBECK $100,000 FOR HER INJURIES AND $300,000 IN PUNITIVE DAMAGES.

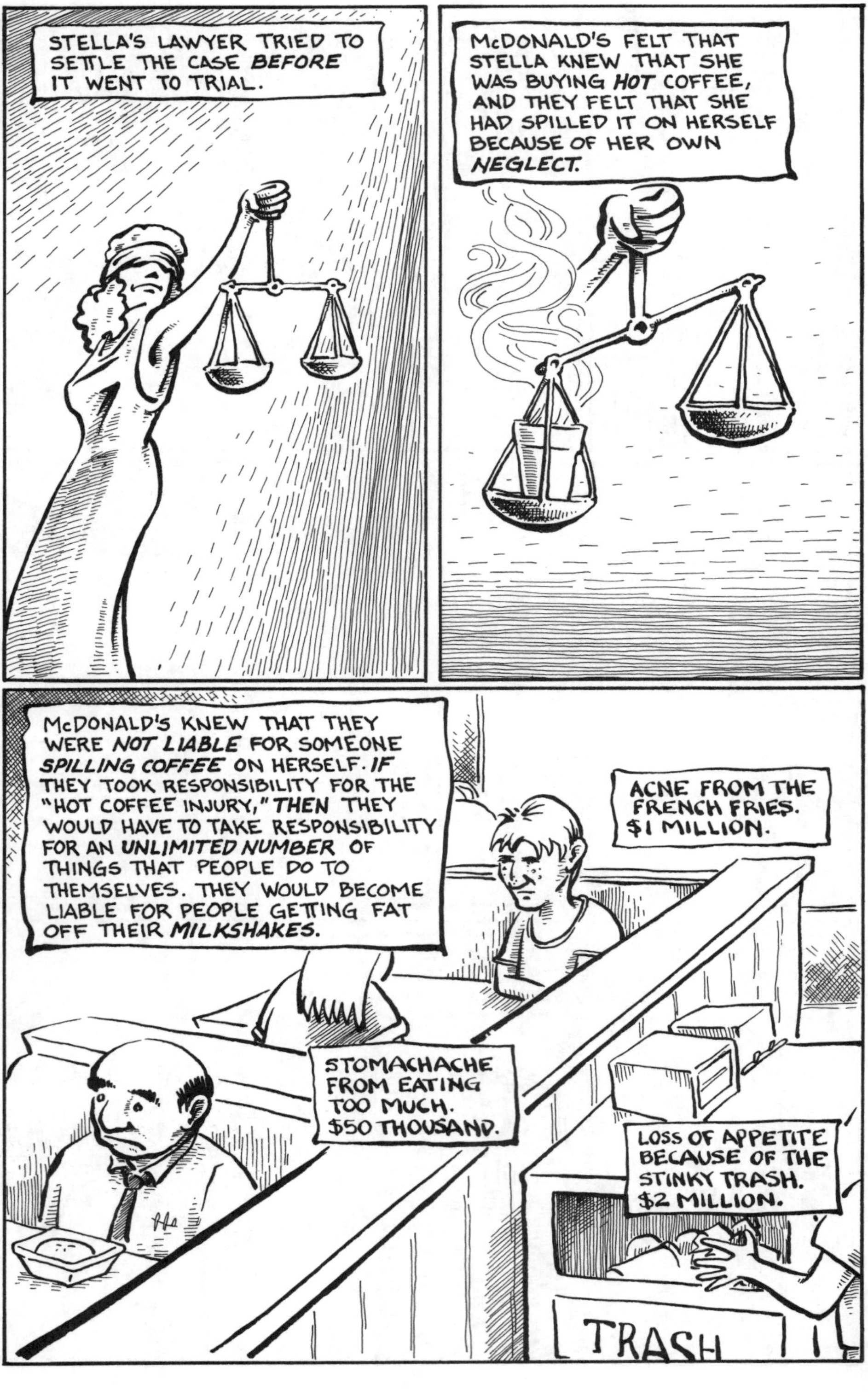
STELLA'S LAWYER TRIED TO SETTLE THE CASE BEFORE IT WENT TO TRIAL.
McDONALD'S FELT THAT STELLA KNEW THAT SHE WAS BUYING HOT COFFEE, AND THEY FELT THAT SHE HAD SPILLED IT ON HERSELF BECAUSE OF HER OWN NEGLECT.
McDONALD'S KNEW THAT THEY WERE NOT LIABLE FOR SOMEONE SPILLING COFFEE ON HERSELF. IF THEY TOOK RESPONSIBILITY FOR THE "HOT COFFEE INJURY," THEN THEY WOULD HAVE TO TAKE RESPONSIBILITY FOR AN UNLIMITED NUMBER OF THINGS THAT PEOPLE DO TO THEMSELVES. THEY WOULD BECOME LIABLE FOR PEOPLE GETTING FAT OFF THEIR MILKSHAKES.
ACNE FROM THE FRENCH FRIES. $1 MILLION.
STOMACHACHE FROM EATING TOO MUCH. $50 THOUSAND.
LOSS OF APPETITE BECAUSE OF THE STINKY TRASH. $2 MILLION.
TRASH

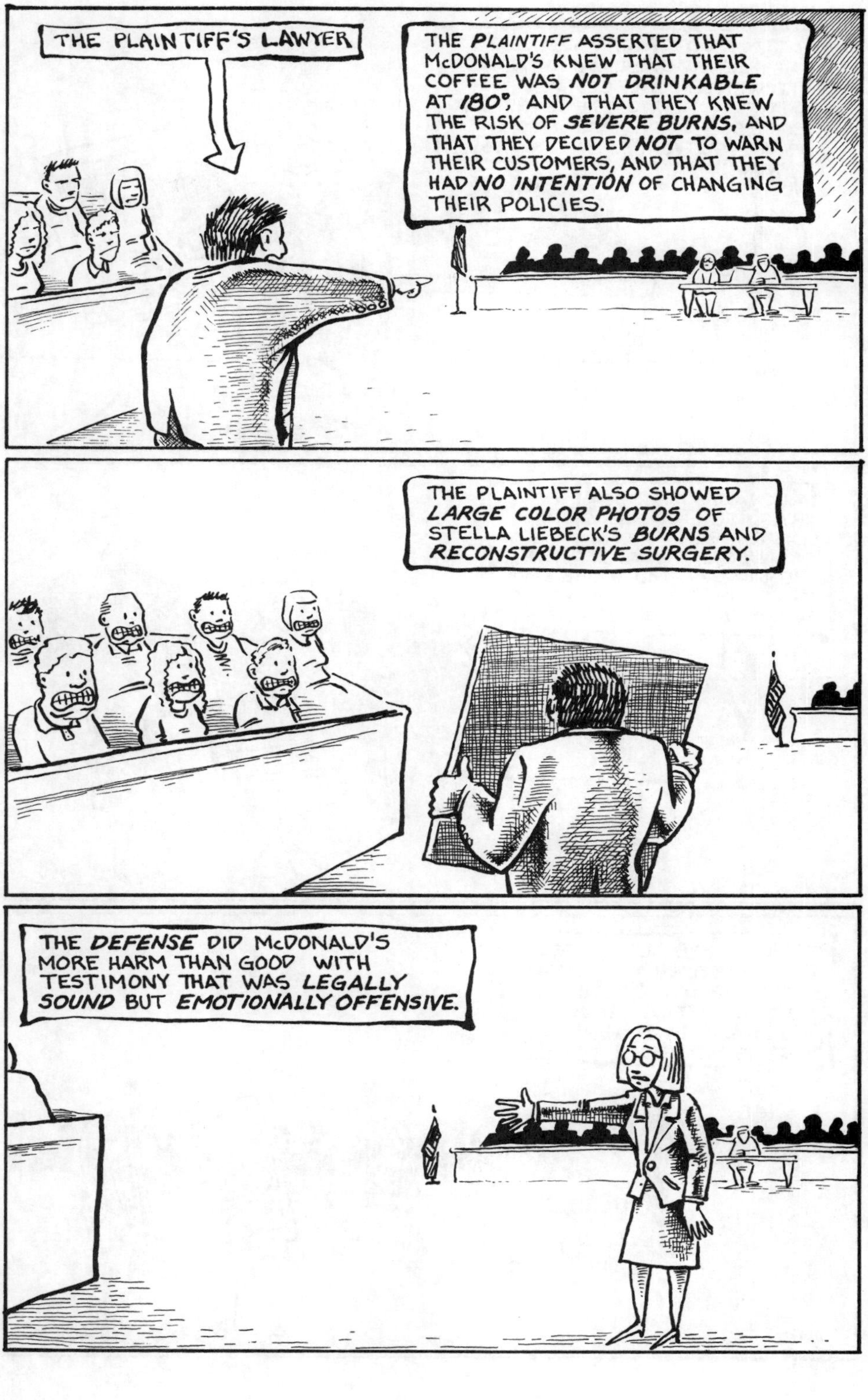
THE PLAINTIFF'S LAWYER
THE PLAINTIFF ASSERTED THAT McDONALD'S KNEW THAT THEIR COFFEE WAS NOT DRINKABLE AT 180°, AND THAT THEY KNEW THE RISK OF SEVERE BURNS, AND THAT THEY DECIDED NOT TO WARN THEIR CUSTOMERS, AND THAT THEY HAD NO INTENTION OF CHANGING THEIR POLICIES.
THE PLAINTIFF ALSO SHOWED LARGE COLOR PHOTOS OF STELLA LIEBECK'S BURNS AND RECONSTRUCTIVE SURGERY.
THE DEFENSE DID McDONALD'S MORE HARM THAN GOOD WITH TESTIMONY THAT WAS LEGALLY SOUND BUT EMOTIONALLY OFFENSIVE.

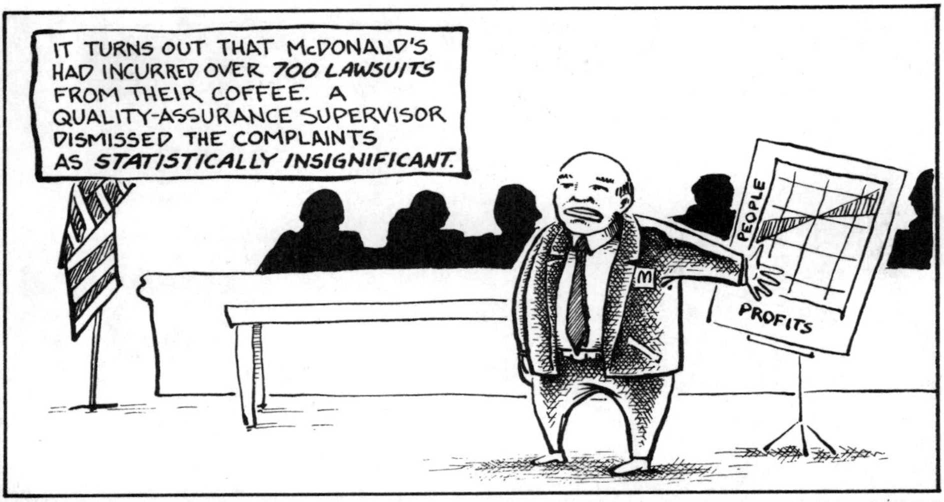
IT TURNS OUT THAT McDONALD'S HAD INCURRED OVER 700 LAWSUITS FROM THEIR COFFEE. A QUALITY-ASSURANCE SUPERVISOR DISMISSED THE COMPLAINTS AS STATISTICALLY INSIGNIFICANT.
PEOPLE
PROFITS

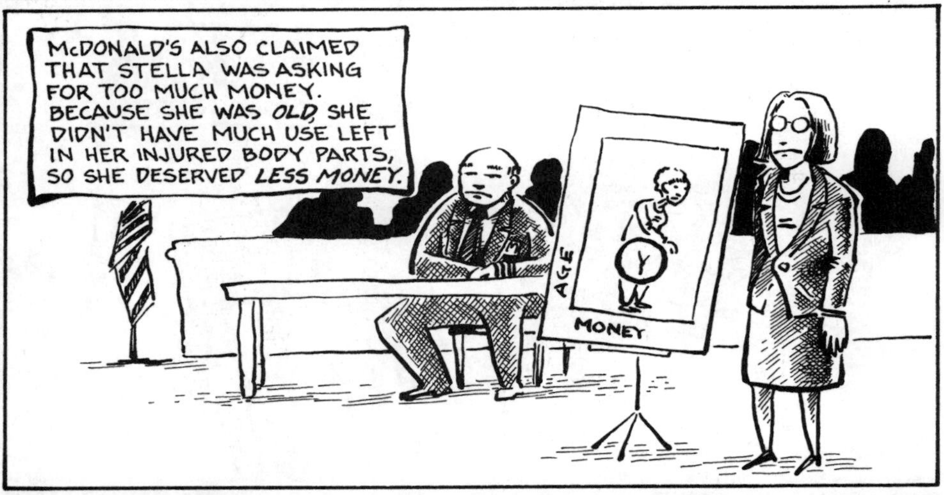
McDONALD'S ALSO CLAIMED THAT STELLA WAS ASKING FOR TOO MUCH MONEY. BECAUSE SHE WAS OLD, SHE DIDN'T HAVE MUCH USE LEFT IN HER INJURED BODY PARTS, SO SHE DESERVED LESS MONEY.
AGE
MONEY

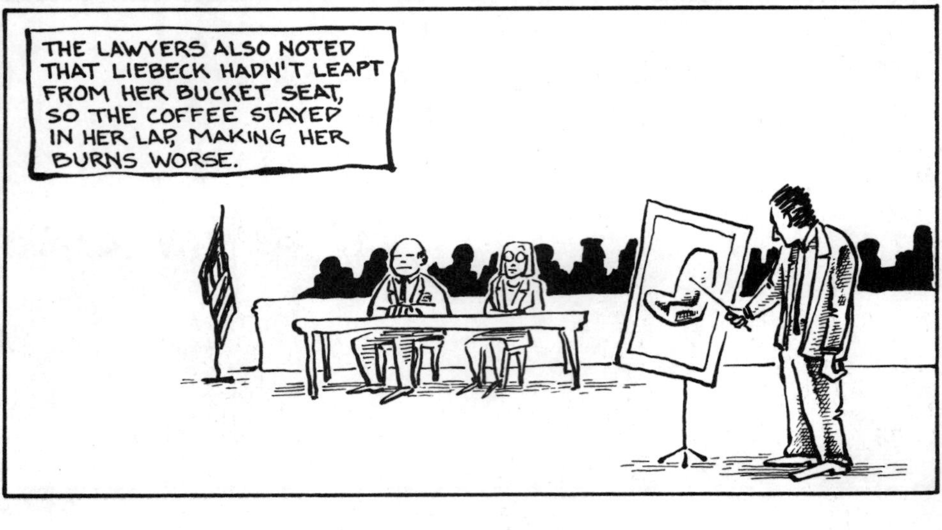
THE LAWYERS ALSO NOTED THAT LIEBECK HADN'T LEAPT FROM HER BUCKET SEAT, SO THE COFFEE STAYED IN HER LAP, MAKING HER BURNS WORSE.

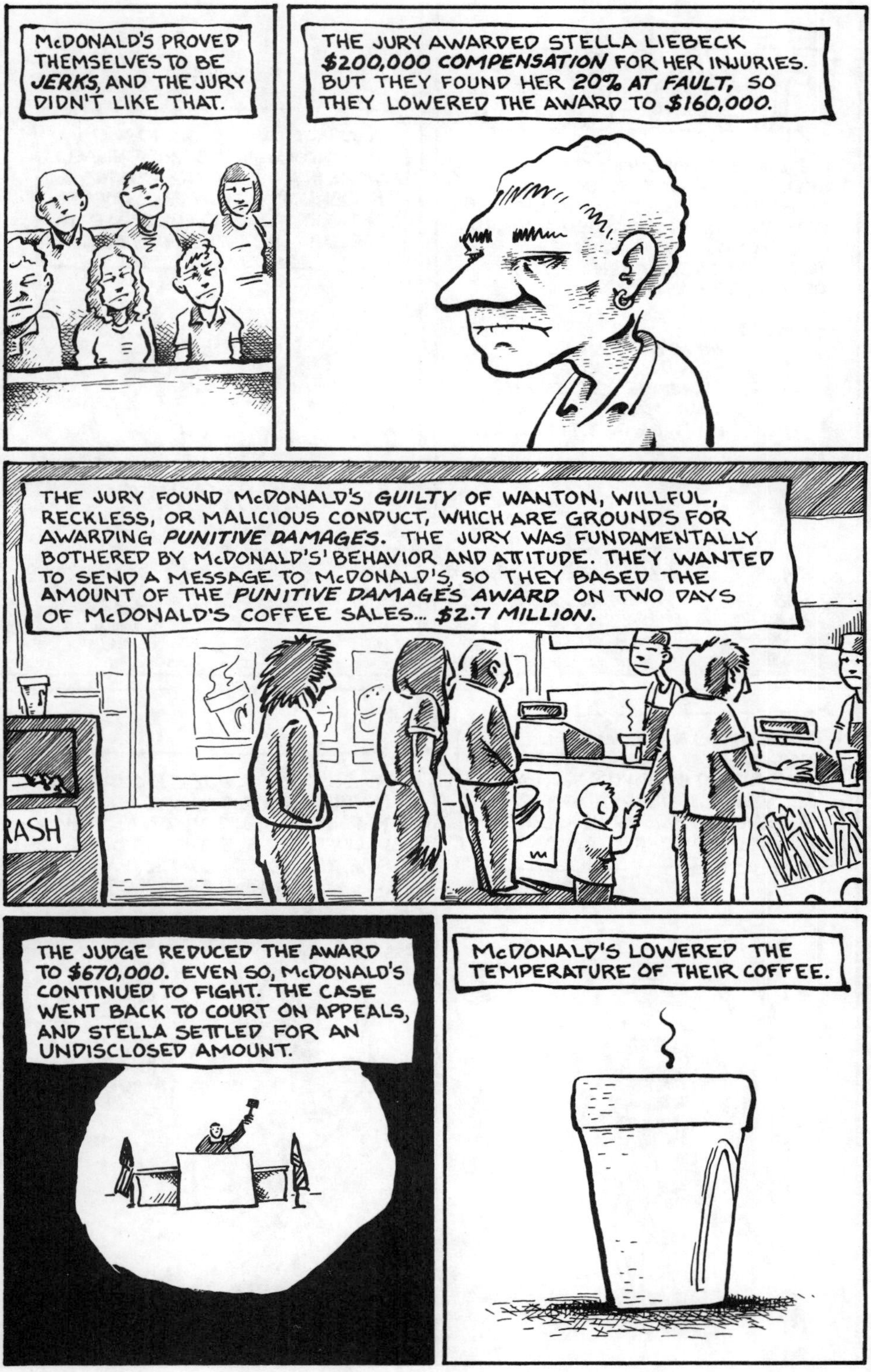
McDONALD'S PROVED THEMSELVES TO BE JERKS, AND THE JURY DIDN'T LIKE THAT.
THE JURY AWARDED STELLA LIEBECK $200,000 COMPENSATION FOR HER INJURIES. BUT THEY FOUND HER 20% AT FAULT, SO THEY LOWERED THE AWARD TO $160,000.
THE JURY FOUND McDONALD'S GUILTY OF WANTON, WILLFUL, RECKLESS, OR MALICIOUS CONDUCT, WHICH ARE GROUNDS FOR AWARDING PUNITIVE DAMAGES. THE JURY WAS FUNDAMENTALLY BOTHERED BY McDONALD'S' BEHAVIOR AND ATTITUDE. THEY WANTED TO SEND A MESSAGE TO McDONALD'S, SO THEY BASED THE AMOUNT OF THE PUNITIVE DAMAGES AWARD ON TWO DAYS OF McDONALD'S COFFEE SALES... $2.7 MILLION.
THE JUDGE REDUCED THE AWARD TO $670,000. EVEN SO, McDONALD'S CONTINUED TO FIGHT. THE CASE WENT BACK TO COURT ON APPEALS, AND STELLA SETTLED FOR AN UNDISCLOSED AMOUNT.
McDONALD'S LOWERED THE TEMPERATURE OF THEIR COFFEE.

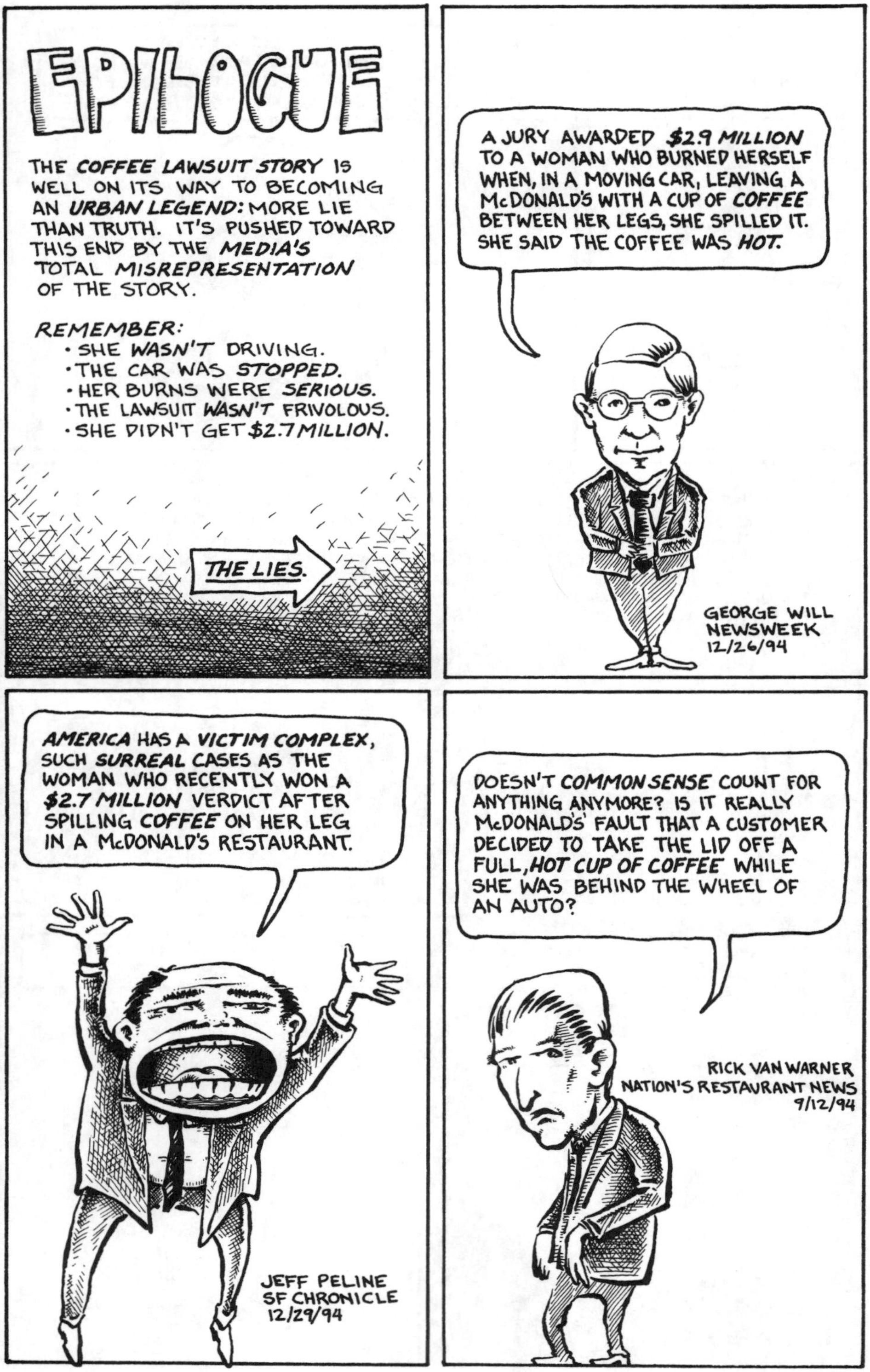
EPILOGUE
THE COFFEE LAWSUIT STORY IS WELL ON ITS WAY TO BECOMING AN URBAN LEGEND: MORE LIE THAN TRUTH. IT'S PUSHED TOWARD THIS END BY THE MEDIA'S TOTAL MISREPRESENTATION OF THE STORY.
REMEMBER:
• SHE WASN'T DRIVING.
• THE CAR WAS STOPPED.
• HER BURNS WERE SERIOUS.
• THE LAWSUIT WASN'T FRIVOLOUS.
• SHE DIDN'T GET $2.7 MILLION.
THE LIES.
A JURY AWARDED $2.9 MILLION TO A WOMAN WHO BURNED HERSELF WHEN, IN A MOVING CAR, LEAVING A McDONALD'S WITH A CUP OF COFFEE BETWEEN HER LEGS, SHE SPILLED IT. SHE SAID THE COFFEE WAS HOT.
GEORGE WILL NEWSWEEK 12/26/94
AMERICA HAS A VICTIM COMPLEX, SUCH SURREAL CASES AS THE WOMAN WHO RECENTLY WON A $2.7 MILLION VERDICT AFTER SPILLING COFFEE ON HER LEG IN A McDONALD'S RESTAURANT.
JEFF PELINE SF CHRONICLE 12/29/94
DOESN'T COMMON SENSE COUNT FOR ANYTHING ANYMORE? IS IT REALLY McDONALDS' FAULT THAT A CUSTOMER DECIDED TO TAKE THE LID OFF A FULL, HOT CUP OF COFFEE WHILE SHE WAS BEHIND THE WHEEL OF AN AUTO?
RICK VAN WARNER NATION'S RESTAURANT NEWS 9/12/94

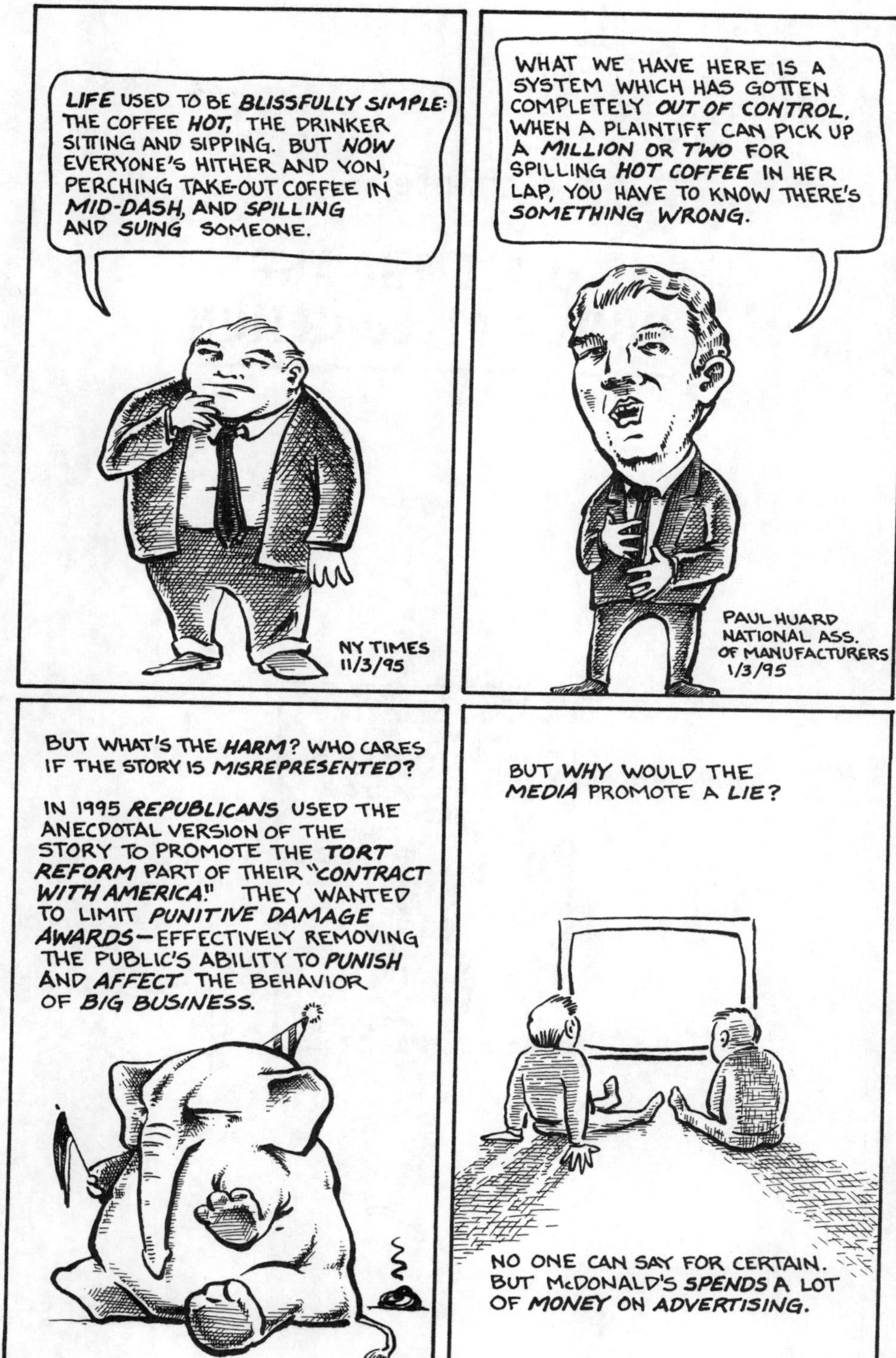
LIFE USED TO BE BLISSFULLY SIMPLE: THE COFFEE HOT, THE DRINKER SITTING AND SIPPING. BUT NOW EVERYONE'S HITHER AND YON, PERCHING TAKE-OUT COFFEE IN MID-DASH, AND SPILLING AND SUING SOMEONE.
NY TIMES 11/3/95
WHAT WE HAVE HERE IS A SYSTEM WHICH HAS GOTTEN COMPLETELY OUT OF CONTROL. WHEN A PLAINTIFF CAN PICK UP A MILLION OR TWO FOR SPILLING HOT COFFEE IN HER LAP, YOU HAVE TO KNOW THERE'S SOMETHING WRONG.
PAUL HUARD NATIONAL ASS. OF MANUFACTURERS 1/3/95
BUT WHAT'S THE HARM? WHO CARES IF THE STORY IS MISREPRESENTED?
IN 1995 REPUBLICANS USED THE ANECDOTAL VERSION OF THE STORY TO PROMOTE THE TORT REFORM PART OF THEIR "CONTRACT WITH AMERICA." THEY WANTED TO LIMIT PUNITIVE DAMAGE AWARDS—EFFECTIVELY REMOVING THE PUBLIC'S ABILITY TO PUNISH AND AFFECT THE BEHAVIOR OF BIG BUSINESS.
BUT WHY WOULD THE MEDIA PROMOTE A LIE?
NO ONE CAN SAY FOR CERTAIN. BUT McDONALD'S SPENDS A LOT OF MONEY ON ADVERTISING.
END.

chapter 5

COFFEE AND THE HUMOR OF ADDICTION

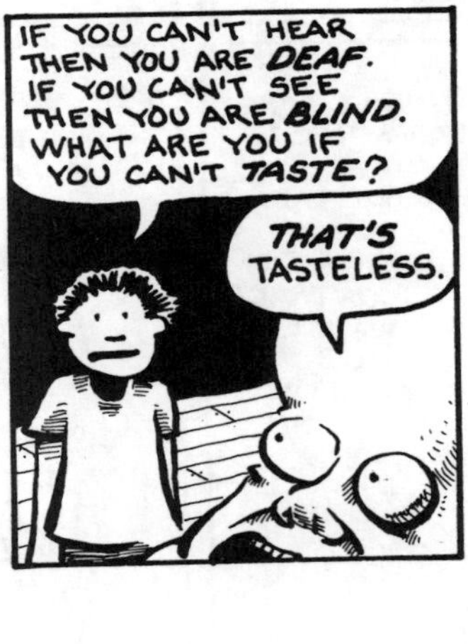
IF YOU CAN'T HEAR THEN YOU ARE DEAF. IF YOU CAN'T SEE THEN YOU ARE BLIND. WHAT ARE YOU IF YOU CAN'T TASTE?
THAT'S TASTELESS.

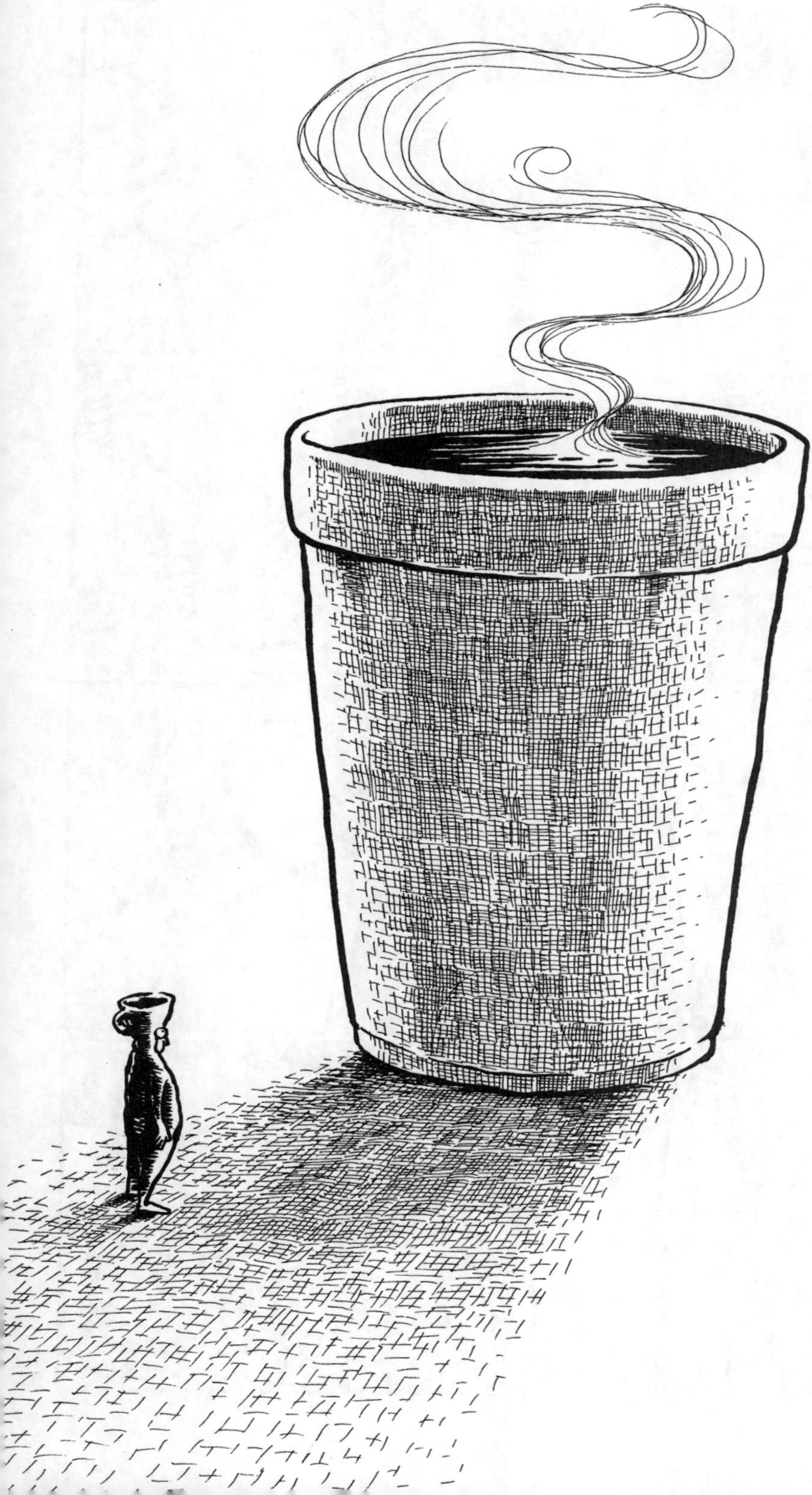

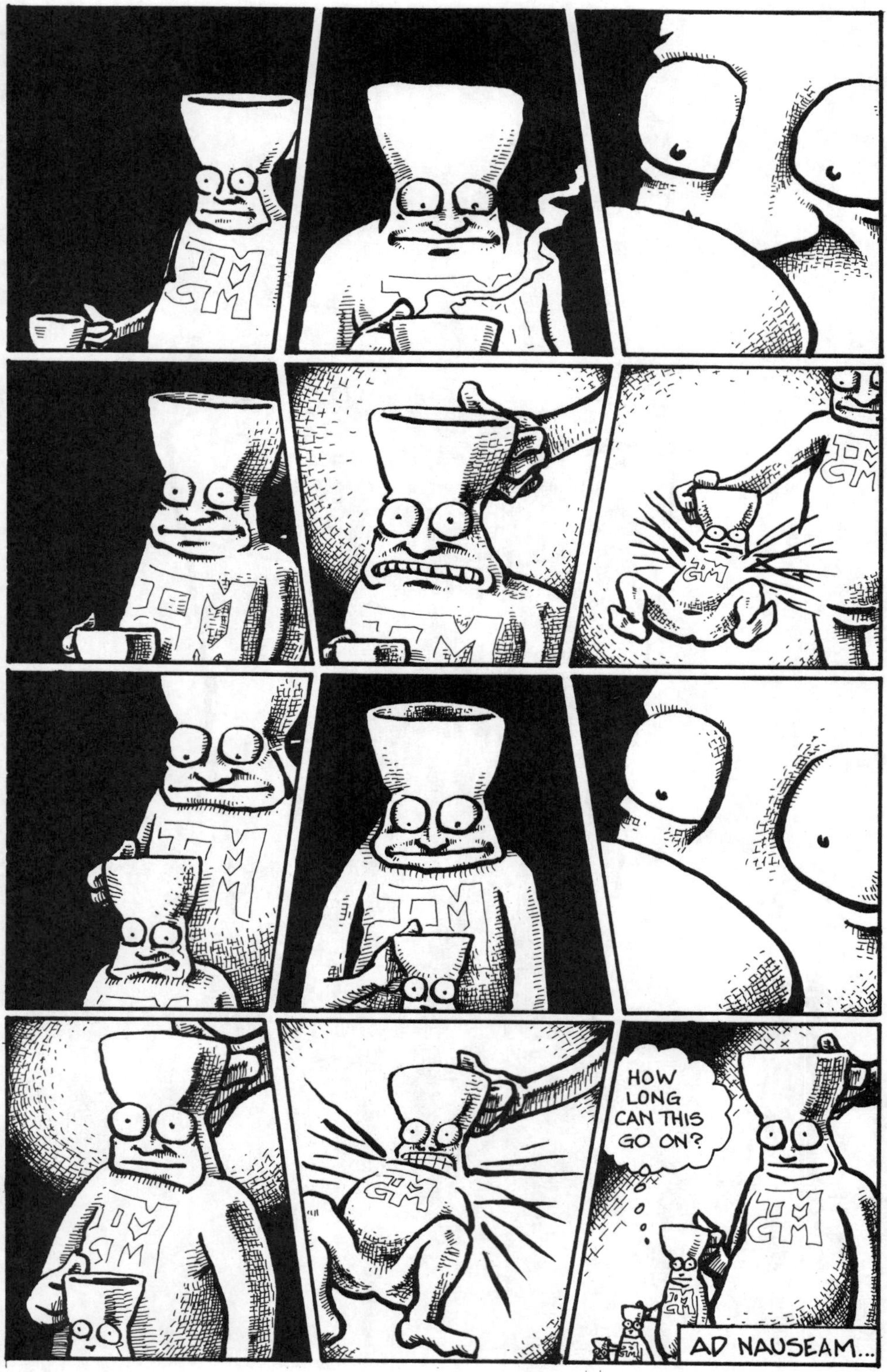
HOW LONG CAN THIS GO ON?
AD NAUSEAM...

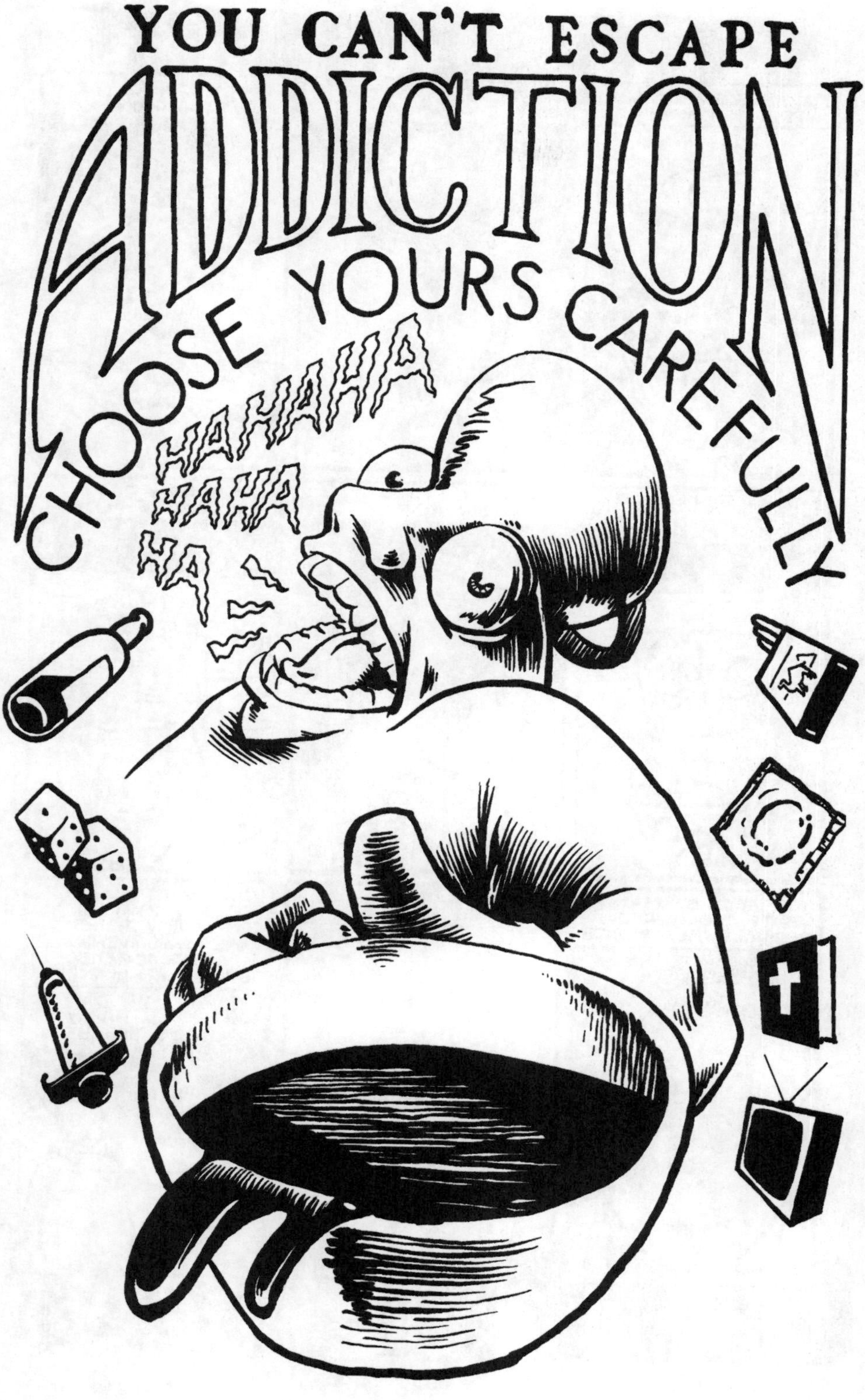
YOU CAN'T ESCAPE
ADDICTION
CHOOSE YOURS CAREFULLY
HAHAHAHA
HAHA
HA

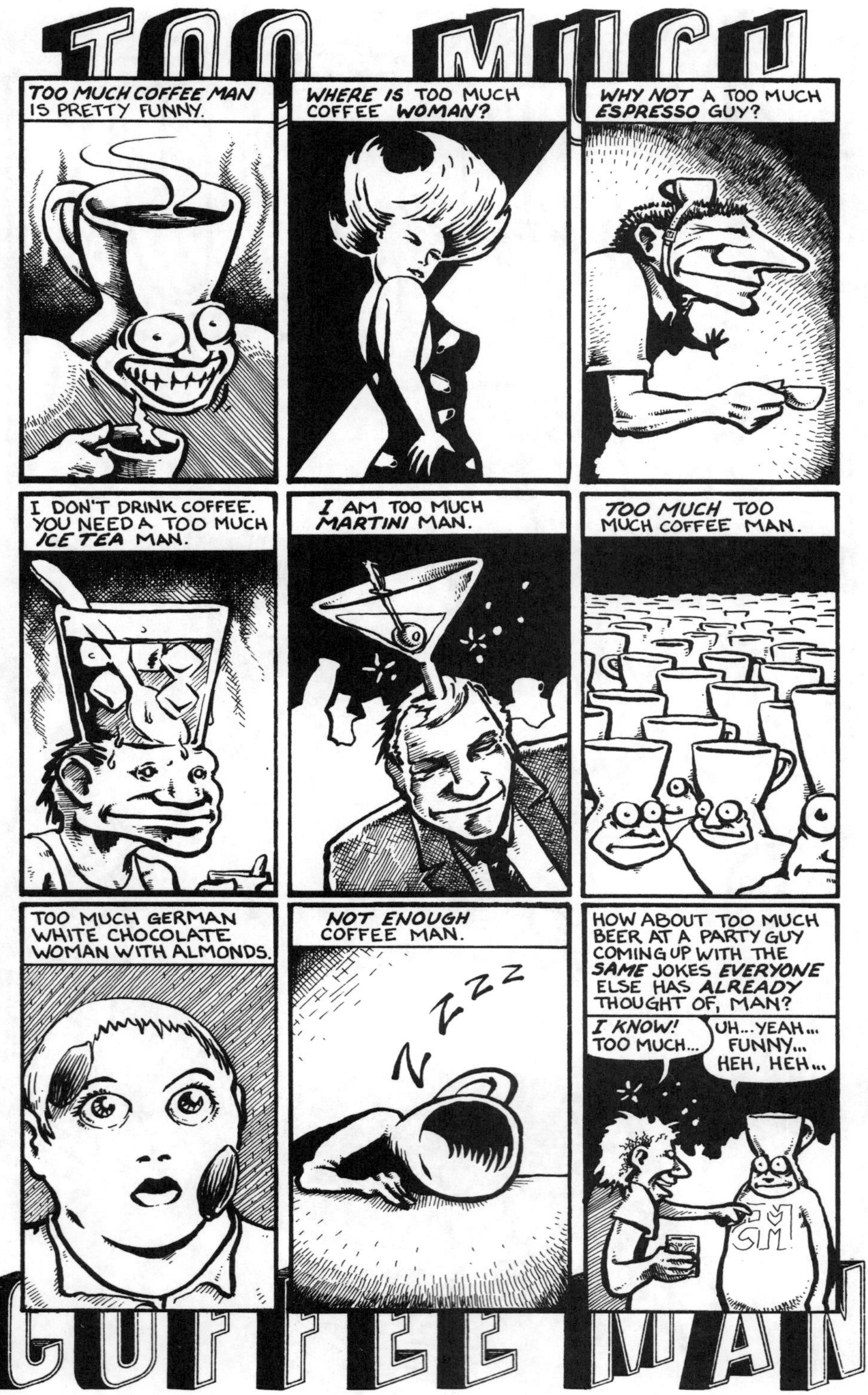
TOO MUCH
TOO MUCH COFFEE MAN IS PRETTY FUNNY.
WHERE IS TOO MUCH COFFEE WOMAN?
WHY NOT A TOO MUCH ESPRESSO GUY?
I DON'T DRINK COFFEE. YOU NEED A TOO MUCH ICE TEA MAN.
I AM TOO MUCH MARTINI MAN.
TOO MUCH TOO MUCH COFFEE MAN.
TOO MUCH GERMAN WHITE CHOCOLATE WOMAN WITH ALMONDS.
NOT ENOUGH COFFEE MAN.
N Z Z Z
HOW ABOUT TOO MUCH BEER AT A PARTY GUY COMING UP WITH THE SAME JOKES EVERYONE ELSE HAS ALREADY THOUGHT OF, MAN?
I KNOW! TOO MUCH...
UH...YEAH... FUNNY... HEH, HEH...
TCM
COFFEE MAN

TOO MUCH COFFEE MAN'S ADVENTURE THEATRE

The hunter sits and waits, knowing that patience is his greatest ally. He also knows that his greatest trial lies ahead and that he can't wait forever.

He moves, slowly, from room to room, careful not to make any noise.

The phone rings.

RING.

It rings again.

RING.

It rings no more.

Again he crawls forward. Every muscle tense.

Suddenly, he leaps. Will this be his last leap? Perhaps he'll be wounded, crippled, never to leap again--forced to live leapless.

He wrestles the beans from the freezer. They're cold to his touch and hard to handle.

Many beans spill on the floor, but equal numbers are coerced into the grinder.

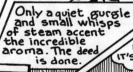

The grinder cuts, hums, buzzes, churns, and cuts the beans into a fine grind.

Orchestrating the beans, water, and filter into the coffee maker is no easy task.

Only a quiet gurgle and small whisps of steam accent the incredible aroma. The deed is done.

DAMN. IT'S DECAF.

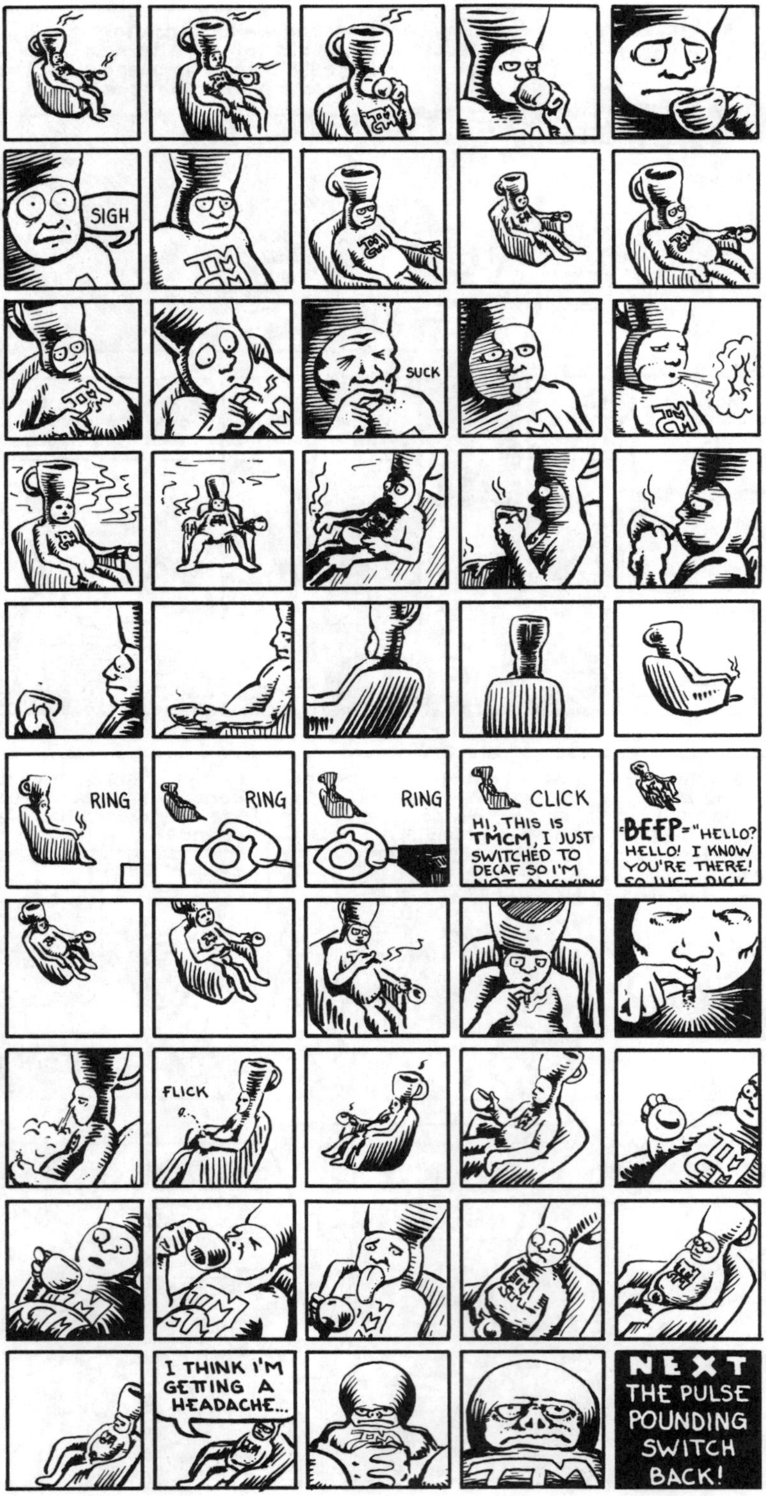
SIGH
SUCK
RING
RING
RING
CLICK
HI, THIS IS TMCM, I JUST SWITCHED TO DECAF SO I'M
BEEP
"HELLO? HELLO! I KNOW YOU'RE THERE!
FLICK
I THINK I'M GETTING A HEADACHE...
NEXT
THE PULSE POUNDING SWITCH BACK!

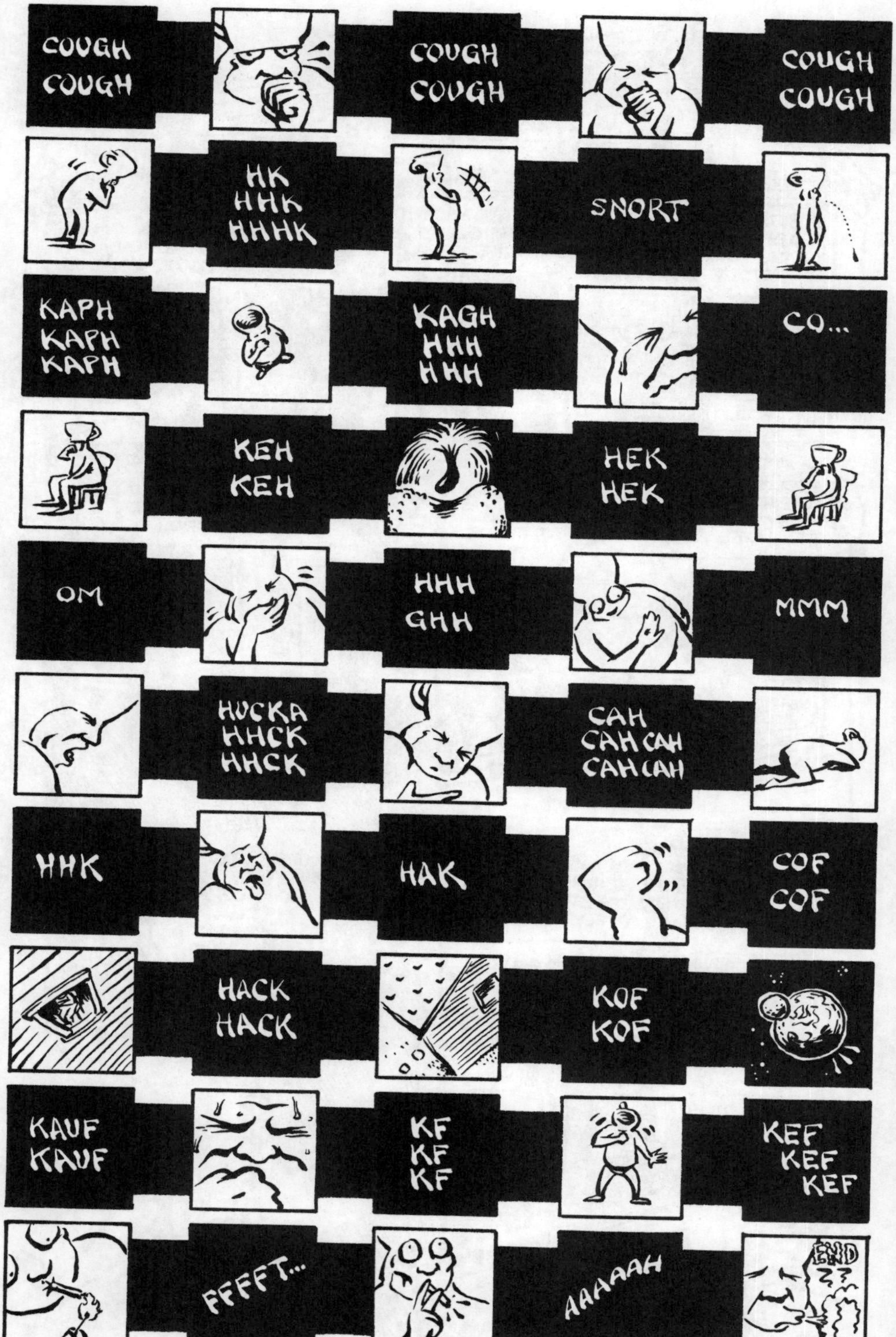
COUGH COUGH
COUGH COUGH
COUGH COUGH
HK HHK HHHK
SNORT
KAPH KAPH KAPH
KAGH HHH HHH
CO...
KEH KEH
HEK HEK
OM
HHH GHH
MMM
HUCKA HHCK HHCK
CAH CAH CAH CAH CAH
HHK
HAK
COF COF
HACK HACK
KOF KOF
KAUF KAUF
KF KF KF
KEF KEF KEF
FFFFT...
AAAAAH
END ??

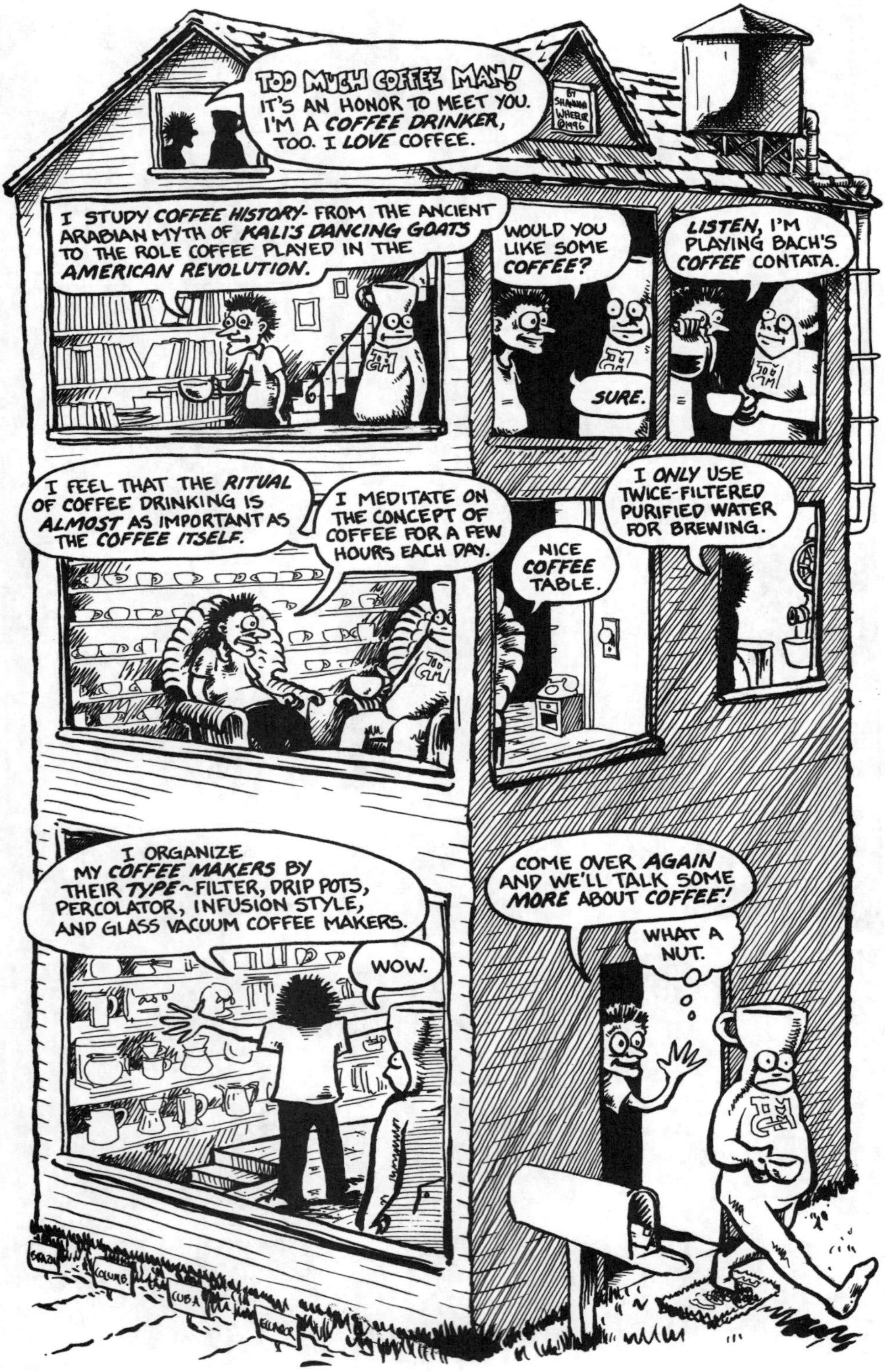

TOO MUCH COFFEE MAN! IT'S AN HONOR TO MEET YOU. I'M A COFFEE DRINKER, TOO. I LOVE COFFEE.
BY SHANNA WHEELER ©1996
I STUDY COFFEE HISTORY- FROM THE ANCIENT ARABIAN MYTH OF KALI'S DANCING GOATS TO THE ROLE COFFEE PLAYED IN THE AMERICAN REVOLUTION.
WOULD YOU LIKE SOME COFFEE?
SURE.
LISTEN, I'M PLAYING BACH'S COFFEE CONTATA.
I FEEL THAT THE RITUAL OF COFFEE DRINKING IS ALMOST AS IMPORTANT AS THE COFFEE ITSELF.
I MEDITATE ON THE CONCEPT OF COFFEE FOR A FEW HOURS EACH DAY.
NICE COFFEE TABLE.
I ONLY USE TWICE-FILTERED PURIFIED WATER FOR BREWING.
I ORGANIZE MY COFFEE MAKERS BY THEIR TYPE~FILTER, DRIP POTS, PERCOLATOR, INFUSION STYLE, AND GLASS VACUUM COFFEE MAKERS.
WOW.
COME OVER AGAIN AND WE'LL TALK SOME MORE ABOUT COFFEE!
WHAT A NUT.

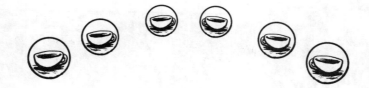

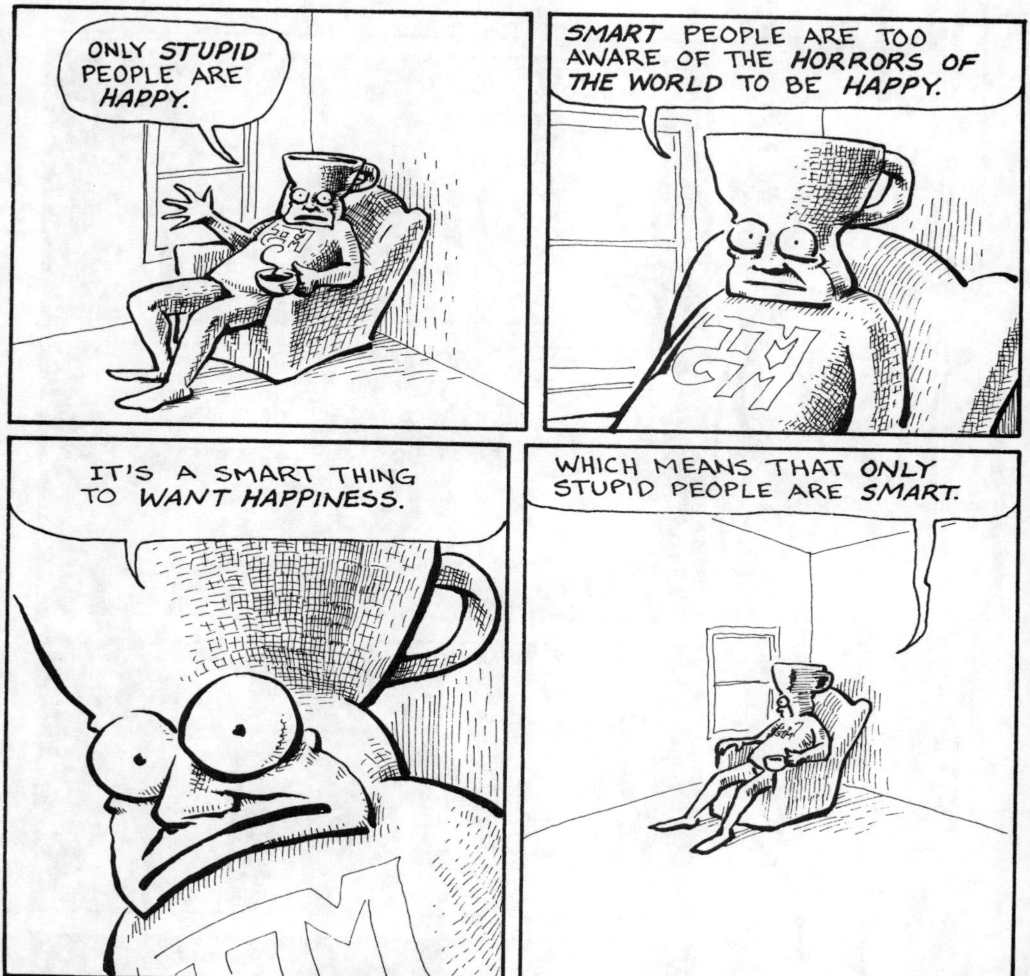
ONLY STUPID PEOPLE ARE HAPPY.
SMART PEOPLE ARE TOO AWARE OF THE HORRORS OF THE WORLD TO BE HAPPY.
IT'S A SMART THING TO WANT HAPPINESS.
WHICH MEANS THAT ONLY STUPID PEOPLE ARE SMART.

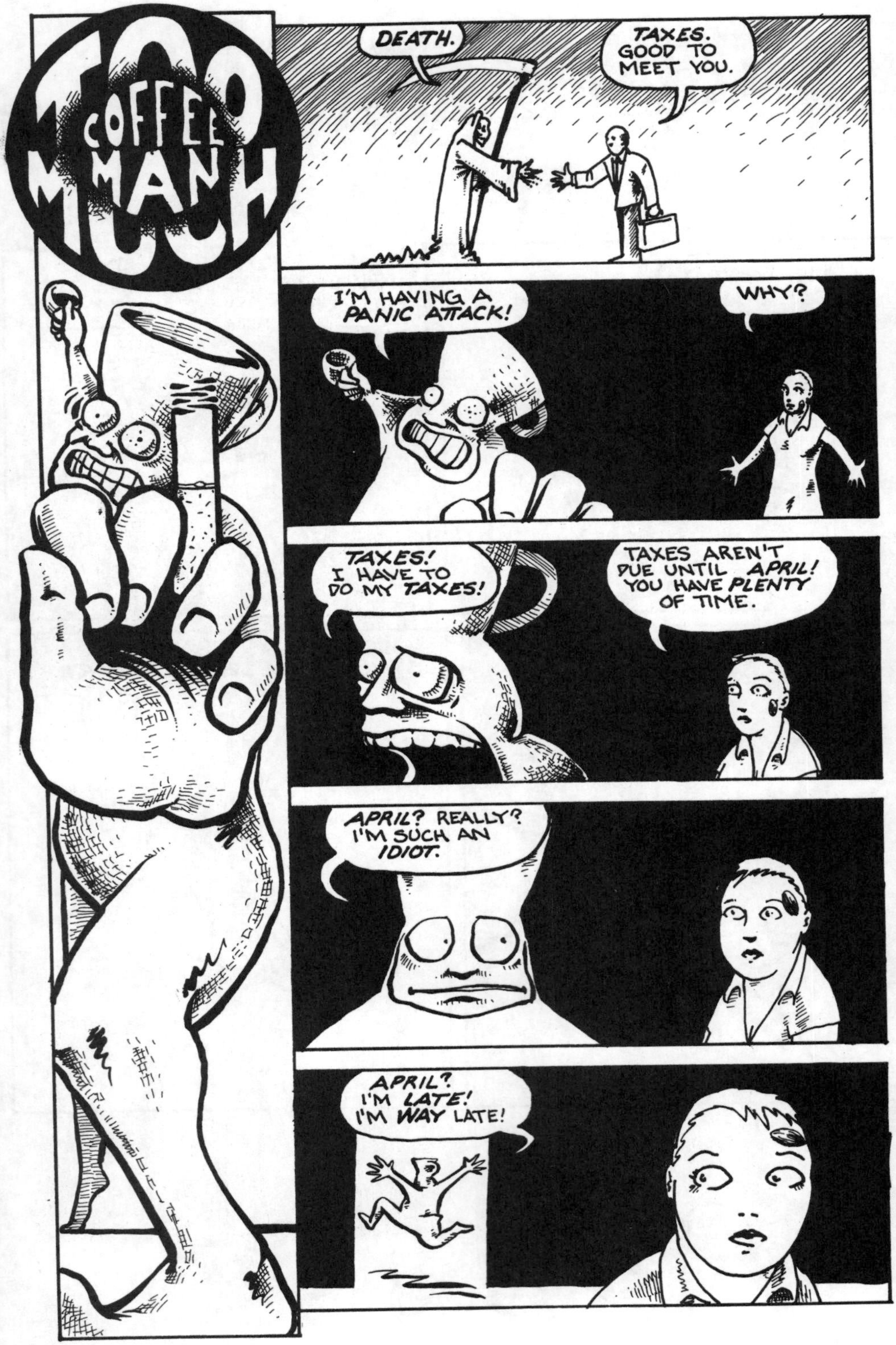
TOO MUCH COFFEE MAN
DEATH.
TAXES. GOOD TO MEET YOU.
I'M HAVING A PANIC ATTACK!
WHY?
TAXES! I HAVE TO DO MY TAXES!
TAXES AREN'T DUE UNTIL APRIL! YOU HAVE PLENTY OF TIME.
APRIL? REALLY? I'M SUCH AN IDIOT.
APRIL? I'M LATE! I'M WAY LATE!

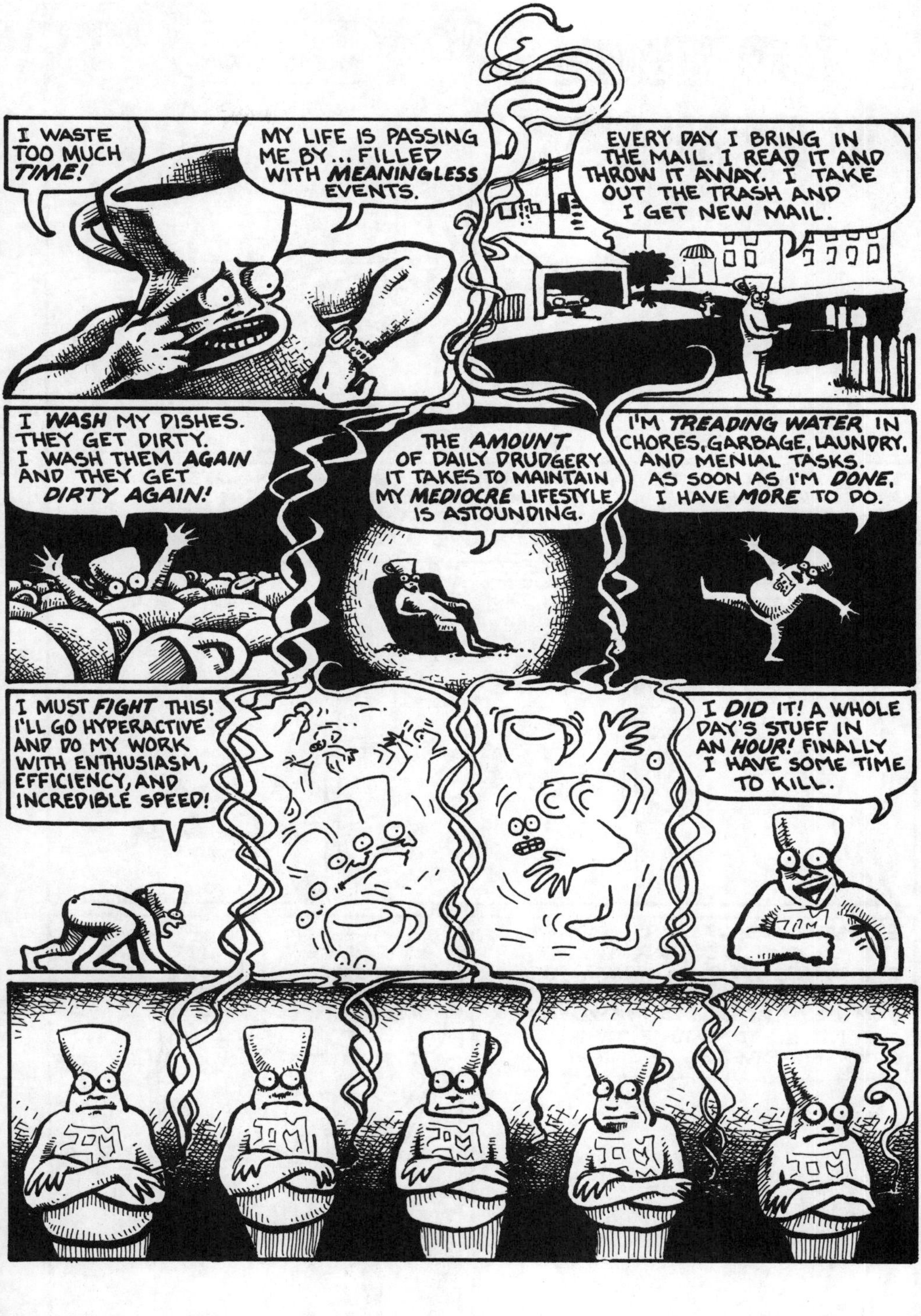
I WASTE TOO MUCH TIME!
MY LIFE IS PASSING ME BY... FILLED WITH MEANINGLESS EVENTS.
EVERY DAY I BRING IN THE MAIL. I READ IT AND THROW IT AWAY. I TAKE OUT THE TRASH AND I GET NEW MAIL.
I WASH MY DISHES. THEY GET DIRTY. I WASH THEM AGAIN AND THEY GET DIRTY AGAIN!
THE AMOUNT OF DAILY DRUDGERY IT TAKES TO MAINTAIN MY MEDIOCRE LIFESTYLE IS ASTOUNDING.
I'M TREADING WATER IN CHORES, GARBAGE, LAUNDRY, AND MENIAL TASKS. AS SOON AS I'M DONE, I HAVE MORE TO DO.
I MUST FIGHT THIS! I'LL GO HYPERACTIVE AND DO MY WORK WITH ENTHUSIASM, EFFICIENCY, AND INCREDIBLE SPEED!
I DID IT! A WHOLE DAY'S STUFF IN AN HOUR! FINALLY I HAVE SOME TIME TO KILL.

TOO MUCH COFFEE MAN

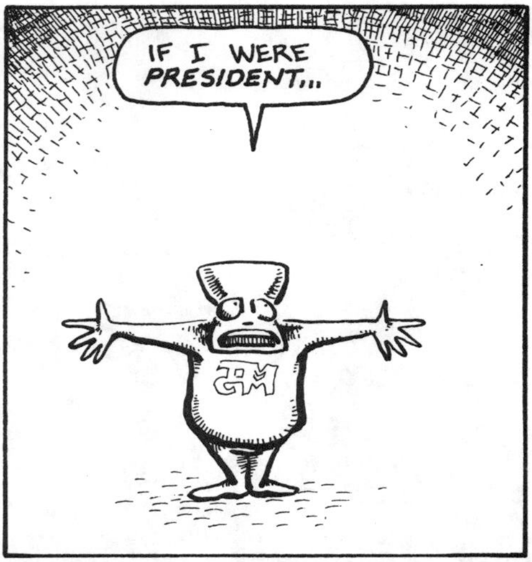
IF I WERE PRESIDENT...

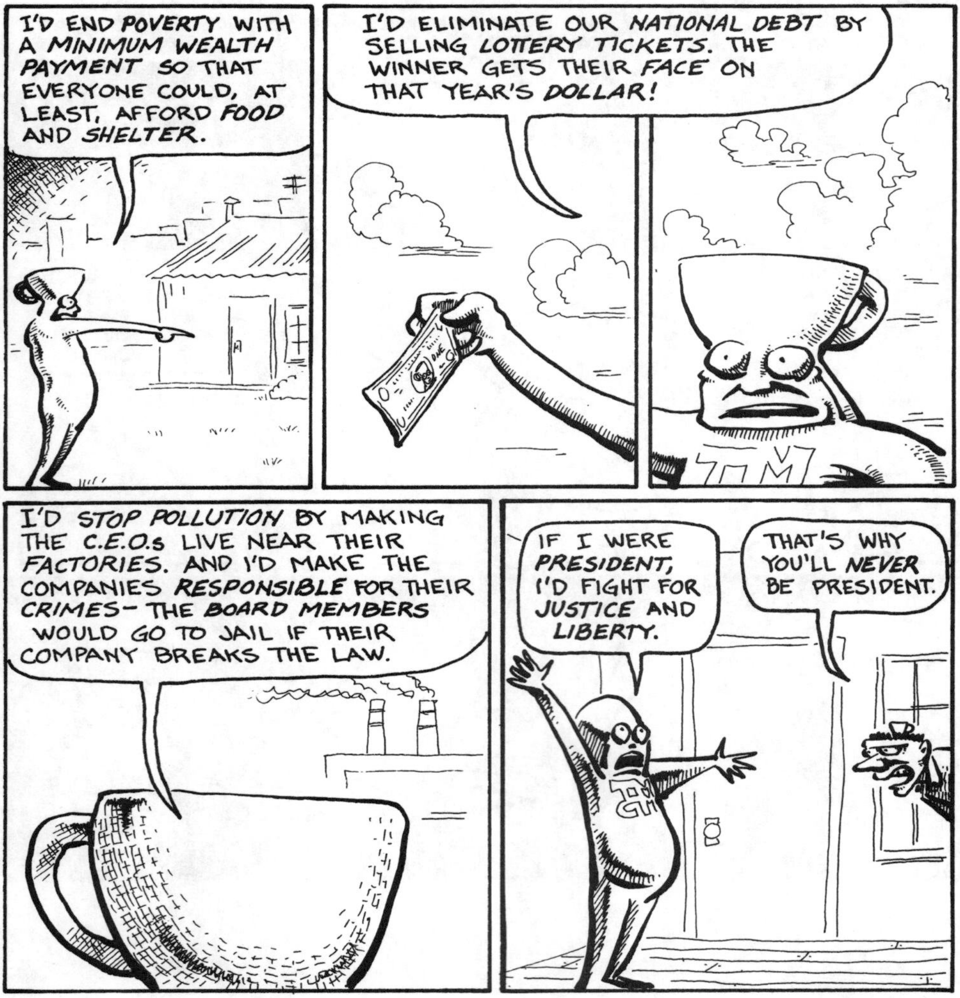
I'D END *POVERTY* WITH A *MINIMUM WEALTH PAYMENT* SO THAT EVERYONE COULD, AT LEAST, AFFORD *FOOD* AND *SHELTER*.
I'D ELIMINATE OUR *NATIONAL DEBT* BY SELLING *LOTTERY TICKETS*. THE WINNER GETS THEIR *FACE* ON THAT YEAR'S *DOLLAR*!
TCM
I'D *STOP POLLUTION* BY MAKING THE C.E.O.s LIVE NEAR THEIR *FACTORIES*. AND I'D MAKE THE COMPANIES *RESPONSIBLE* FOR THEIR *CRIMES*– THE *BOARD MEMBERS* WOULD GO TO JAIL IF THEIR COMPANY BREAKS THE LAW.
IF I WERE *PRESIDENT*, I'D FIGHT FOR *JUSTICE* AND *LIBERTY*.
THAT'S WHY YOU'LL *NEVER* BE PRESIDENT.

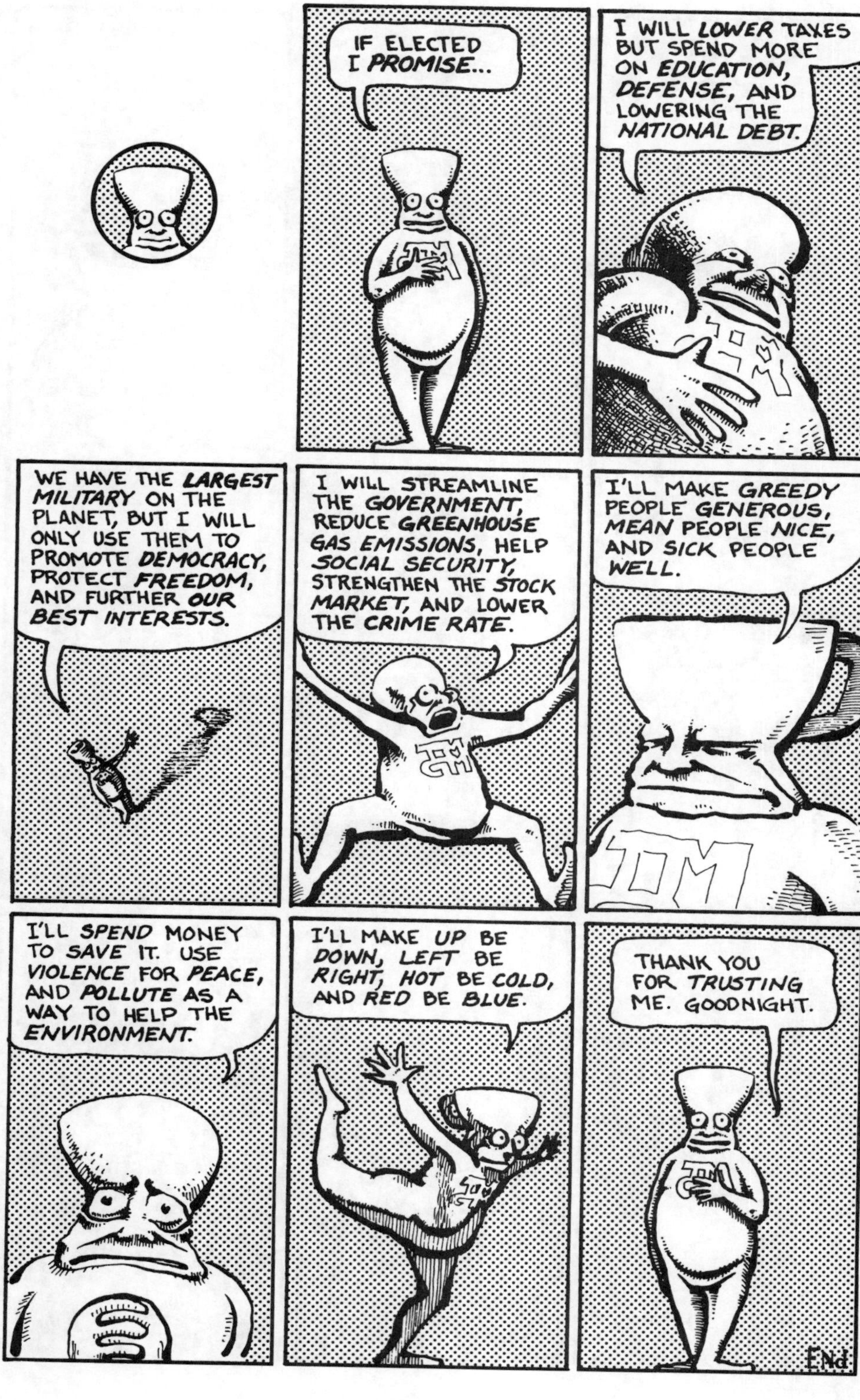
IF ELECTED I PROMISE...
I WILL LOWER TAXES BUT SPEND MORE ON EDUCATION, DEFENSE, AND LOWERING THE NATIONAL DEBT.
WE HAVE THE LARGEST MILITARY ON THE PLANET, BUT I WILL ONLY USE THEM TO PROMOTE DEMOCRACY, PROTECT FREEDOM, AND FURTHER OUR BEST INTERESTS.
I WILL STREAMLINE THE GOVERNMENT, REDUCE GREENHOUSE GAS EMISSIONS, HELP SOCIAL SECURITY, STRENGTHEN THE STOCK MARKET, AND LOWER THE CRIME RATE.
I'LL MAKE GREEDY PEOPLE GENEROUS, MEAN PEOPLE NICE, AND SICK PEOPLE WELL.
I'LL SPEND MONEY TO SAVE IT. USE VIOLENCE FOR PEACE, AND POLLUTE AS A WAY TO HELP THE ENVIRONMENT.
I'LL MAKE UP BE DOWN, LEFT BE RIGHT, HOT BE COLD, AND RED BE BLUE.
THANK YOU FOR TRUSTING ME. GOODNIGHT.
END

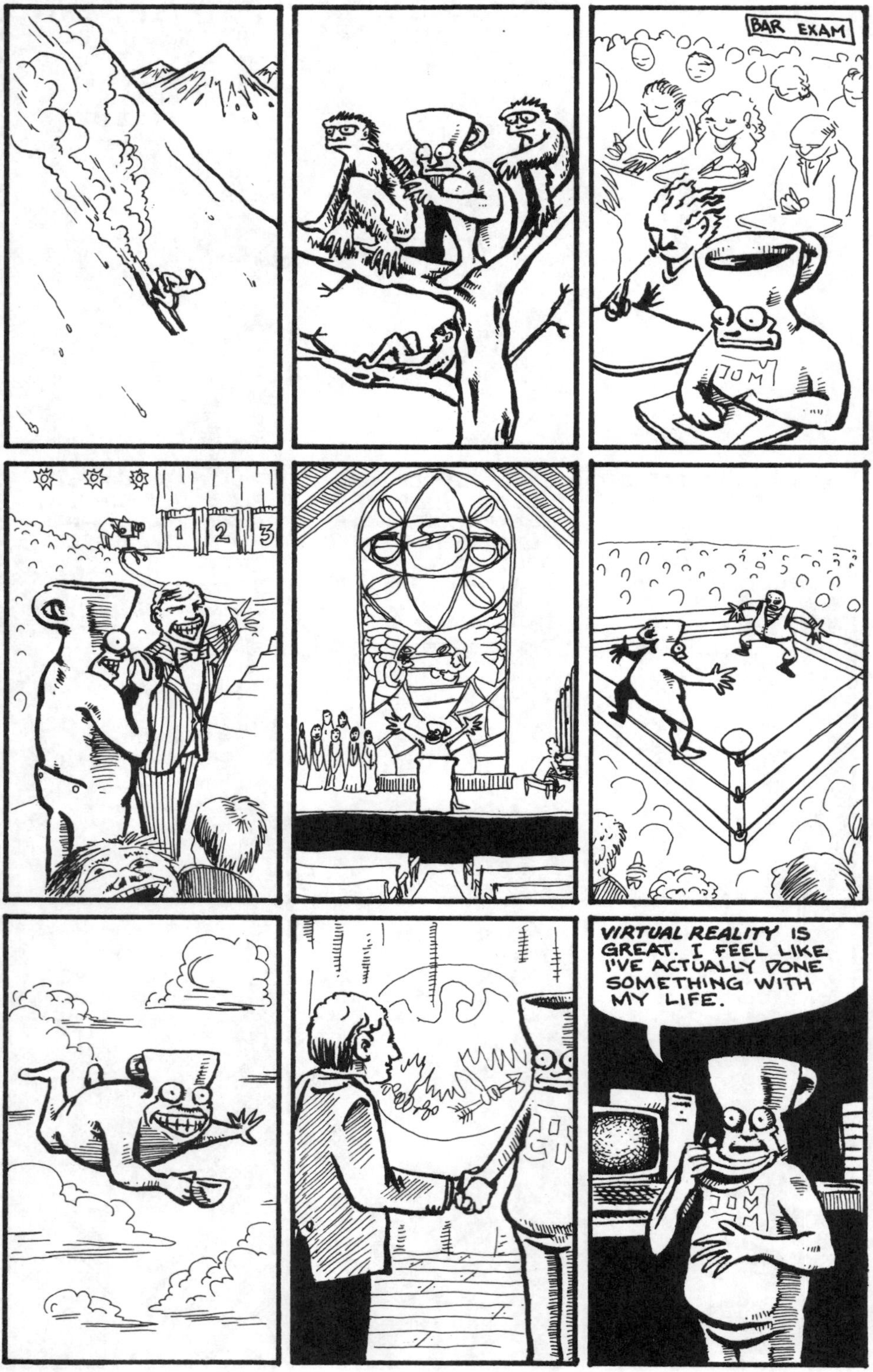
BAR EXAM
1
2
3
JOM
VIRTUAL REALITY IS GREAT. I FEEL LIKE I'VE ACTUALLY DONE SOMETHING WITH MY LIFE.

TOO MUCH COFFEE MAN

SUPERHERO

I AM A SUPERHERO!

I AM STRONG, AND I AM MIGHTY, AND I HAVE A CAPE!

BACK HOME, IN MY SECRET "COFFEE HOUSE," I HAVE HIGH-TECH GADGETRY TO HELP ME.

EVER VIGILANT, I LOOK FOR SUPER-VILLAINS.

THERE SURE AREN'T TOO MANY SUPER-VILLAINS AROUND.

WHY DON'T YOU FIGHT SOMETHING REAL, LIKE POLLUTION, SEXISM, GLOBAL WARMING, OR OVERPOPULATION?

GRRRRRR!!! YES! I'LL FIGHT THOSE THINGS WITH EVERY FIBER OF MY BEING!

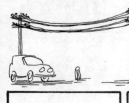

I DON'T THINK SUPERHEROES WERE MADE TO FIGHT REAL PROBLEMS.

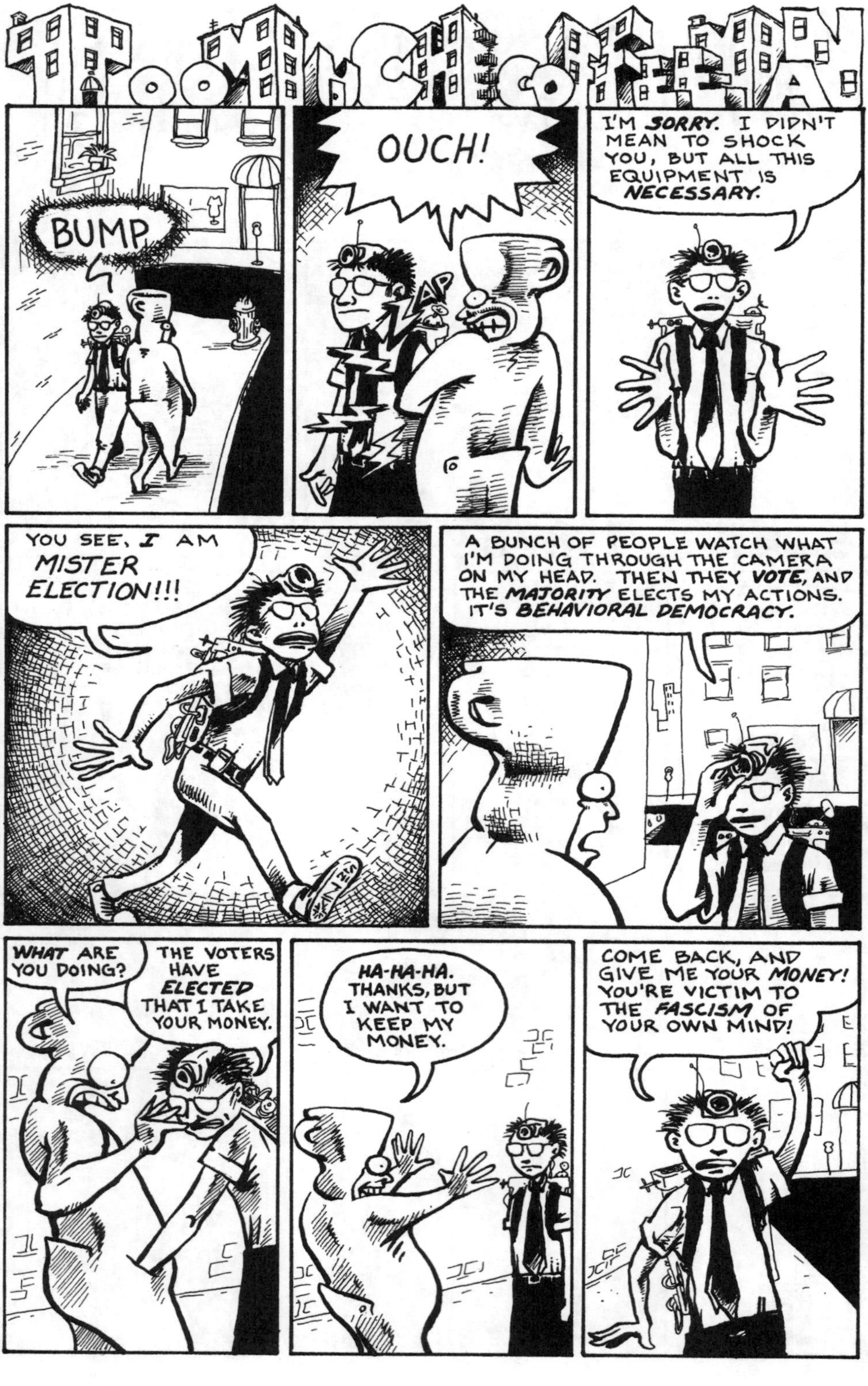
TOO MUCH COFFEE MAN
BUMP
OUCH!
ZAP
I'M SORRY. I DIDN'T MEAN TO SHOCK YOU, BUT ALL THIS EQUIPMENT IS NECESSARY.
YOU SEE, I AM MISTER ELECTION!!!
A BUNCH OF PEOPLE WATCH WHAT I'M DOING THROUGH THE CAMERA ON MY HEAD. THEN THEY VOTE, AND THE MAJORITY ELECTS MY ACTIONS. IT'S BEHAVIORAL DEMOCRACY.
WHAT ARE YOU DOING?
THE VOTERS HAVE ELECTED THAT I TAKE YOUR MONEY.
HA-HA-HA. THANKS, BUT I WANT TO KEEP MY MONEY.
COME BACK, AND GIVE ME YOUR MONEY! YOU'RE VICTIM TO THE FASCISM OF YOUR OWN MIND!

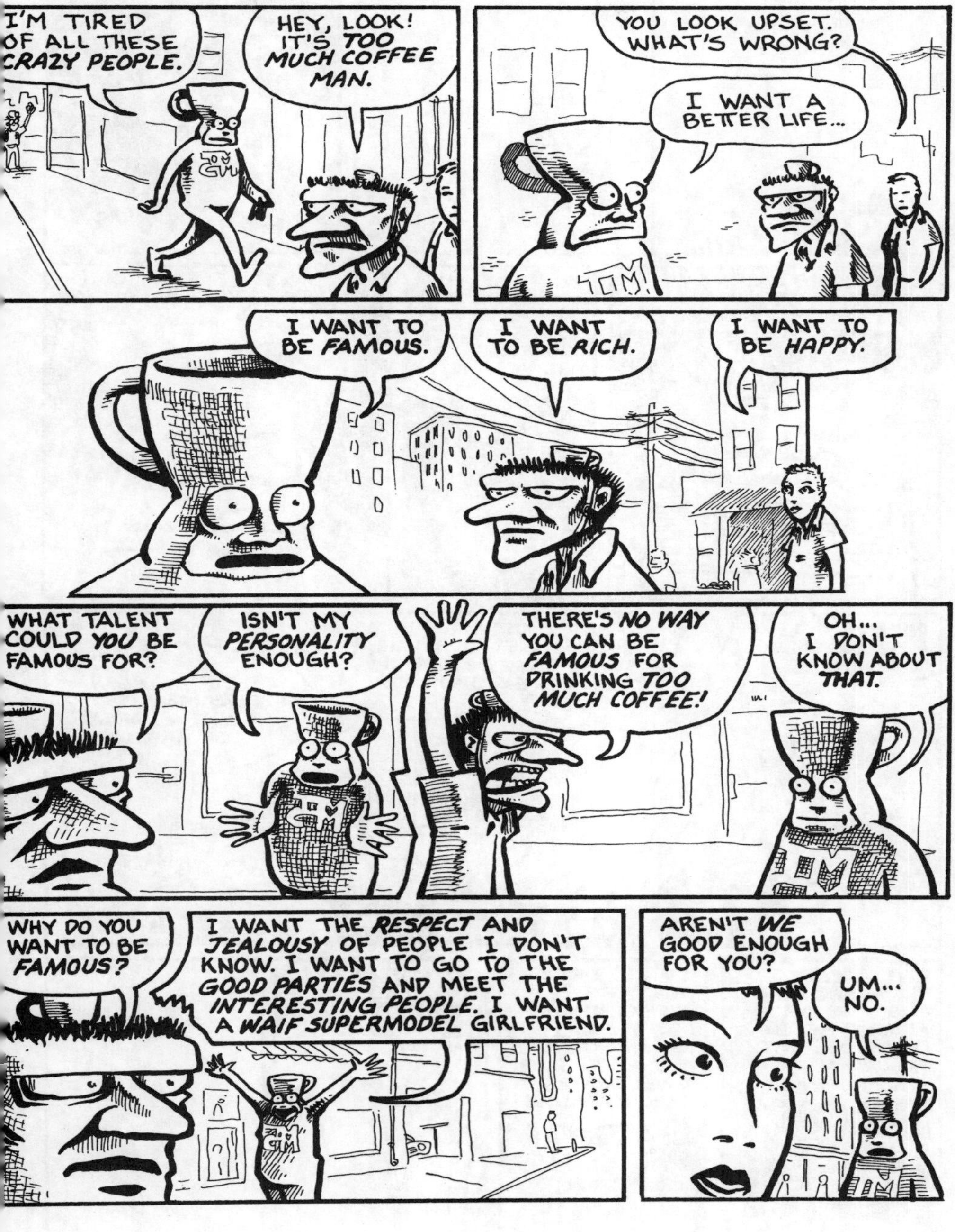
I'M TIRED OF ALL THESE CRAZY PEOPLE.
HEY, LOOK! IT'S TOO MUCH COFFEE MAN.
YOU LOOK UPSET. WHAT'S WRONG?
I WANT A BETTER LIFE...
I WANT TO BE FAMOUS.
I WANT TO BE RICH.
I WANT TO BE HAPPY.
WHAT TALENT COULD YOU BE FAMOUS FOR?
ISN'T MY PERSONALITY ENOUGH?
THERE'S NO WAY YOU CAN BE FAMOUS FOR DRINKING TOO MUCH COFFEE!
OH... I DON'T KNOW ABOUT THAT.
WHY DO YOU WANT TO BE FAMOUS?
I WANT THE RESPECT AND JEALOUSY OF PEOPLE I DON'T KNOW. I WANT TO GO TO THE GOOD PARTIES AND MEET THE INTERESTING PEOPLE. I WANT A WAIF SUPERMODEL GIRLFRIEND.
AREN'T WE GOOD ENOUGH FOR YOU?
UM... NO.

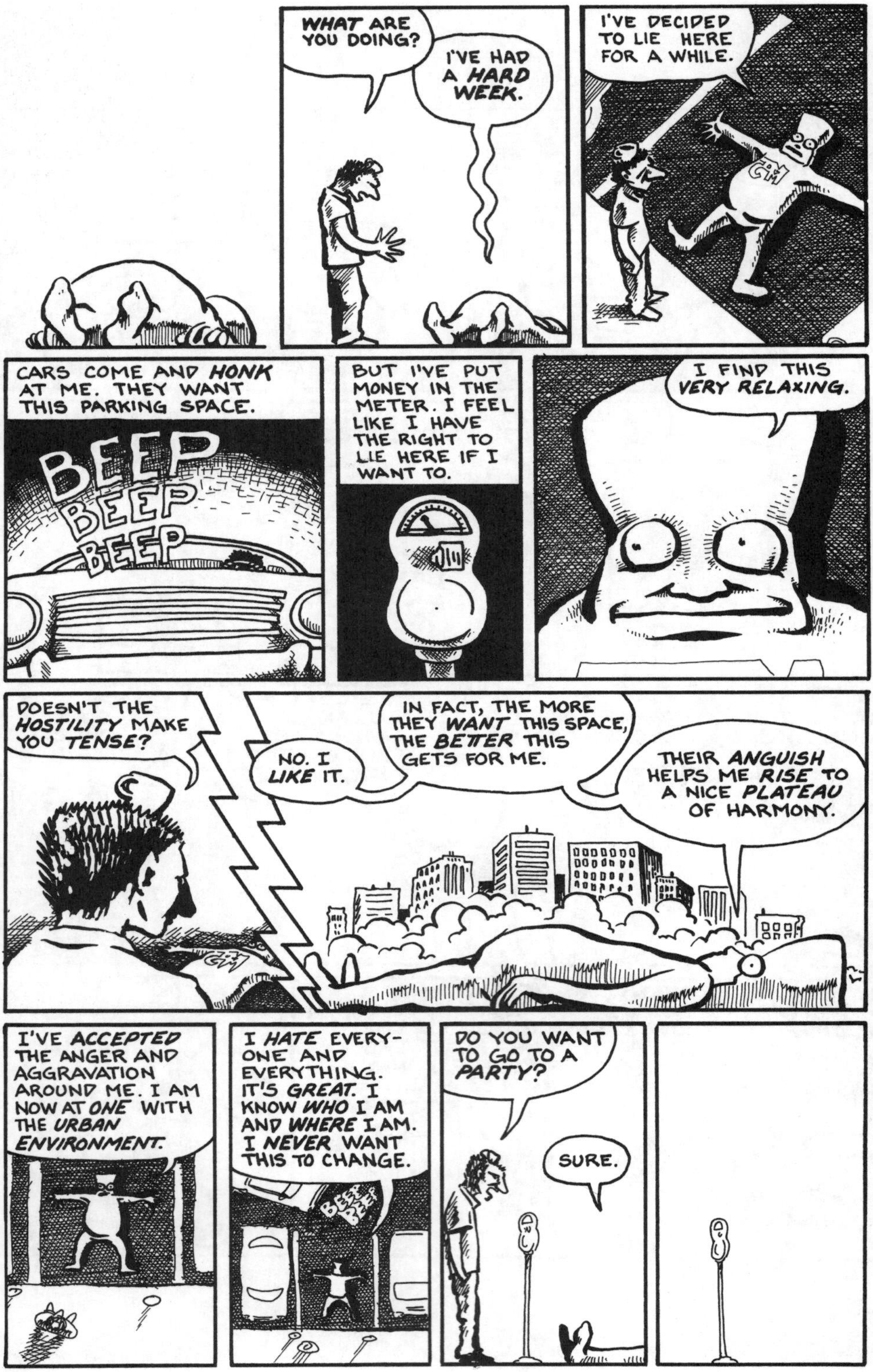

WHAT ARE YOU DOING?
I'VE HAD A HARD WEEK.
I'VE DECIDED TO LIE HERE FOR A WHILE.
CARS COME AND HONK AT ME. THEY WANT THIS PARKING SPACE.
BEEP BEEP BEEP
BUT I'VE PUT MONEY IN THE METER. I FEEL LIKE I HAVE THE RIGHT TO LIE HERE IF I WANT TO.
I FIND THIS VERY RELAXING.
DOESN'T THE HOSTILITY MAKE YOU TENSE?
NO. I LIKE IT.
IN FACT, THE MORE THEY WANT THIS SPACE, THE BETTER THIS GETS FOR ME.
THEIR ANGUISH HELPS ME RISE TO A NICE PLATEAU OF HARMONY.
I'VE ACCEPTED THE ANGER AND AGGRAVATION AROUND ME. I AM NOW AT ONE WITH THE URBAN ENVIRONMENT.
I HATE EVERYONE AND EVERYTHING. IT'S GREAT. I KNOW WHO I AM AND WHERE I AM. I NEVER WANT THIS TO CHANGE.
DO YOU WANT TO GO TO A PARTY?
SURE.

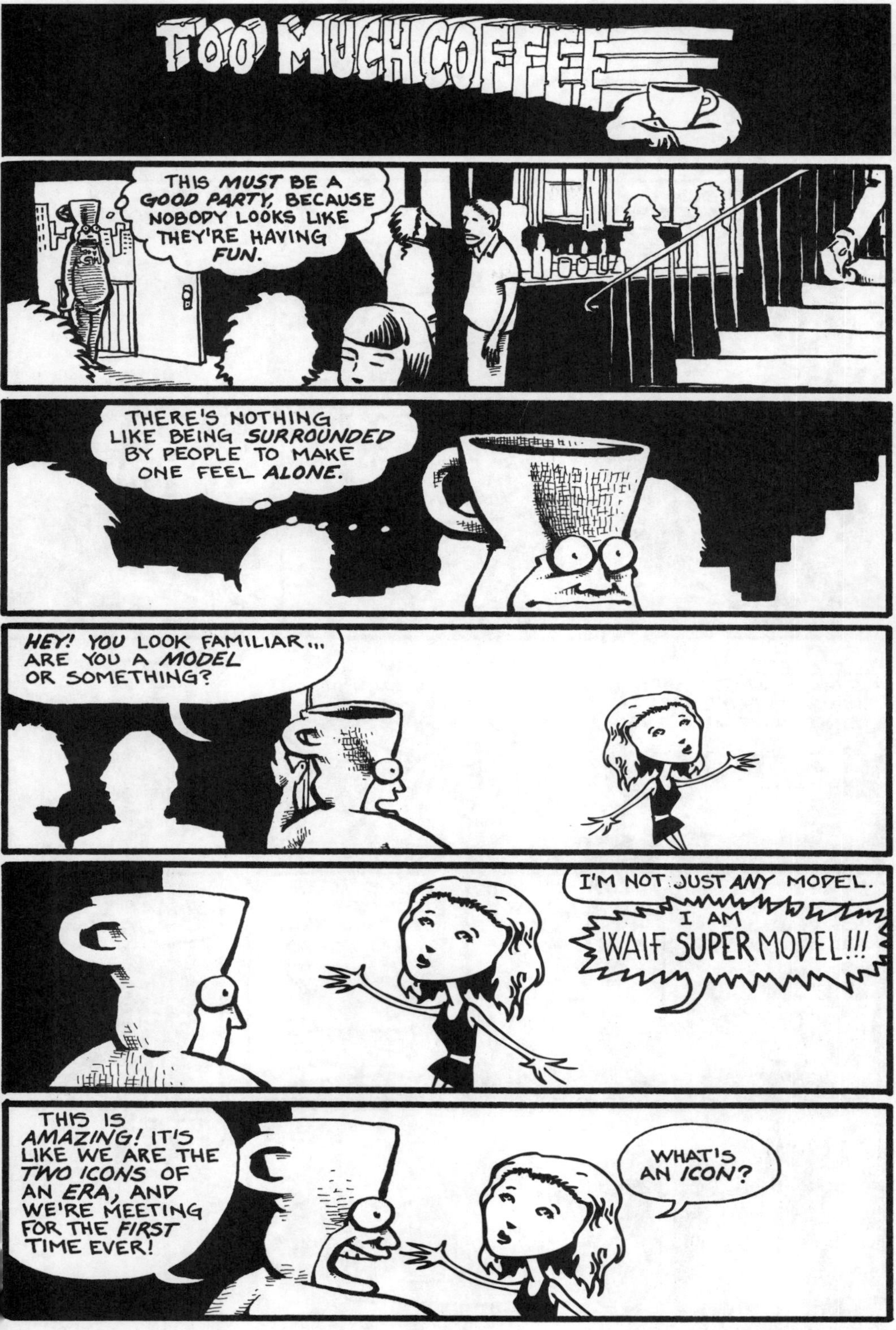
TOO MUCH COFFEE
THIS MUST BE A GOOD PARTY, BECAUSE NOBODY LOOKS LIKE THEY'RE HAVING FUN.
THERE'S NOTHING LIKE BEING SURROUNDED BY PEOPLE TO MAKE ONE FEEL ALONE.
HEY! YOU LOOK FAMILIAR... ARE YOU A MODEL OR SOMETHING?
I'M NOT JUST ANY MODEL.
I AM WAIF SUPER MODEL!!!
THIS IS AMAZING! IT'S LIKE WE ARE THE TWO ICONS OF AN ERA, AND WE'RE MEETING FOR THE FIRST TIME EVER!
WHAT'S AN ICON?

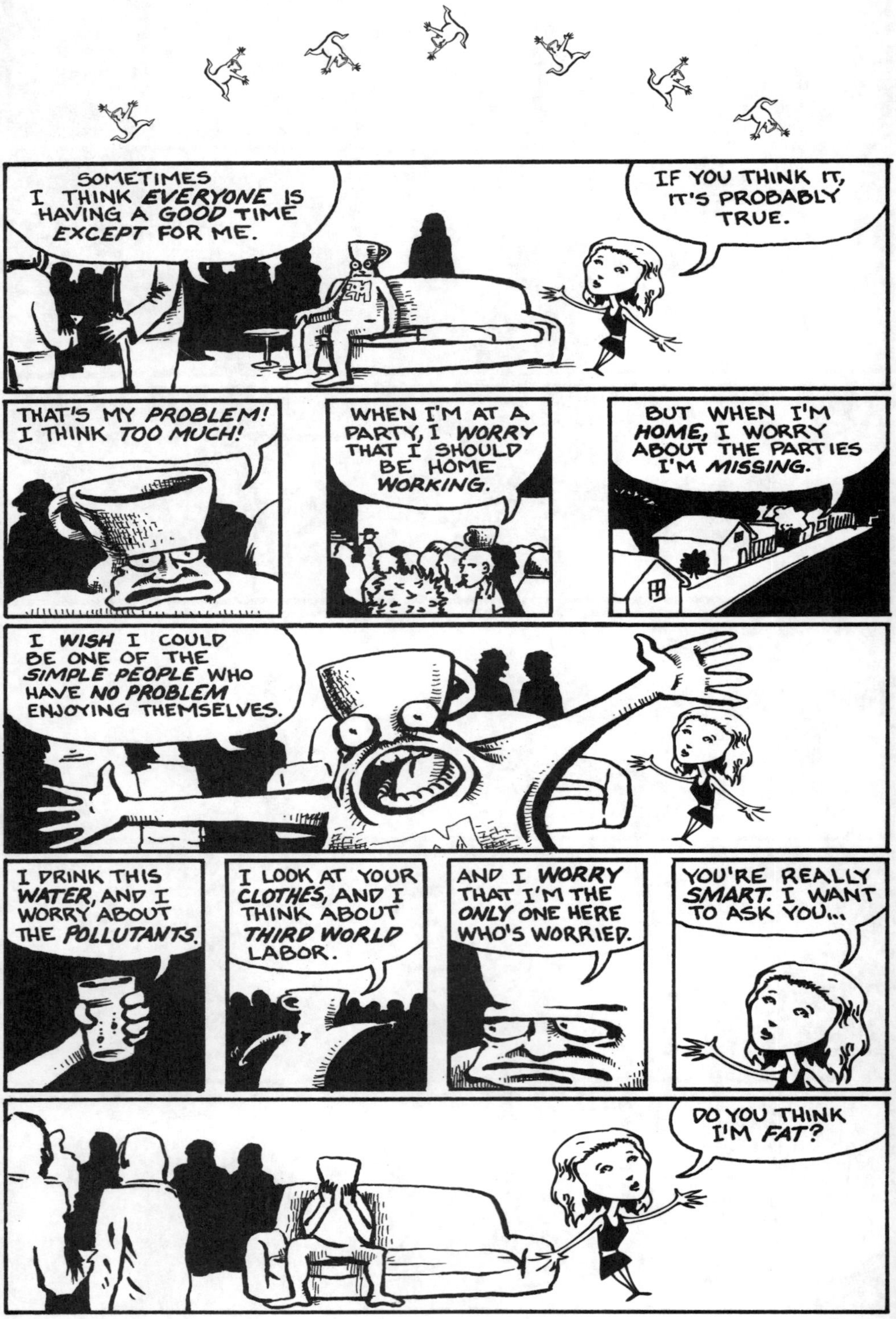
SOMETIMES I THINK EVERYONE IS HAVING A GOOD TIME EXCEPT FOR ME.
IF YOU THINK IT, IT'S PROBABLY TRUE.
THAT'S MY PROBLEM! I THINK TOO MUCH!
WHEN I'M AT A PARTY, I WORRY THAT I SHOULD BE HOME WORKING.
BUT WHEN I'M HOME, I WORRY ABOUT THE PARTIES I'M MISSING.
I WISH I COULD BE ONE OF THE SIMPLE PEOPLE WHO HAVE NO PROBLEM ENJOYING THEMSELVES.
I DRINK THIS WATER, AND I WORRY ABOUT THE POLLUTANTS.
I LOOK AT YOUR CLOTHES, AND I THINK ABOUT THIRD WORLD LABOR.
AND I WORRY THAT I'M THE ONLY ONE HERE WHO'S WORRIED.
YOU'RE REALLY SMART. I WANT TO ASK YOU...
DO YOU THINK I'M FAT?

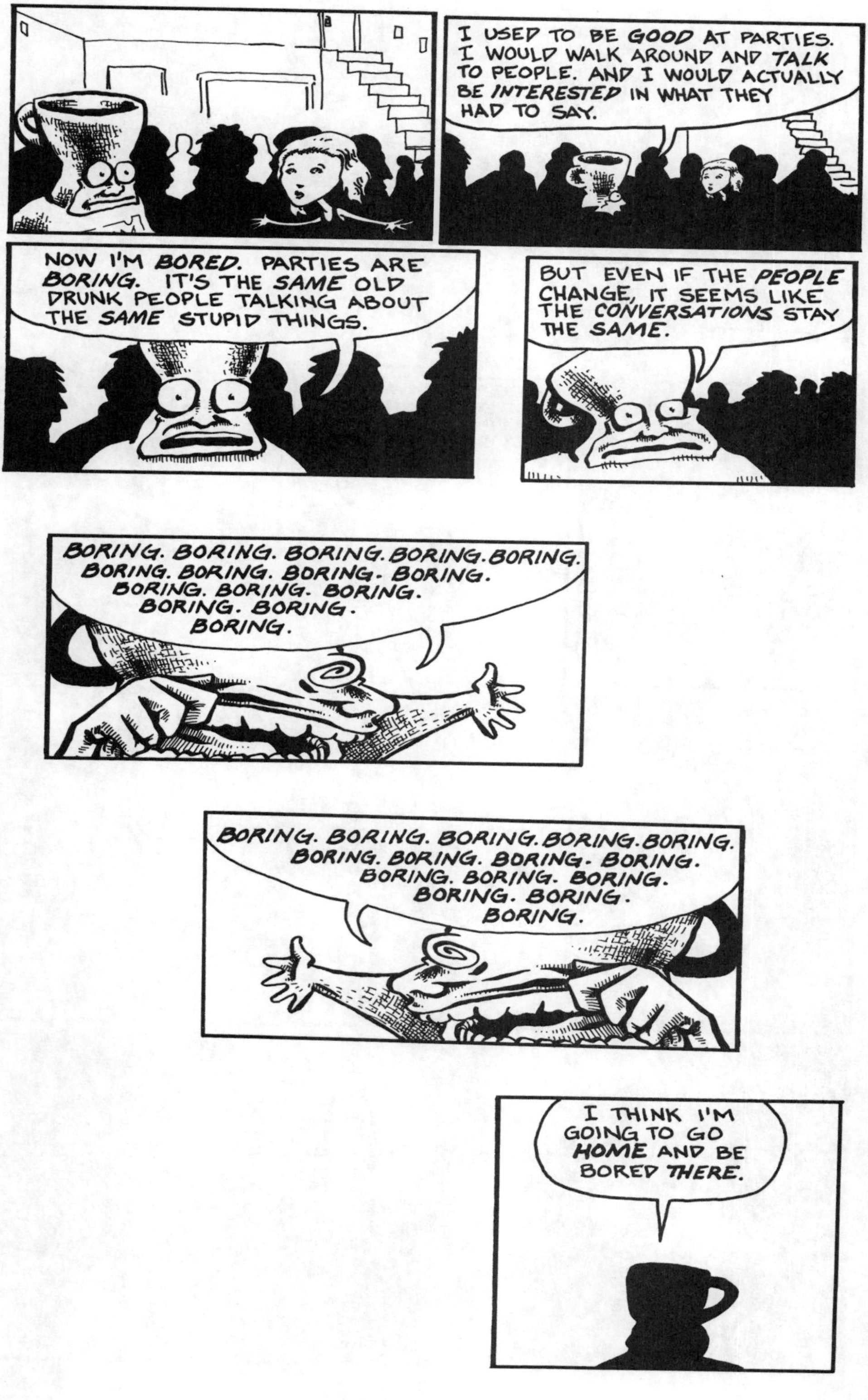
I USED TO BE GOOD AT PARTIES. I WOULD WALK AROUND AND TALK TO PEOPLE. AND I WOULD ACTUALLY BE INTERESTED IN WHAT THEY HAD TO SAY.
NOW I'M BORED. PARTIES ARE BORING. IT'S THE SAME OLD DRUNK PEOPLE TALKING ABOUT THE SAME STUPID THINGS.
BUT EVEN IF THE PEOPLE CHANGE, IT SEEMS LIKE THE CONVERSATIONS STAY THE SAME.
BORING. BORING. BORING. BORING. BORING. BORING. BORING. BORING. BORING. BORING. BORING. BORING. BORING. BORING. BORING.
BORING. BORING. BORING. BORING. BORING. BORING. BORING. BORING. BORING. BORING. BORING. BORING. BORING. BORING. BORING.
I THINK I'M GOING TO GO HOME AND BE BORED THERE.

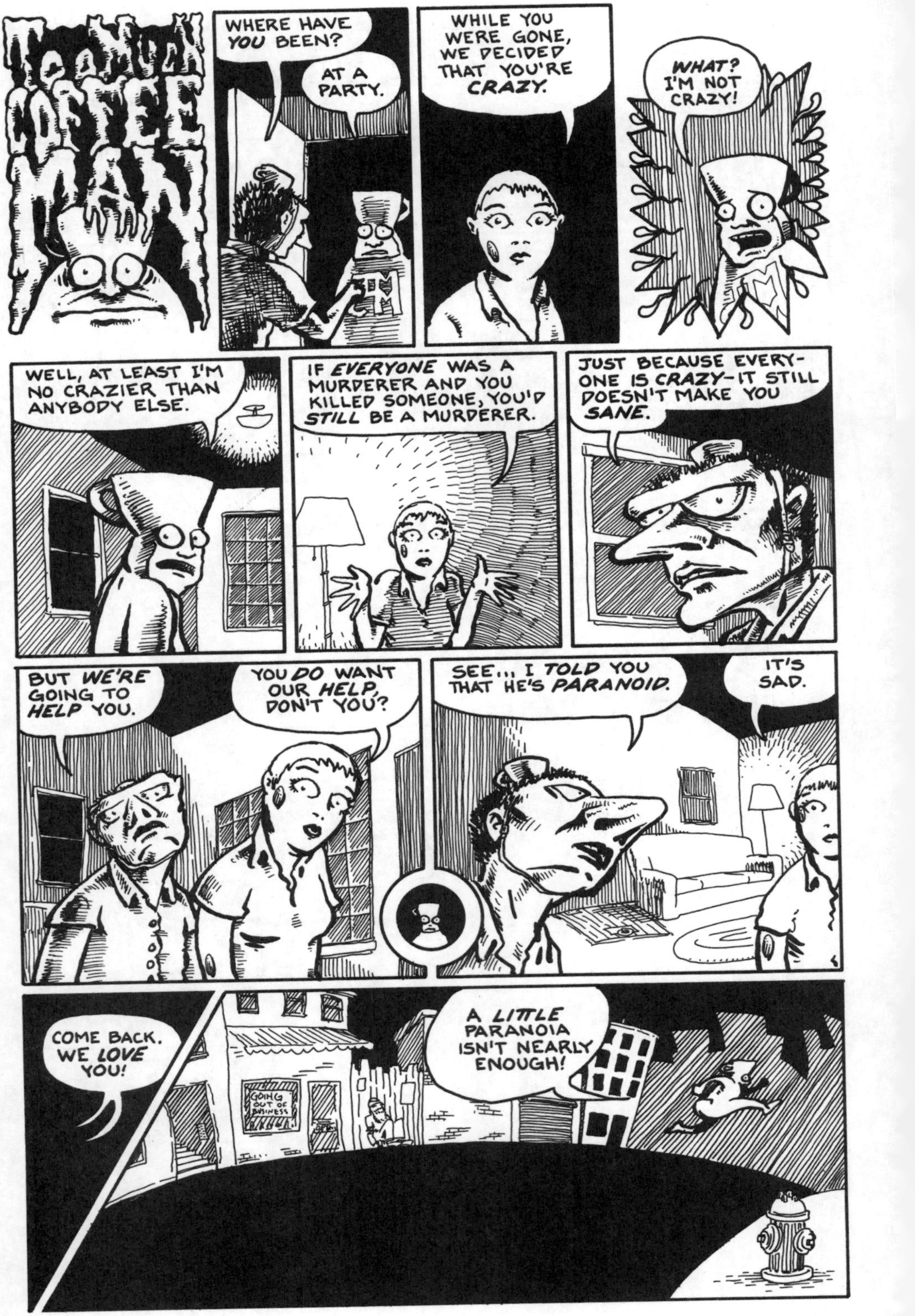
TOO MUCH COFFEE MAN
WHERE HAVE YOU BEEN?
AT A PARTY.
WHILE YOU WERE GONE, WE DECIDED THAT YOU'RE CRAZY.
WHAT? I'M NOT CRAZY!
WELL, AT LEAST I'M NO CRAZIER THAN ANYBODY ELSE.
IF EVERYONE WAS A MURDERER AND YOU KILLED SOMEONE, YOU'D STILL BE A MURDERER.
JUST BECAUSE EVERY-ONE IS CRAZY- IT STILL DOESN'T MAKE YOU SANE.
BUT WE'RE GOING TO HELP YOU.
YOU DO WANT OUR HELP, DON'T YOU?
SEE... I TOLD YOU THAT HE'S PARANOID.
IT'S SAD.
COME BACK. WE LOVE YOU!
A LITTLE PARANOIA ISN'T NEARLY ENOUGH!
GOING OUT OF BUSINESS

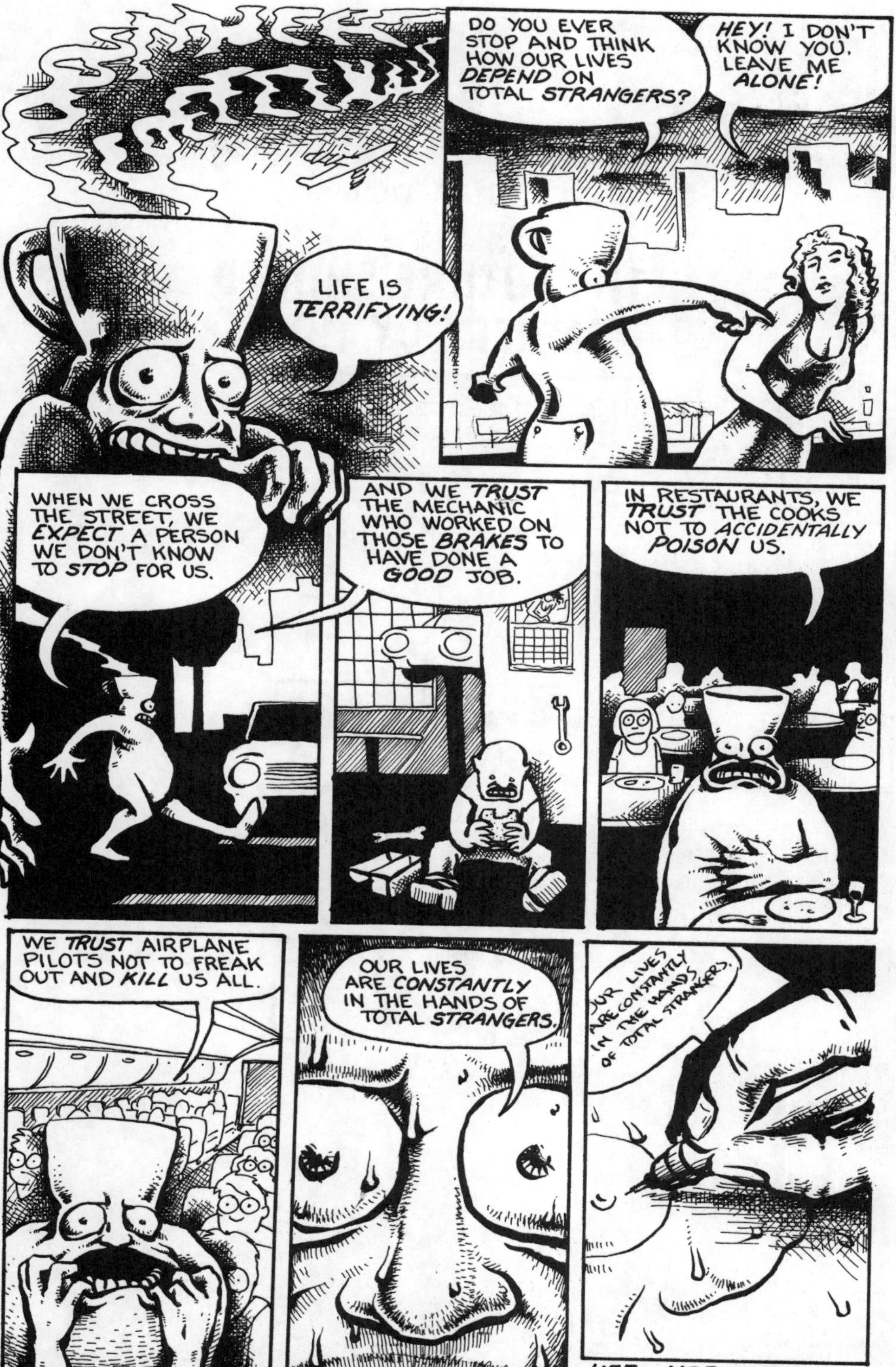
DO YOU EVER STOP AND THINK HOW OUR LIVES DEPEND ON TOTAL STRANGERS?
HEY! I DON'T KNOW YOU. LEAVE ME ALONE!
LIFE IS TERRIFYING!
WHEN WE CROSS THE STREET, WE EXPECT A PERSON WE DON'T KNOW TO STOP FOR US.
AND WE TRUST THE MECHANIC WHO WORKED ON THOSE BRAKES TO HAVE DONE A GOOD JOB.
IN RESTAURANTS, WE TRUST THE COOKS NOT TO ACCIDENTALLY POISON US.
WE TRUST AIRPLANE PILOTS NOT TO FREAK OUT AND KILL US ALL.
OUR LIVES ARE CONSTANTLY IN THE HANDS OF TOTAL STRANGERS.
OUR LIVES ARE CONSTANTLY IN THE HANDS OF TOTAL STRANGERS.
HEE... HEE... HEE...

chapter 6

THE FUTURE SHOULD BE HERE BY NOW

God is an atheist, and other realizations

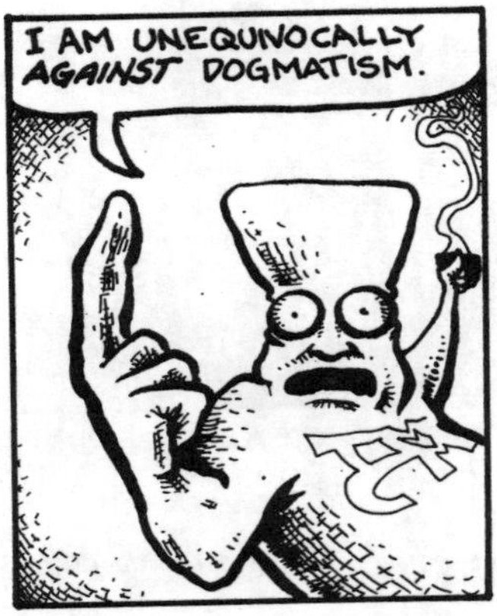
I AM UNEQUIVOCALLY AGAINST DOGMATISM.

WHOEVER SAID THAT *KNOWLEDGE* IS *POWER* IS A *FOOL.*

WHAT ARE YOU TALKING ABOUT?

THE *MORE* KNOWLEDGE I HAVE ABOUT FOOD, THE *LESS* I'M ABLE TO EAT.

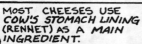
MOST CHEESES USE *COW'S STOMACH LINING* (RENNET) AS A *MAIN* INGREDIENT.

I WOULDN'T DRINK A *WOMAN'S* BREAST MILK, BUT IT'S *NORMAL* TO DRINK COWS' *BREAST MILK.*

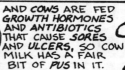
AND *COWS* ARE FED *GROWTH HORMONES* AND *ANTIBIOTICS* THAT CAUSE *SORES* AND *ULCERS,* SO COW MILK HAS A FAIR BIT OF *PUS* IN IT.

GROSS.

MOO.

IT'S NOT MY FAULT.

WITH THE WAY THAT ANIMALS ARE *RAISED* AND *SLAUGHTERED,* IT'S NO WONDER THAT *SALMONELLA,* E.COLI, LISTERIA, AND *MAD COW* (WITH ITS 16-YEAR LATENCY IN HUMANS) ARE *RAMPANT.*

VEGETABLES ARE NO BETTER THAN *MEAT.* MOST OF THEM ARE *IRRADIATED,* BATHED IN *PESTICIDES,* AND *WAXED* TO LOOK MORE *NATURAL.* AND THE *GENETICALLY MODIFIED FOODS* AREN'T EVEN LABELED.

I KNOW *TOO MUCH!* I'M *POWERLESS* TO EAT THIS JUNK!

KNOWLEDGE IS *NAUSEA.*

93

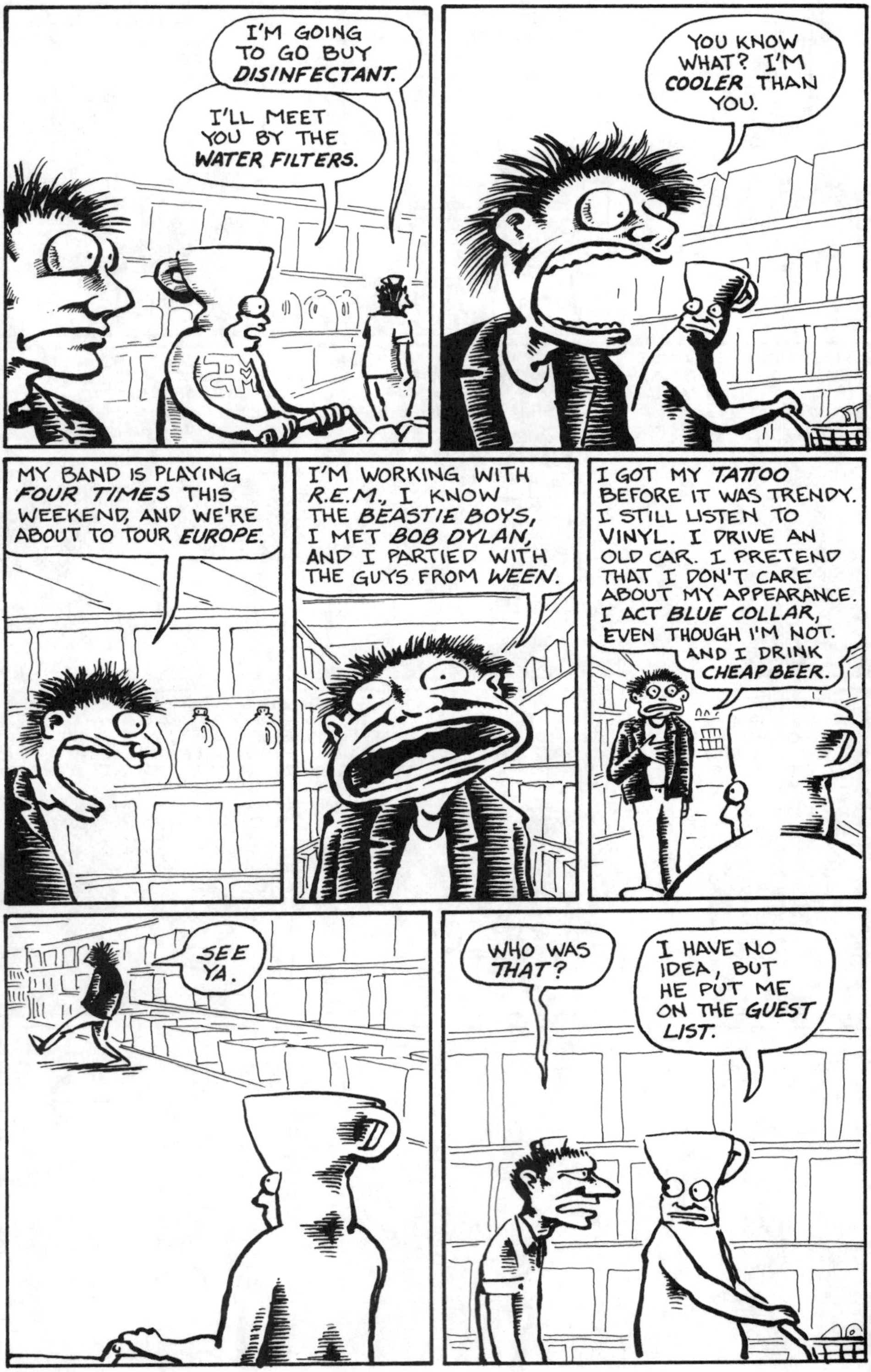
I'M GOING TO GO BUY DISINFECTANT.
I'LL MEET YOU BY THE WATER FILTERS.
YOU KNOW WHAT? I'M COOLER THAN YOU.
MY BAND IS PLAYING FOUR TIMES THIS WEEKEND, AND WE'RE ABOUT TO TOUR EUROPE.
I'M WORKING WITH R.E.M., I KNOW THE BEASTIE BOYS, I MET BOB DYLAN, AND I PARTIED WITH THE GUYS FROM WEEN.
I GOT MY TATTOO BEFORE IT WAS TRENDY. I STILL LISTEN TO VINYL. I DRIVE AN OLD CAR. I PRETEND THAT I DON'T CARE ABOUT MY APPEARANCE. I ACT BLUE COLLAR, EVEN THOUGH I'M NOT. AND I DRINK CHEAP BEER.
SEE YA.
WHO WAS THAT?
I HAVE NO IDEA, BUT HE PUT ME ON THE GUEST LIST.

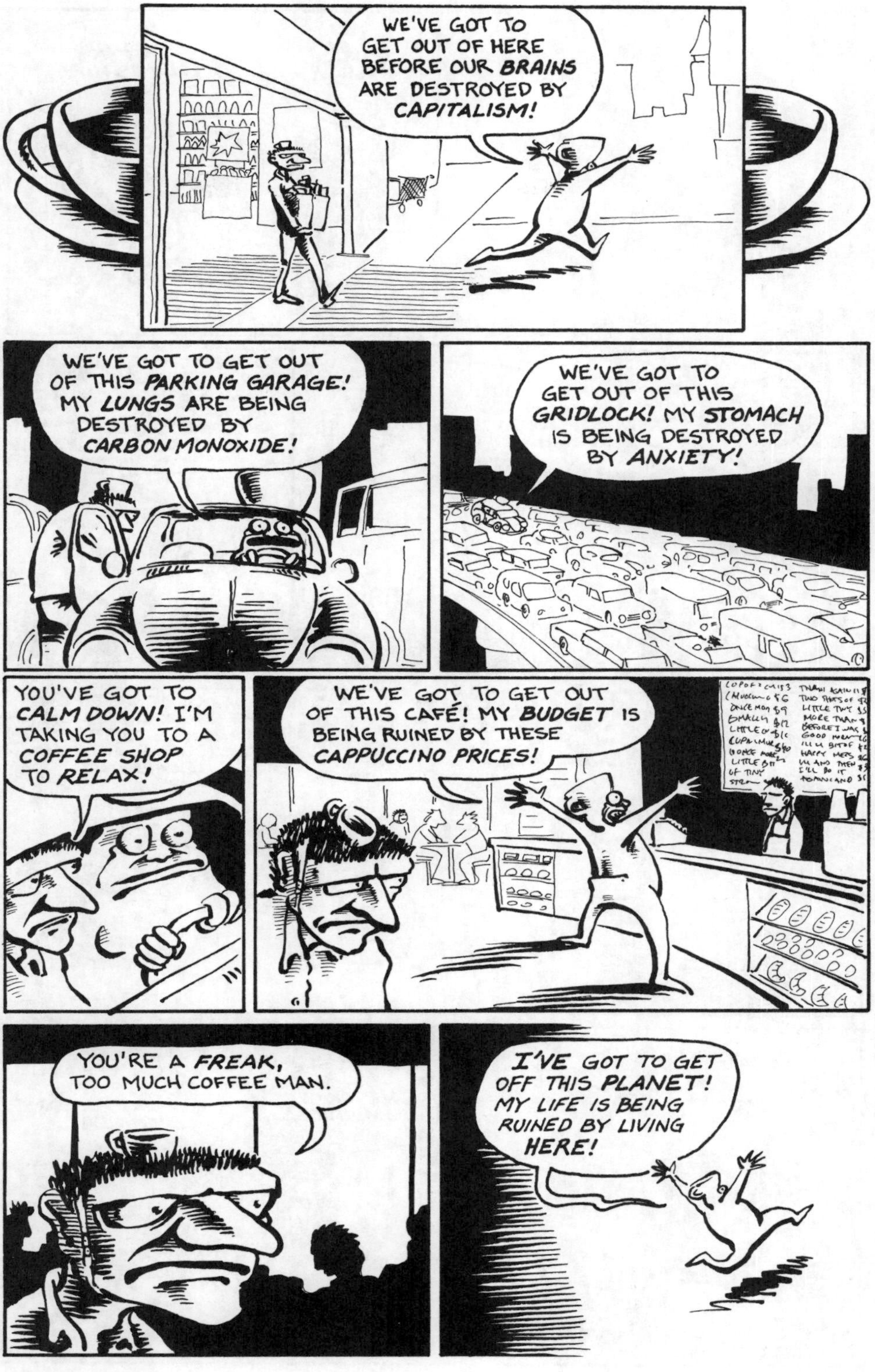
WE'VE GOT TO GET OUT OF HERE BEFORE OUR BRAINS ARE DESTROYED BY CAPITALISM!
WE'VE GOT TO GET OUT OF THIS PARKING GARAGE! MY LUNGS ARE BEING DESTROYED BY CARBON MONOXIDE!
WE'VE GOT TO GET OUT OF THIS GRIDLOCK! MY STOMACH IS BEING DESTROYED BY ANXIETY!
YOU'VE GOT TO CALM DOWN! I'M TAKING YOU TO A COFFEE SHOP TO RELAX!
WE'VE GOT TO GET OUT OF THIS CAFÉ! MY BUDGET IS BEING RUINED BY THESE CAPPUCCINO PRICES!
YOU'RE A FREAK, TOO MUCH COFFEE MAN.
I'VE GOT TO GET OFF THIS PLANET! MY LIFE IS BEING RUINED BY LIVING HERE!

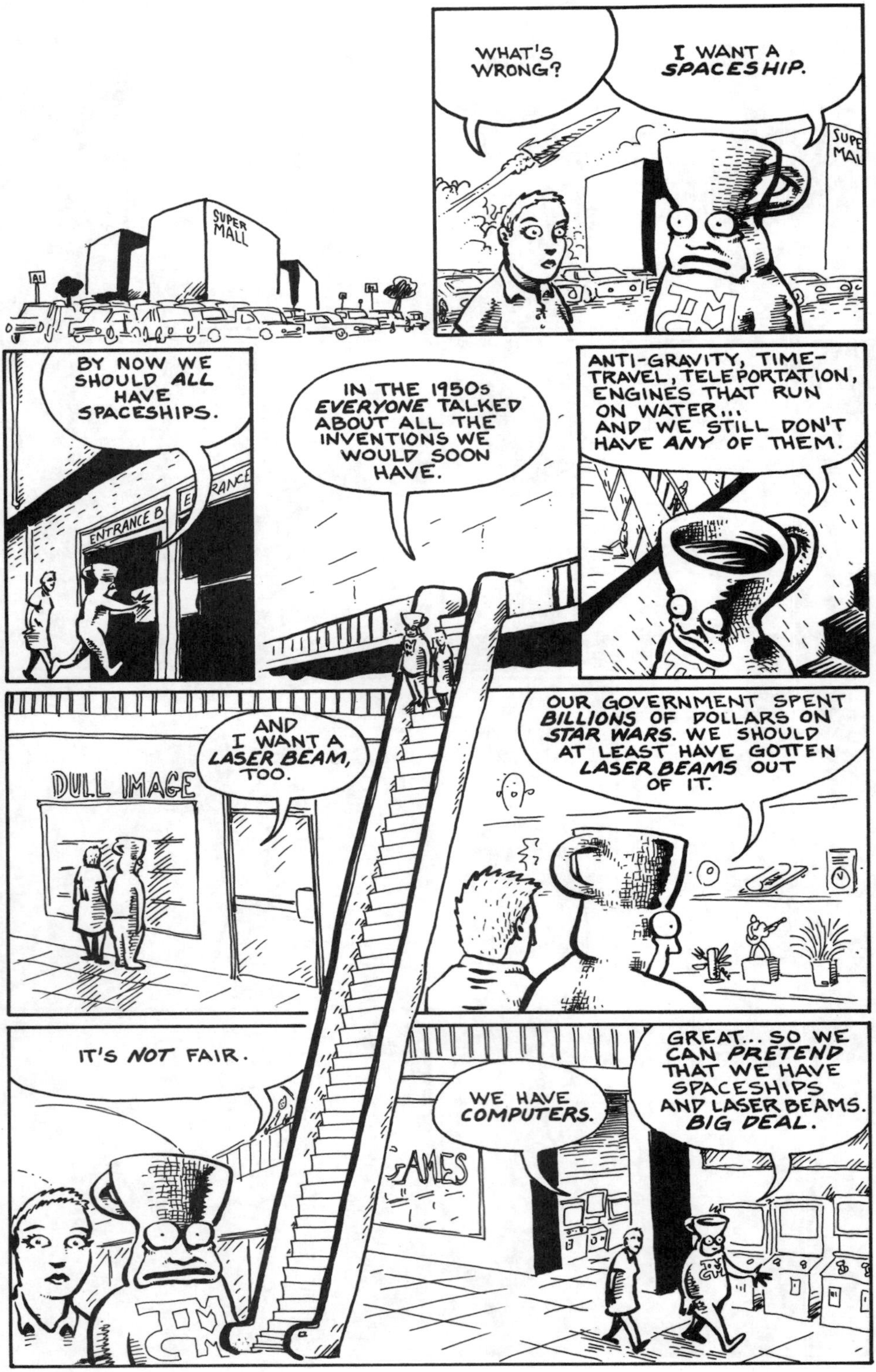
SUPER MALL
WHAT'S WRONG?
I WANT A *SPACESHIP*.
SUPER MALL
BY NOW WE SHOULD *ALL* HAVE SPACESHIPS.
ENTRANCE B
IN THE 1950s *EVERYONE* TALKED ABOUT ALL THE INVENTIONS WE WOULD SOON HAVE.
ANTI-GRAVITY, TIME-TRAVEL, TELEPORTATION, ENGINES THAT RUN ON WATER... AND WE STILL DON'T HAVE *ANY* OF THEM.
DULL IMAGE
AND I WANT A *LASER BEAM*, TOO.
OUR GOVERNMENT SPENT *BILLIONS* OF DOLLARS ON *STAR WARS*. WE SHOULD AT LEAST HAVE GOTTEN *LASER BEAMS* OUT OF IT.
IT'S *NOT* FAIR.
WE HAVE *COMPUTERS*.
GREAT... SO WE CAN *PRETEND* THAT WE HAVE SPACESHIPS AND LASER BEAMS. *BIG DEAL*.

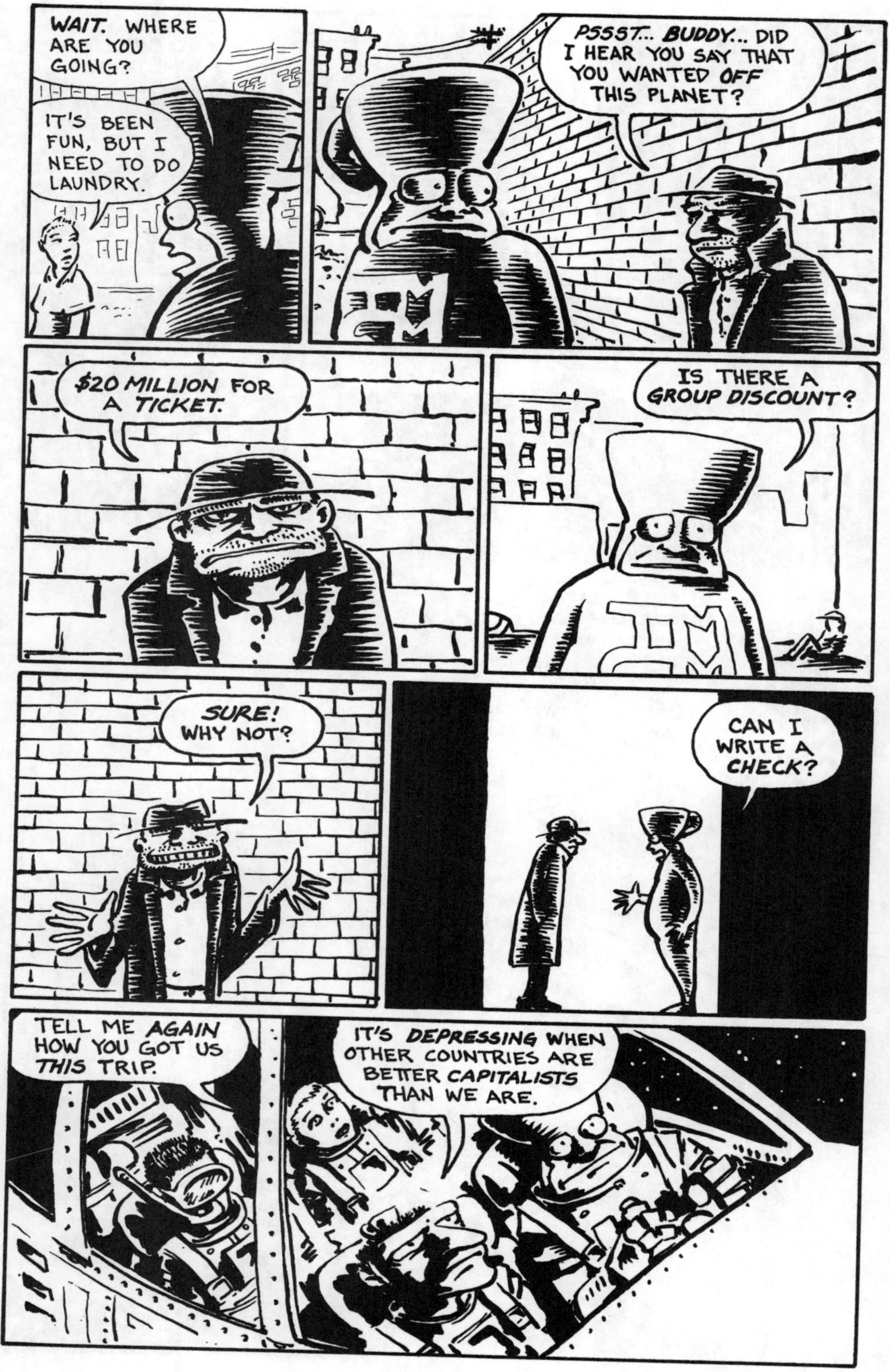
WAIT. WHERE ARE YOU GOING?
IT'S BEEN FUN, BUT I NEED TO DO LAUNDRY.
PSSST... BUDDY... DID I HEAR YOU SAY THAT YOU WANTED OFF THIS PLANET?
$20 MILLION FOR A TICKET.
IS THERE A GROUP DISCOUNT?
SURE! WHY NOT?
CAN I WRITE A CHECK?
TELL ME AGAIN HOW YOU GOT US THIS TRIP.
IT'S DEPRESSING WHEN OTHER COUNTRIES ARE BETTER CAPITALISTS THAN WE ARE.

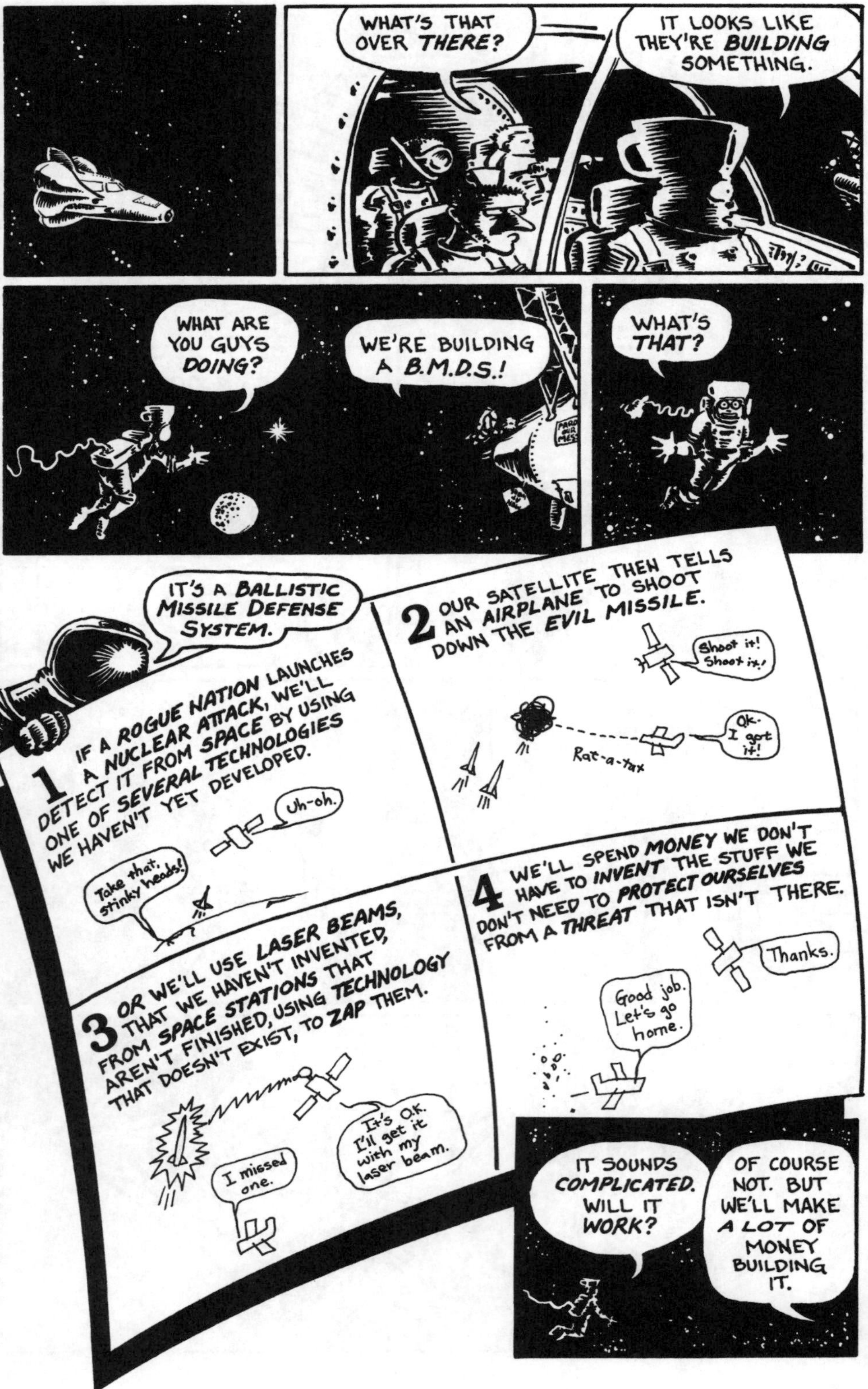
WHAT'S THAT OVER *THERE*?
IT LOOKS LIKE THEY'RE *BUILDING* SOMETHING.
WHAT ARE YOU GUYS *DOING*?
WE'RE BUILDING A *B.M.D.S.*!
WHAT'S *THAT*?
IT'S A *BALLISTIC MISSILE DEFENSE SYSTEM.*
1 IF A *ROGUE NATION* LAUNCHES A *NUCLEAR ATTACK*, WE'LL DETECT IT FROM *SPACE* BY USING ONE OF *SEVERAL TECHNOLOGIES* WE HAVEN'T YET DEVELOPED.
Uh-oh.
Take that, stinky heads!
2 OUR SATELLITE THEN TELLS AN *AIRPLANE* TO SHOOT DOWN THE *EVIL MISSILE*.
Shoot it! Shoot it!
O.K. I got it!
Rat-a-tat
3 *OR* WE'LL USE *LASER BEAMS*, THAT WE HAVEN'T INVENTED, FROM *SPACE STATIONS* THAT AREN'T FINISHED, USING *TECHNOLOGY* THAT DOESN'T EXIST, TO *ZAP* THEM.
It's O.K. I'll get it with my laser beam.
I missed one.
4 WE'LL SPEND *MONEY* WE DON'T HAVE TO *INVENT* THE STUFF WE DON'T NEED TO *PROTECT OURSELVES* FROM A *THREAT* THAT ISN'T THERE.
Thanks.
Good job. Let's go home.
IT SOUNDS *COMPLICATED*. WILL IT *WORK*?
OF COURSE NOT. BUT WE'LL MAKE *A LOT* OF MONEY BUILDING IT.

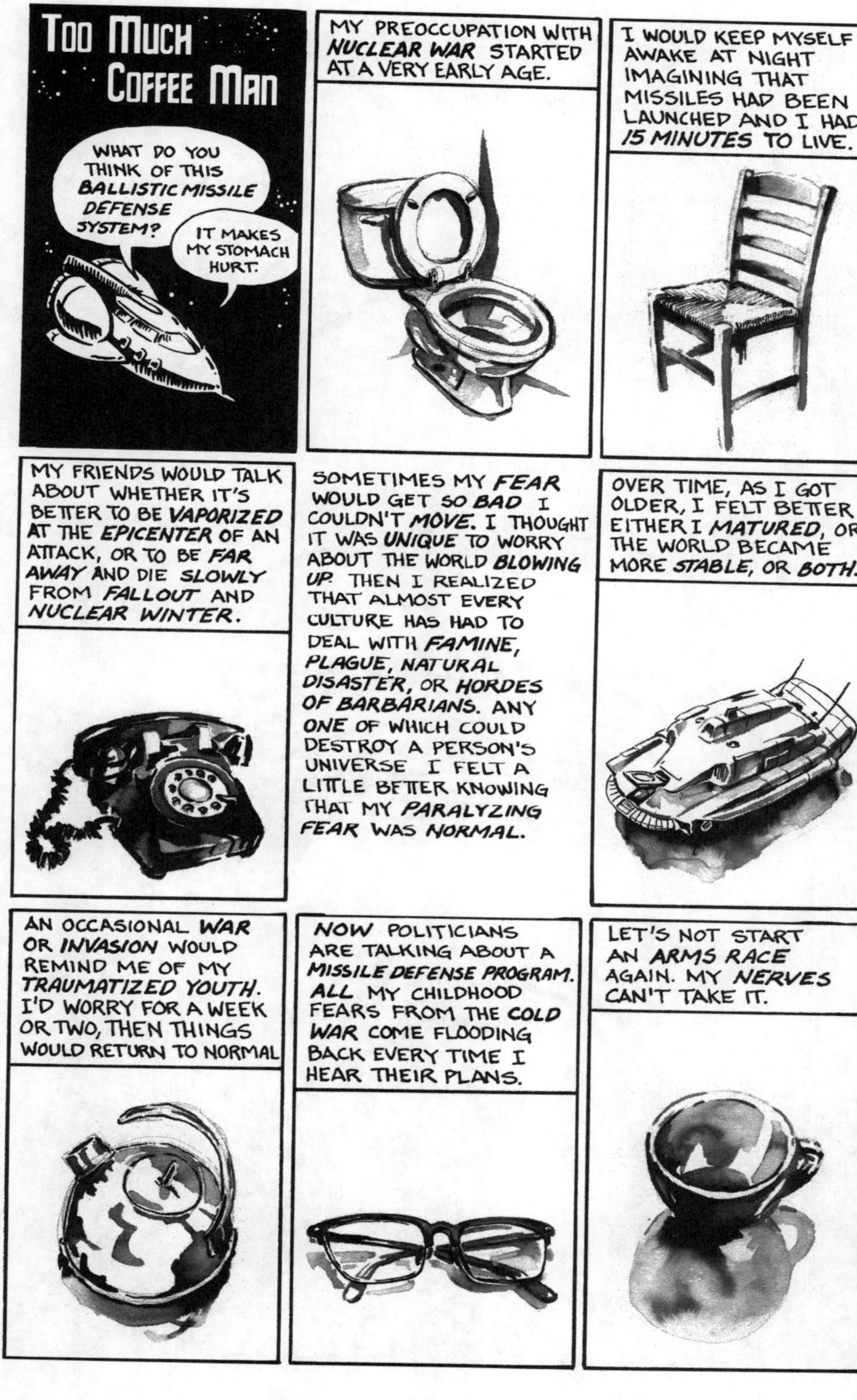
TOO MUCH COFFEE MAN
WHAT DO YOU THINK OF THIS BALLISTIC MISSILE DEFENSE SYSTEM?
IT MAKES MY STOMACH HURT.
MY PREOCCUPATION WITH NUCLEAR WAR STARTED AT A VERY EARLY AGE.
I WOULD KEEP MYSELF AWAKE AT NIGHT IMAGINING THAT MISSILES HAD BEEN LAUNCHED AND I HAD 15 MINUTES TO LIVE.
MY FRIENDS WOULD TALK ABOUT WHETHER IT'S BETTER TO BE VAPORIZED AT THE EPICENTER OF AN ATTACK, OR TO BE FAR AWAY AND DIE SLOWLY FROM FALLOUT AND NUCLEAR WINTER.
SOMETIMES MY FEAR WOULD GET SO BAD I COULDN'T MOVE. I THOUGHT IT WAS UNIQUE TO WORRY ABOUT THE WORLD BLOWING UP. THEN I REALIZED THAT ALMOST EVERY CULTURE HAS HAD TO DEAL WITH FAMINE, PLAGUE, NATURAL DISASTER, OR HORDES OF BARBARIANS. ANY ONE OF WHICH COULD DESTROY A PERSON'S UNIVERSE. I FELT A LITTLE BETTER KNOWING THAT MY PARALYZING FEAR WAS NORMAL.
OVER TIME, AS I GOT OLDER, I FELT BETTER. EITHER I MATURED, OR THE WORLD BECAME MORE STABLE, OR BOTH.
AN OCCASIONAL WAR OR INVASION WOULD REMIND ME OF MY TRAUMATIZED YOUTH. I'D WORRY FOR A WEEK OR TWO, THEN THINGS WOULD RETURN TO NORMAL
NOW POLITICIANS ARE TALKING ABOUT A MISSILE DEFENSE PROGRAM. ALL MY CHILDHOOD FEARS FROM THE COLD WAR COME FLOODING BACK EVERY TIME I HEAR THEIR PLANS.
LET'S NOT START AN ARMS RACE AGAIN. MY NERVES CAN'T TAKE IT.

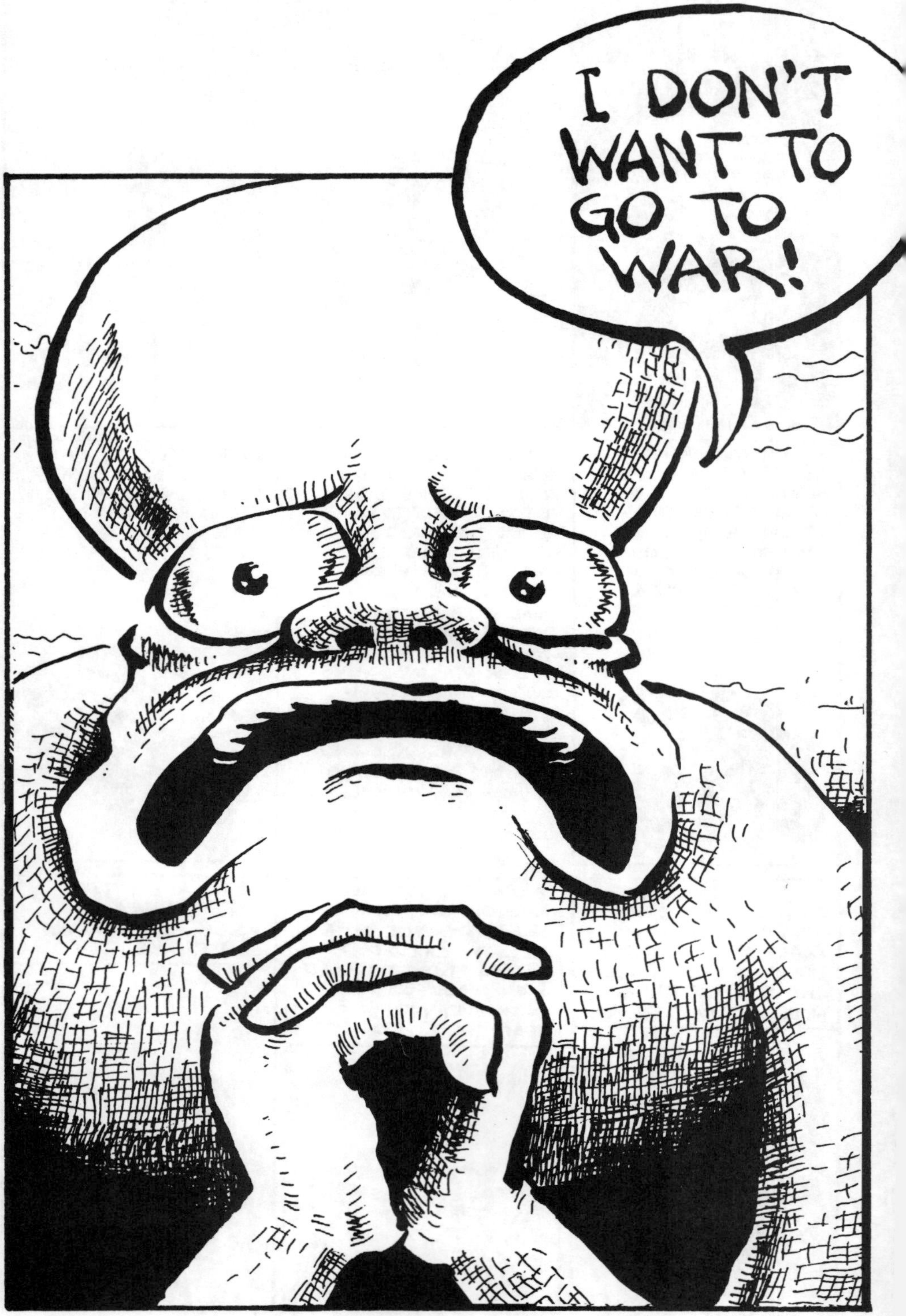
I DON'T WANT TO GO TO WAR!

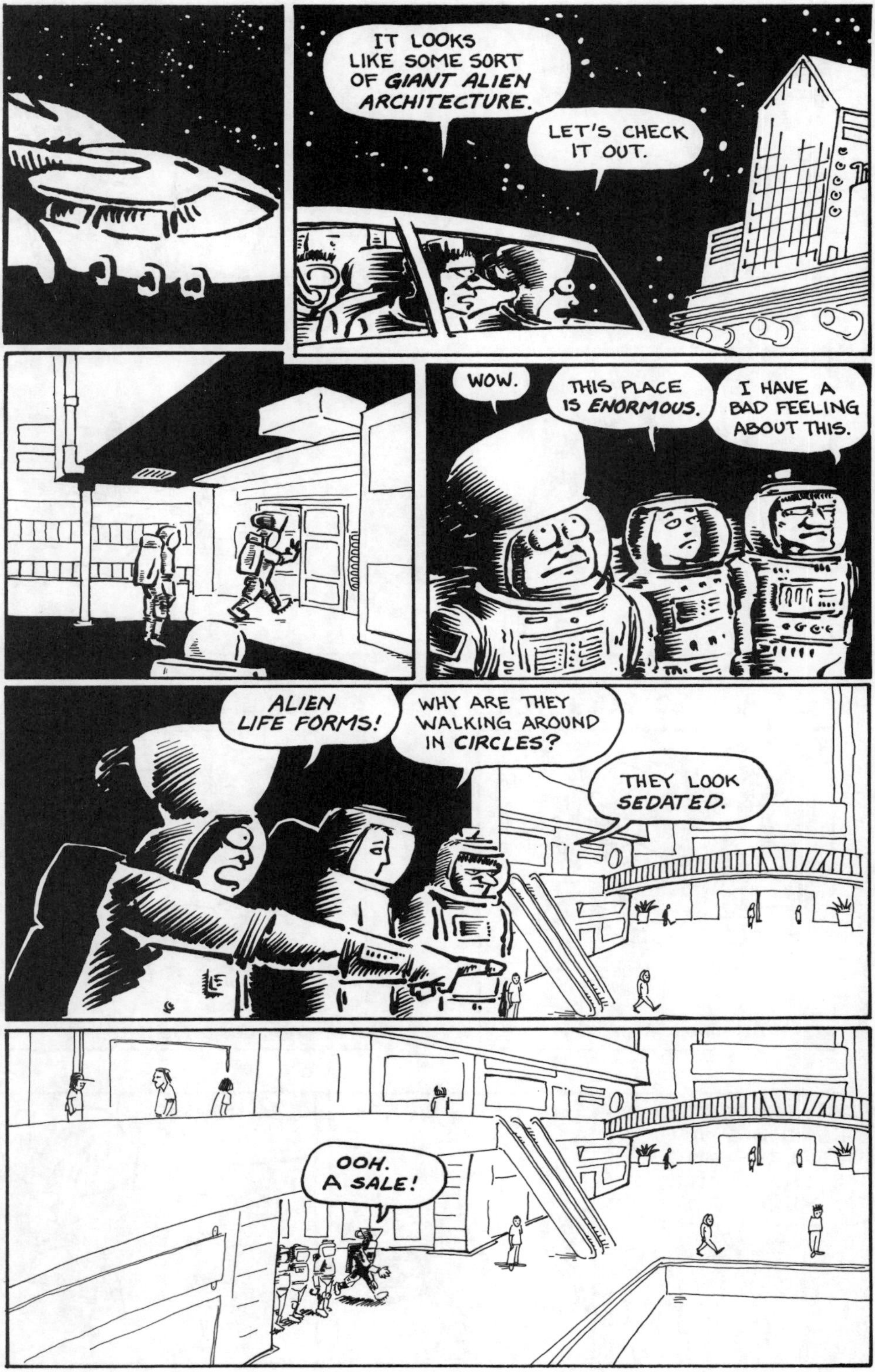
IT LOOKS LIKE SOME SORT OF GIANT ALIEN ARCHITECTURE.
LET'S CHECK IT OUT.
WOW.
THIS PLACE IS ENORMOUS.
I HAVE A BAD FEELING ABOUT THIS.
ALIEN LIFE FORMS!
WHY ARE THEY WALKING AROUND IN CIRCLES?
THEY LOOK SEDATED.
OOH. A SALE!

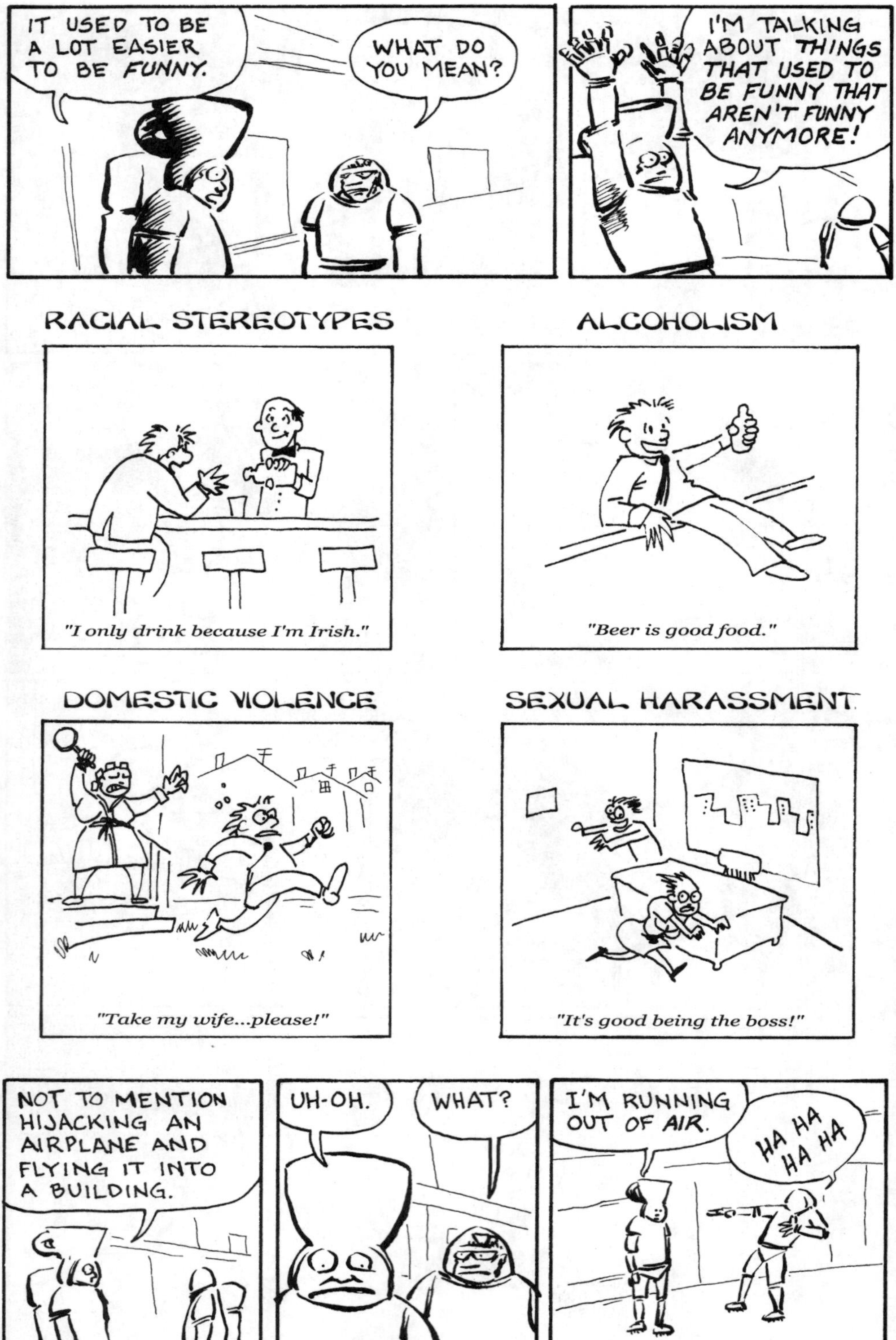
IT USED TO BE A LOT EASIER TO BE FUNNY.
WHAT DO YOU MEAN?
I'M TALKING ABOUT THINGS THAT USED TO BE FUNNY THAT AREN'T FUNNY ANYMORE!
RACIAL STEREOTYPES
"I only drink because I'm Irish."
ALCOHOLISM
"Beer is good food."
DOMESTIC VIOLENCE
"Take my wife...please!"
SEXUAL HARASSMENT
"It's good being the boss!"
NOT TO MENTION HIJACKING AN AIRPLANE AND FLYING IT INTO A BUILDING.
UH-OH.
WHAT?
I'M RUNNING OUT OF AIR.
HA HA HA HA

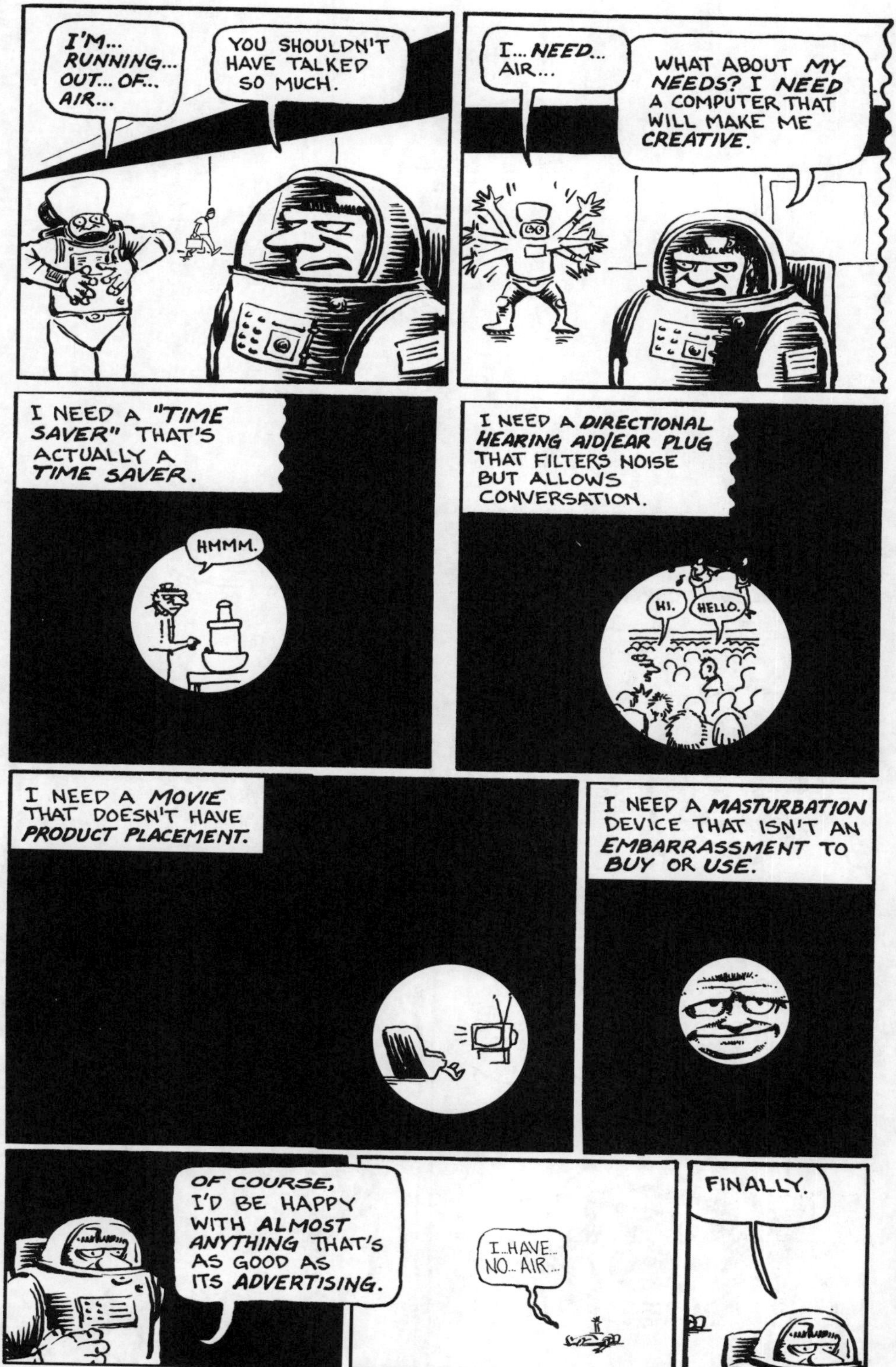
I'M... RUNNING... OUT... OF... AIR...
YOU SHOULDN'T HAVE TALKED SO MUCH.
I... NEED... AIR...
WHAT ABOUT MY NEEDS? I NEED A COMPUTER THAT WILL MAKE ME CREATIVE.
I NEED A "TIME SAVER" THAT'S ACTUALLY A TIME SAVER.
HMMM.
I NEED A DIRECTIONAL HEARING AID/EAR PLUG THAT FILTERS NOISE BUT ALLOWS CONVERSATION.
HI.
HELLO.
I NEED A MOVIE THAT DOESN'T HAVE PRODUCT PLACEMENT.
I NEED A MASTURBATION DEVICE THAT ISN'T AN EMBARRASSMENT TO BUY OR USE.
OF COURSE, I'D BE HAPPY WITH ALMOST ANYTHING THAT'S AS GOOD AS ITS ADVERTISING.
I...HAVE... NO... AIR...
FINALLY.

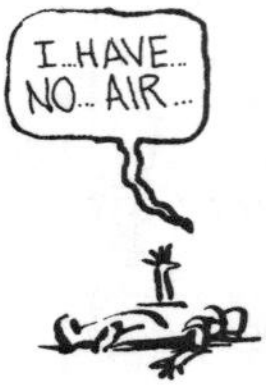
I...HAVE...
NO... AIR...

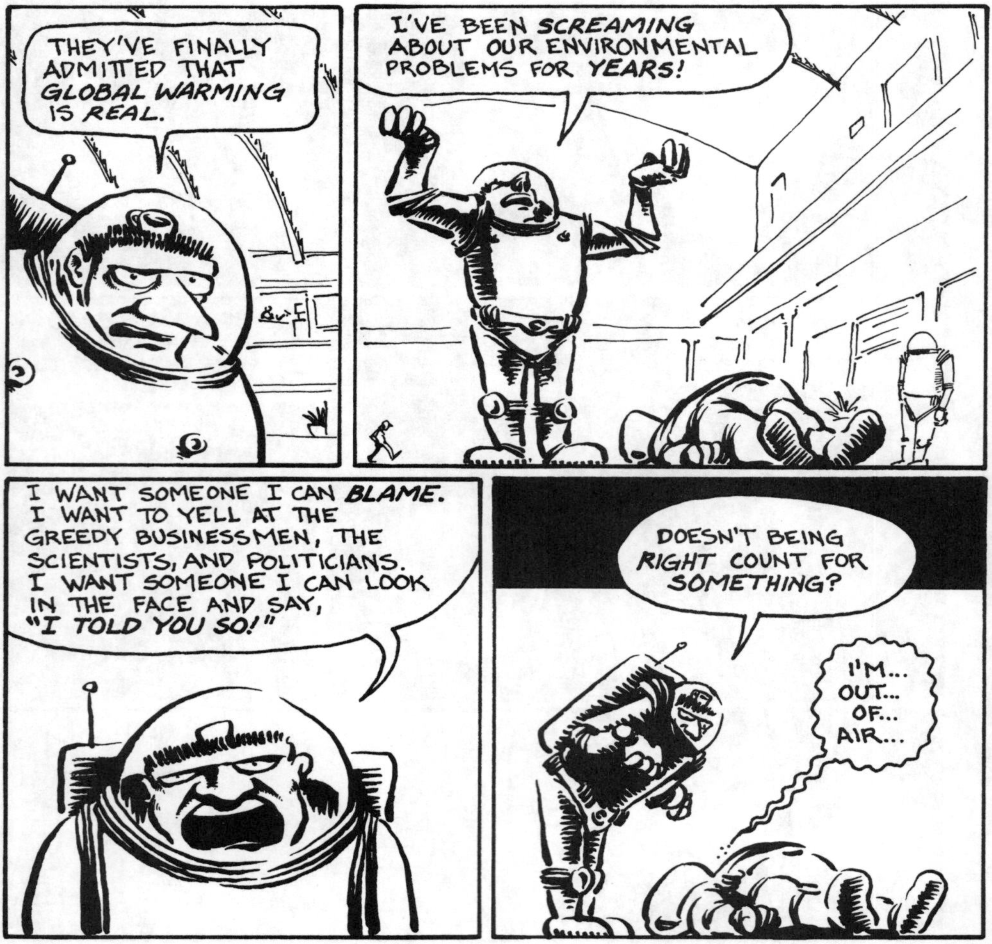
THEY'VE FINALLY ADMITTED THAT GLOBAL WARMING IS REAL.
I'VE BEEN SCREAMING ABOUT OUR ENVIRONMENTAL PROBLEMS FOR YEARS!
I WANT SOMEONE I CAN BLAME. I WANT TO YELL AT THE GREEDY BUSINESSMEN, THE SCIENTISTS, AND POLITICIANS. I WANT SOMEONE I CAN LOOK IN THE FACE AND SAY, "I TOLD YOU SO!"
DOESN'T BEING RIGHT COUNT FOR SOMETHING?
I'M... OUT... OF... AIR...

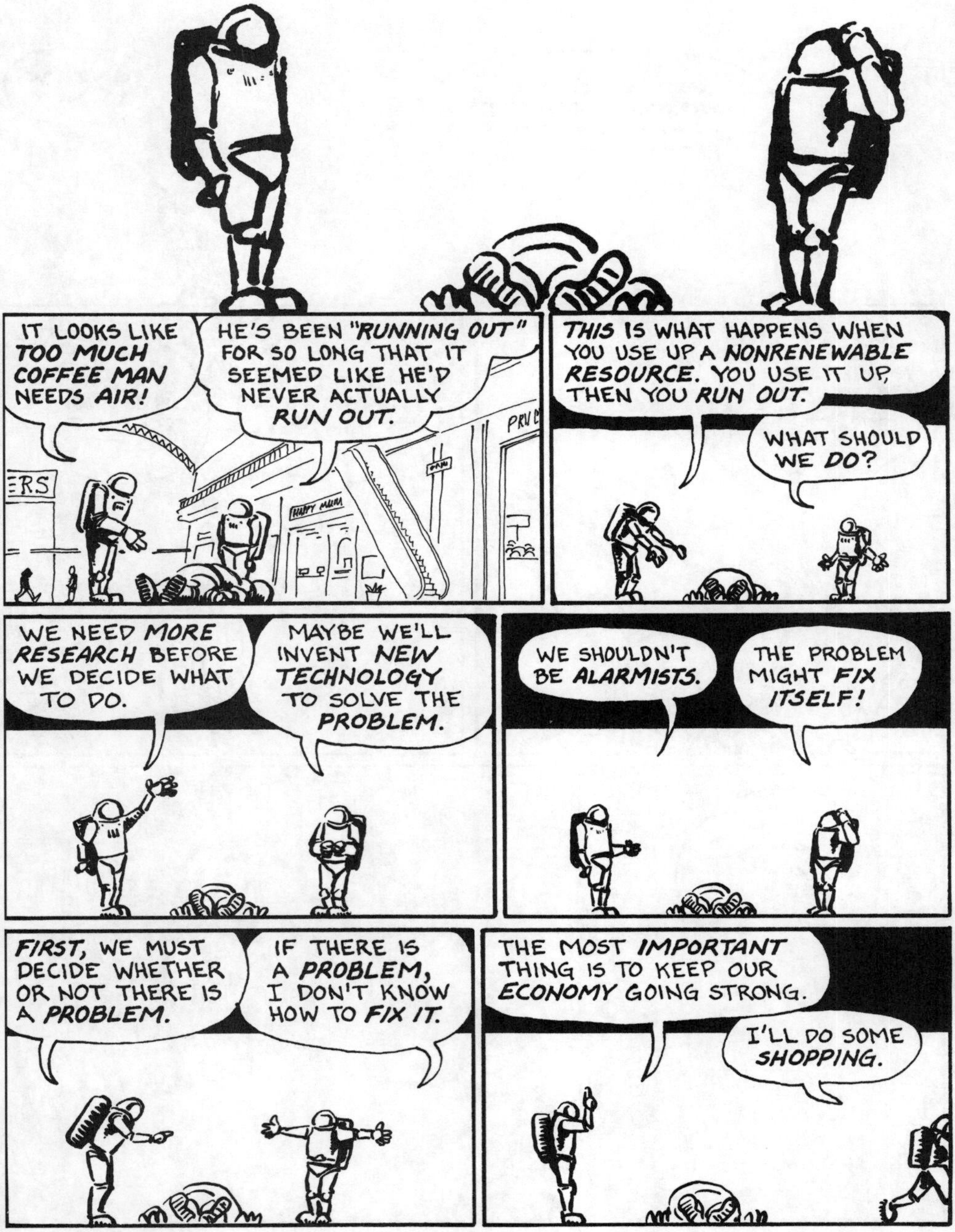

IT LOOKS LIKE TOO MUCH COFFEE MAN NEEDS AIR!
HE'S BEEN "RUNNING OUT" FOR SO LONG THAT IT SEEMED LIKE HE'D NEVER ACTUALLY RUN OUT.
ERS
HAPPY MUMU
PRV
THIS IS WHAT HAPPENS WHEN YOU USE UP A NONRENEWABLE RESOURCE. YOU USE IT UP, THEN YOU RUN OUT.
WHAT SHOULD WE DO?
WE NEED MORE RESEARCH BEFORE WE DECIDE WHAT TO DO.
MAYBE WE'LL INVENT NEW TECHNOLOGY TO SOLVE THE PROBLEM.
WE SHOULDN'T BE ALARMISTS.
THE PROBLEM MIGHT FIX ITSELF!
FIRST, WE MUST DECIDE WHETHER OR NOT THERE IS A PROBLEM.
IF THERE IS A PROBLEM, I DON'T KNOW HOW TO FIX IT.
THE MOST IMPORTANT THING IS TO KEEP OUR ECONOMY GOING STRONG.
I'LL DO SOME SHOPPING.

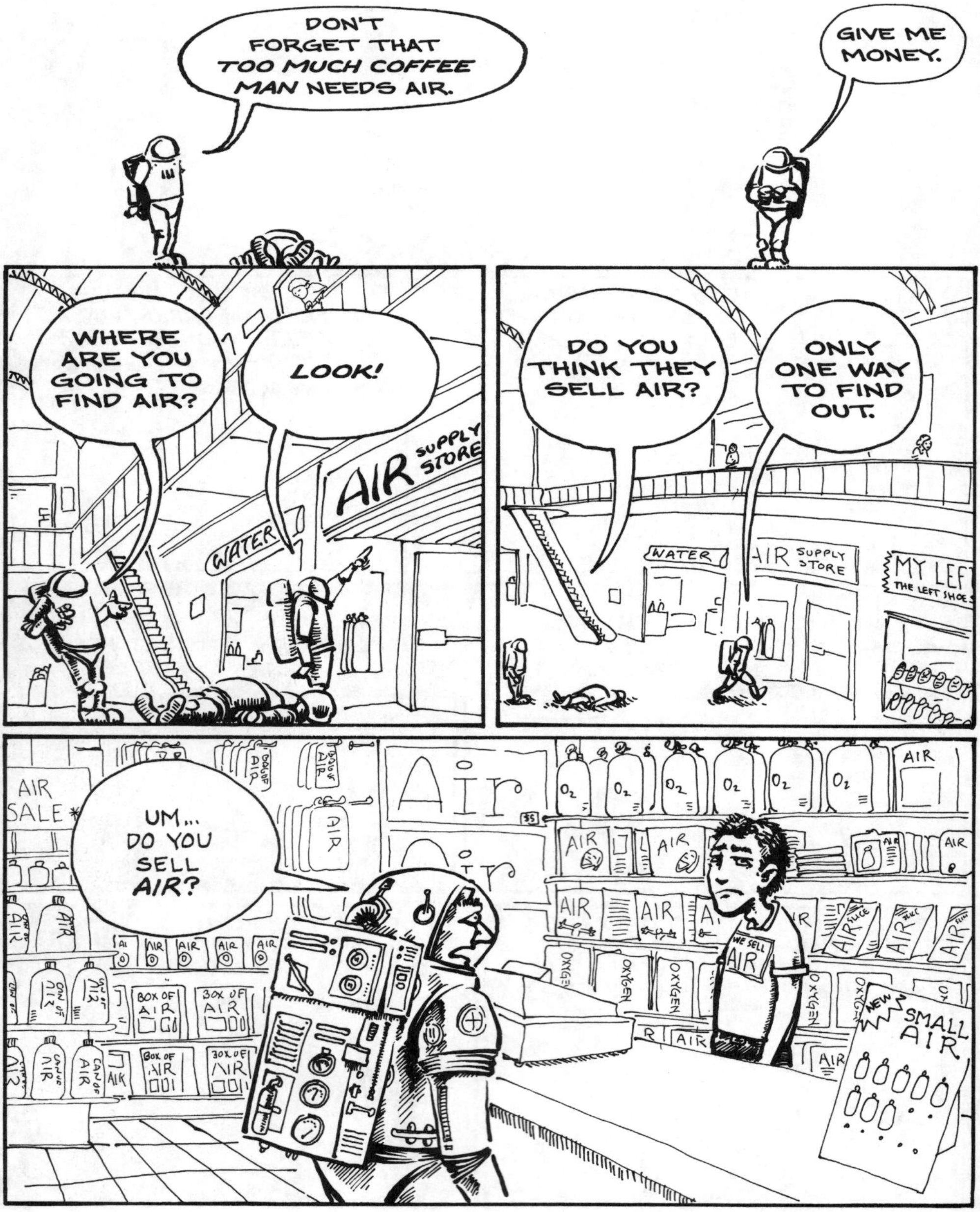
DON'T FORGET THAT TOO MUCH COFFEE MAN NEEDS AIR.
GIVE ME MONEY.
WHERE ARE YOU GOING TO FIND AIR?
LOOK!
AIR SUPPLY STORE
WATER
DO YOU THINK THEY SELL AIR?
ONLY ONE WAY TO FIND OUT.
WATER
AIR SUPPLY STORE
AIR SALE
UM... DO YOU SELL AIR?
WE SELL AIR
NEW SMALL AIR

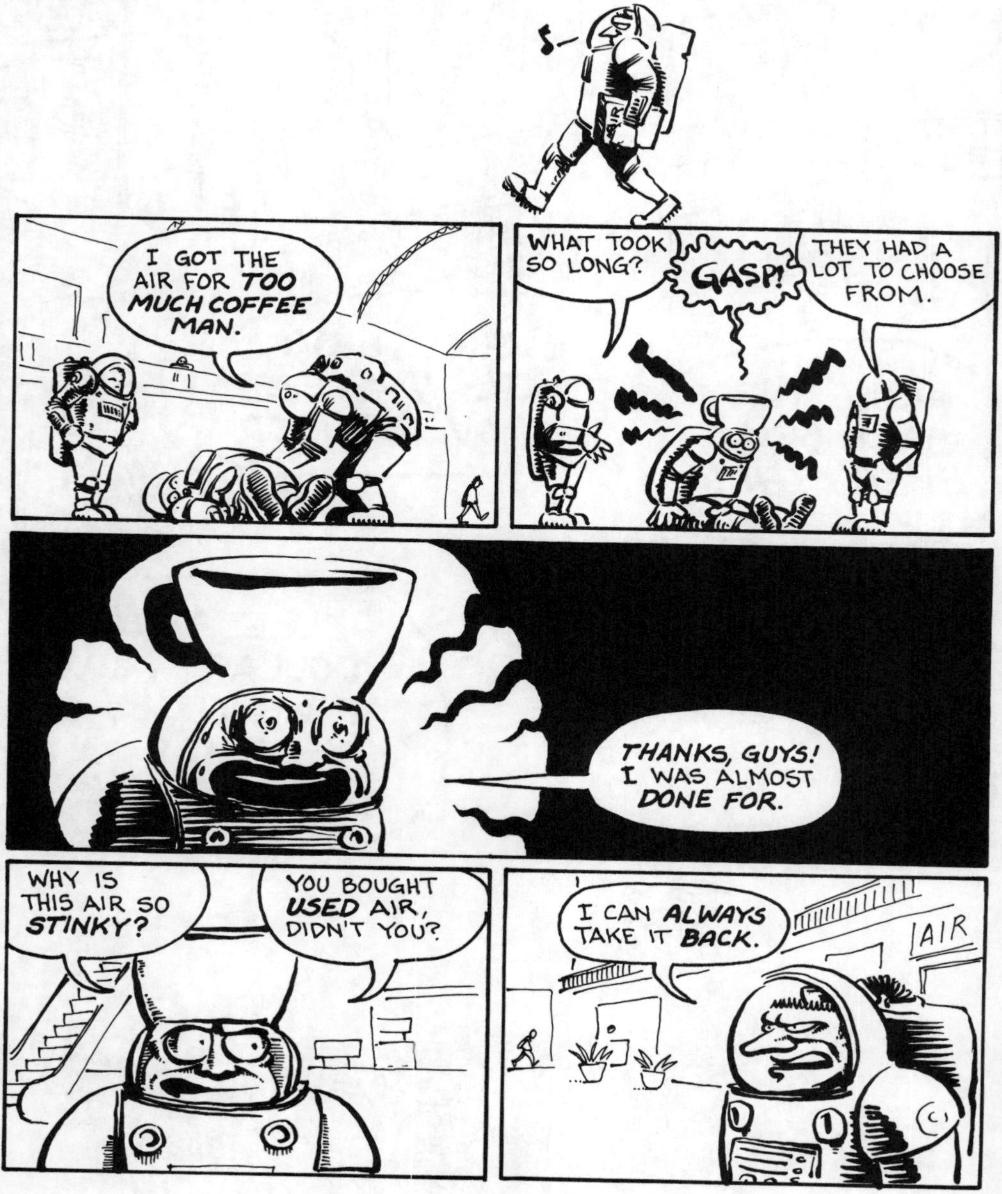
AIR
I GOT THE AIR FOR TOO MUCH COFFEE MAN.
WHAT TOOK SO LONG?
GASP!
THEY HAD A LOT TO CHOOSE FROM.
THANKS, GUYS! I WAS ALMOST DONE FOR.
WHY IS THIS AIR SO STINKY?
YOU BOUGHT USED AIR, DIDN'T YOU?
I CAN ALWAYS TAKE IT BACK.
AIR

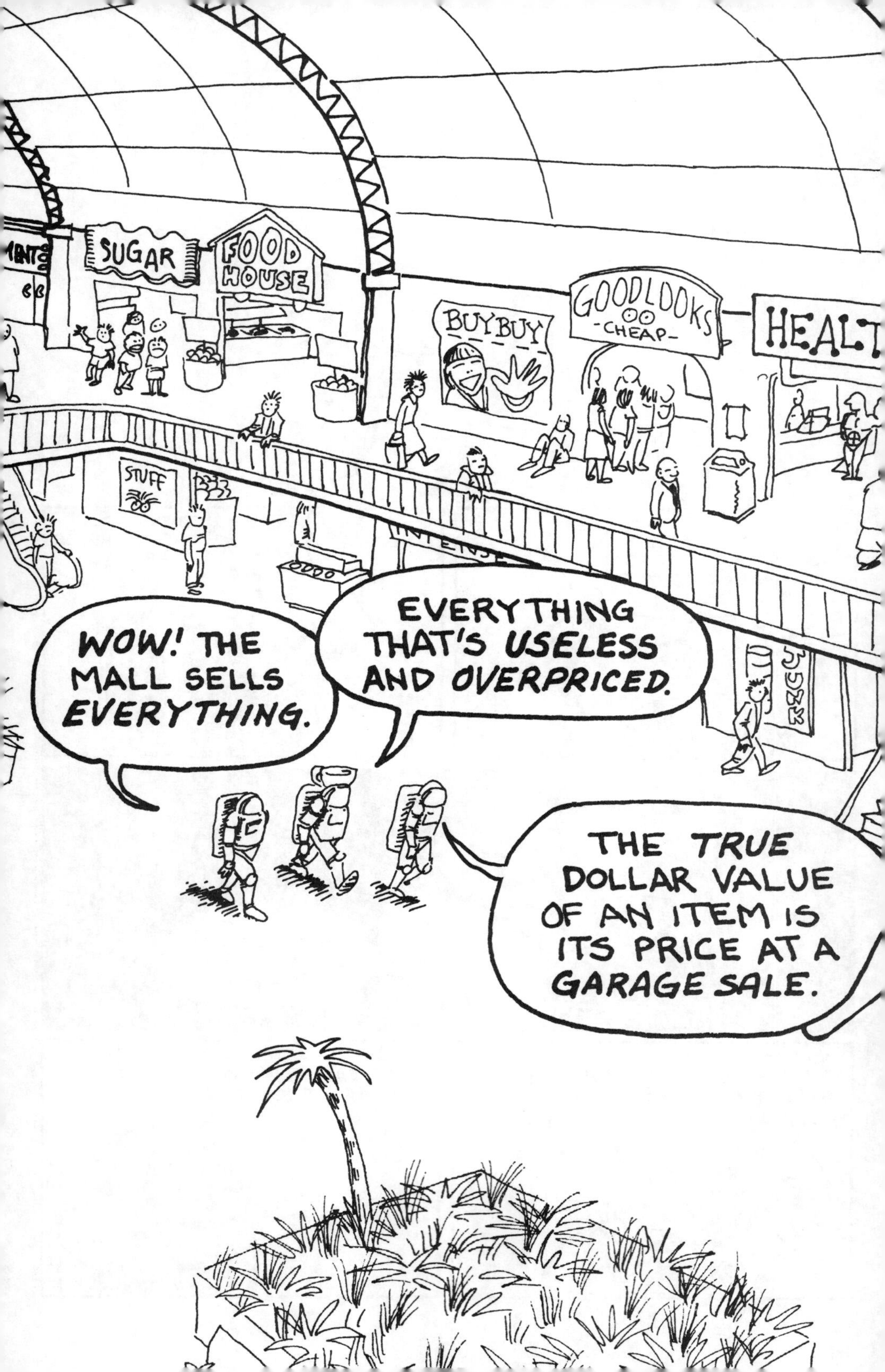
SUGAR
FOOD HOUSE
BUYBUY
GOODLOOKS
CHEAP
HEALT
STUFF
JUNK
WOW! THE MALL SELLS EVERYTHING.
EVERYTHING THAT'S USELESS AND OVERPRICED.
THE TRUE DOLLAR VALUE OF AN ITEM IS ITS PRICE AT A GARAGE SALE.

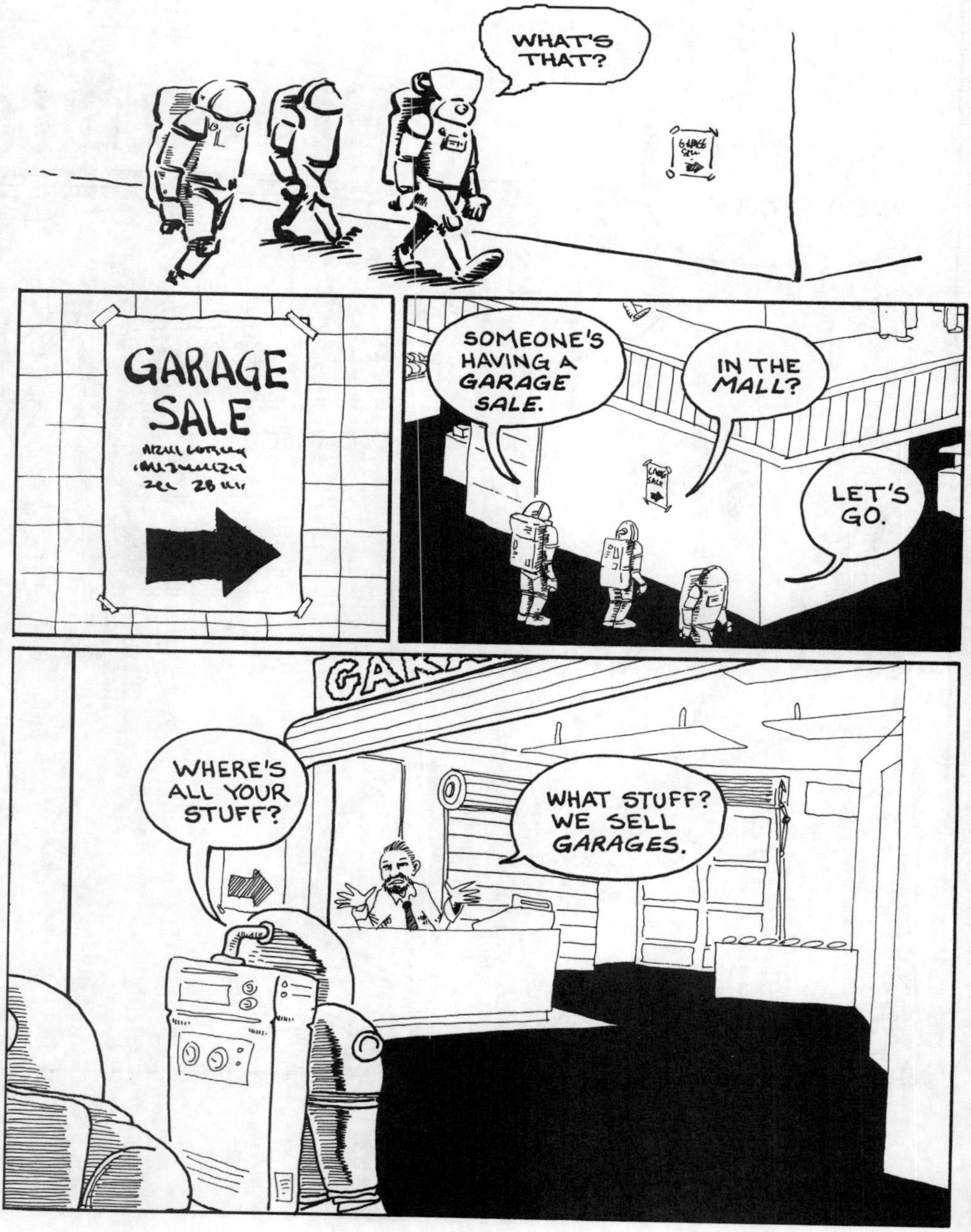
WHAT'S THAT?
GARAGE SALE
SOMEONE'S HAVING A GARAGE SALE.
IN THE MALL?
LET'S GO.
WHERE'S ALL YOUR STUFF?
WHAT STUFF? WE SELL GARAGES.

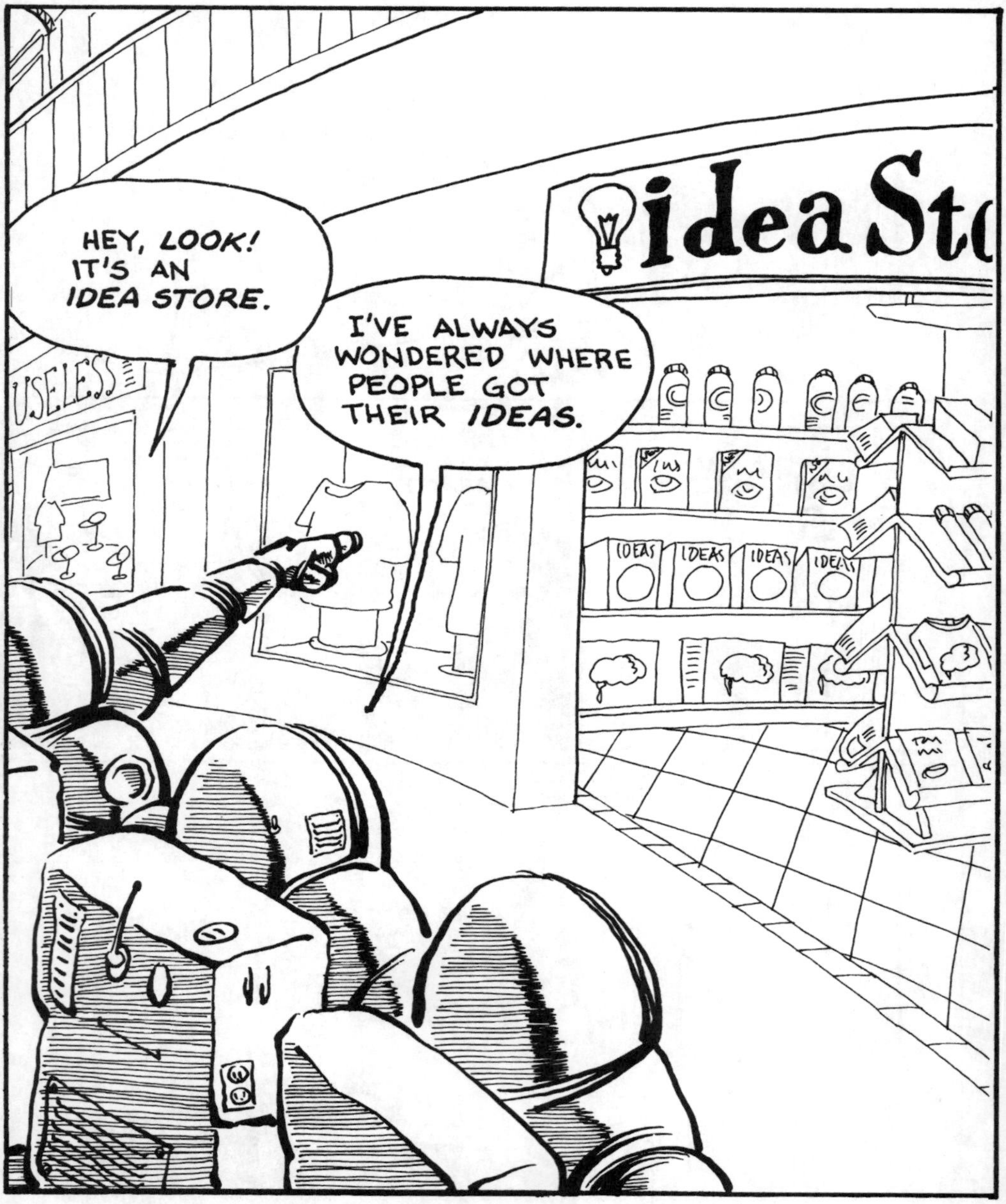
idea
USELESS
HEY, LOOK! IT'S AN IDEA STORE.
I'VE ALWAYS WONDERED WHERE PEOPLE GOT THEIR IDEAS.
IDEAS

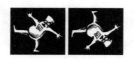

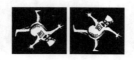

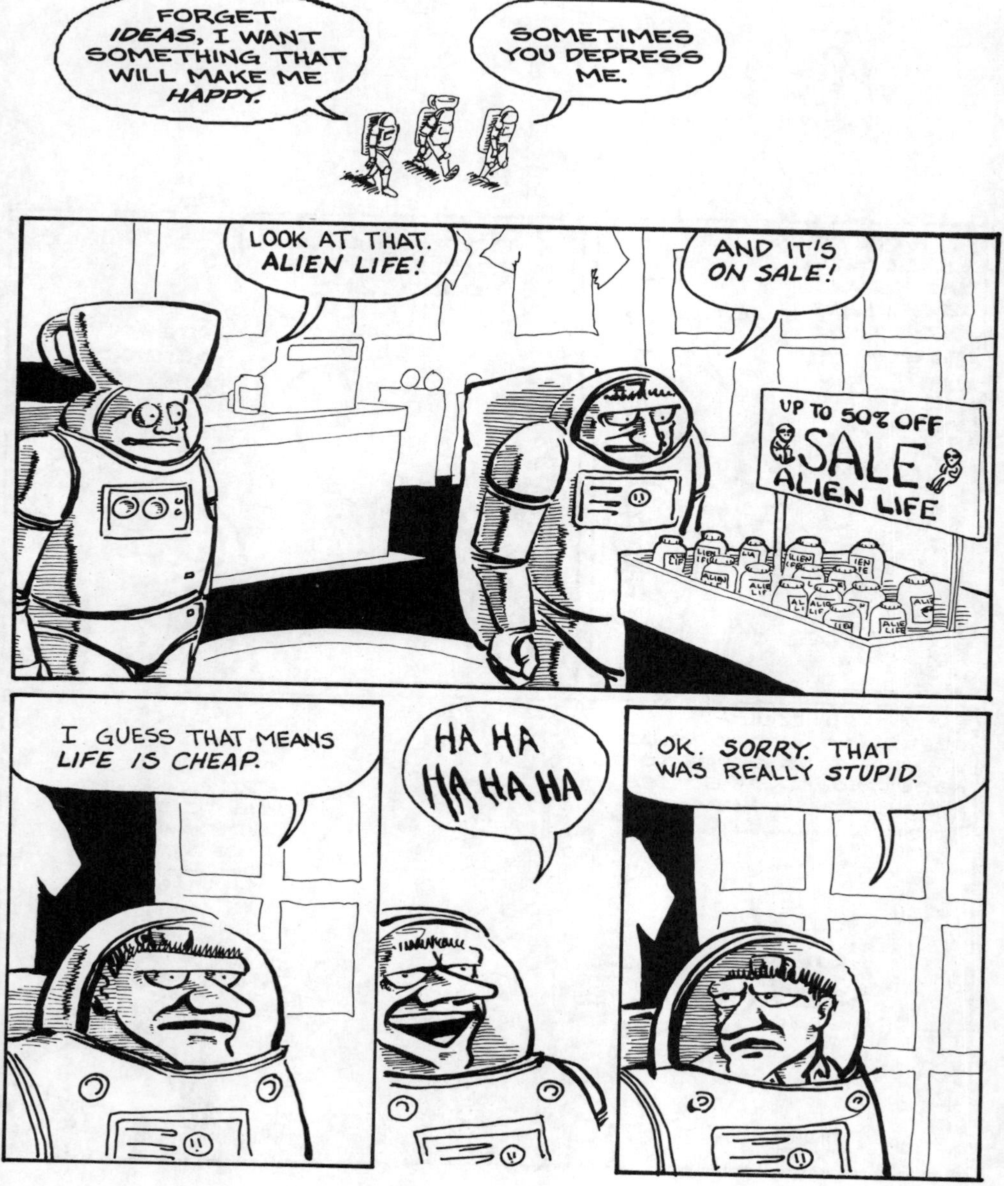
FORGET IDEAS, I WANT SOMETHING THAT WILL MAKE ME HAPPY.
SOMETIMES YOU DEPRESS ME.
LOOK AT THAT. ALIEN LIFE!
AND IT'S ON SALE!
UP TO 50% OFF
SALE
ALIEN LIFE
I GUESS THAT MEANS LIFE IS CHEAP.
HA HA HA HA HA
OK. SORRY. THAT WAS REALLY STUPID.

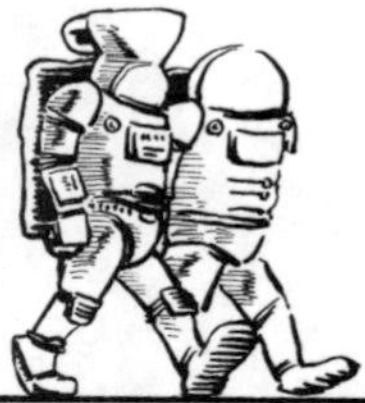

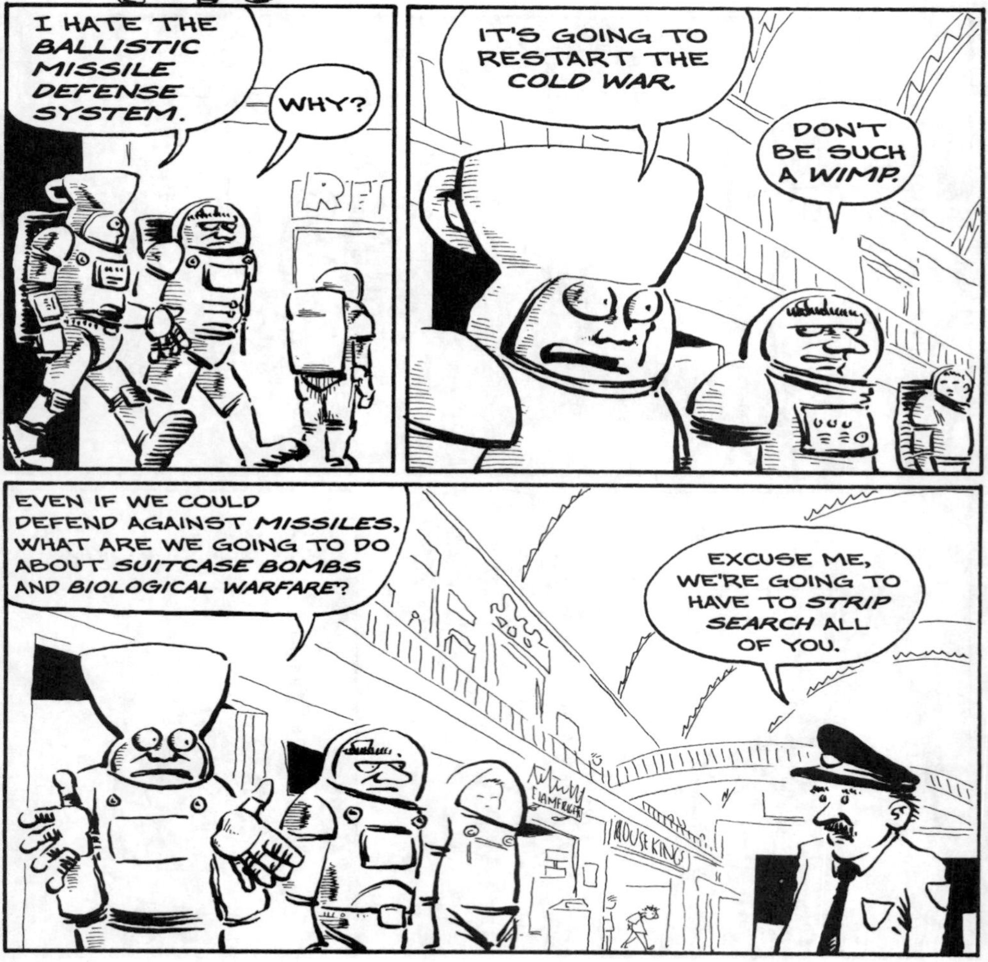

I HATE THE *BALLISTIC MISSILE DEFENSE SYSTEM.*
WHY?
IT'S GOING TO RESTART THE *COLD WAR.*
DON'T BE SUCH A *WIMP.*
EVEN IF WE COULD DEFEND AGAINST *MISSILES,* WHAT ARE WE GOING TO DO ABOUT *SUITCASE BOMBS* AND *BIOLOGICAL WARFARE?*
EXCUSE ME, WE'RE GOING TO HAVE TO *STRIP SEARCH* ALL OF YOU.

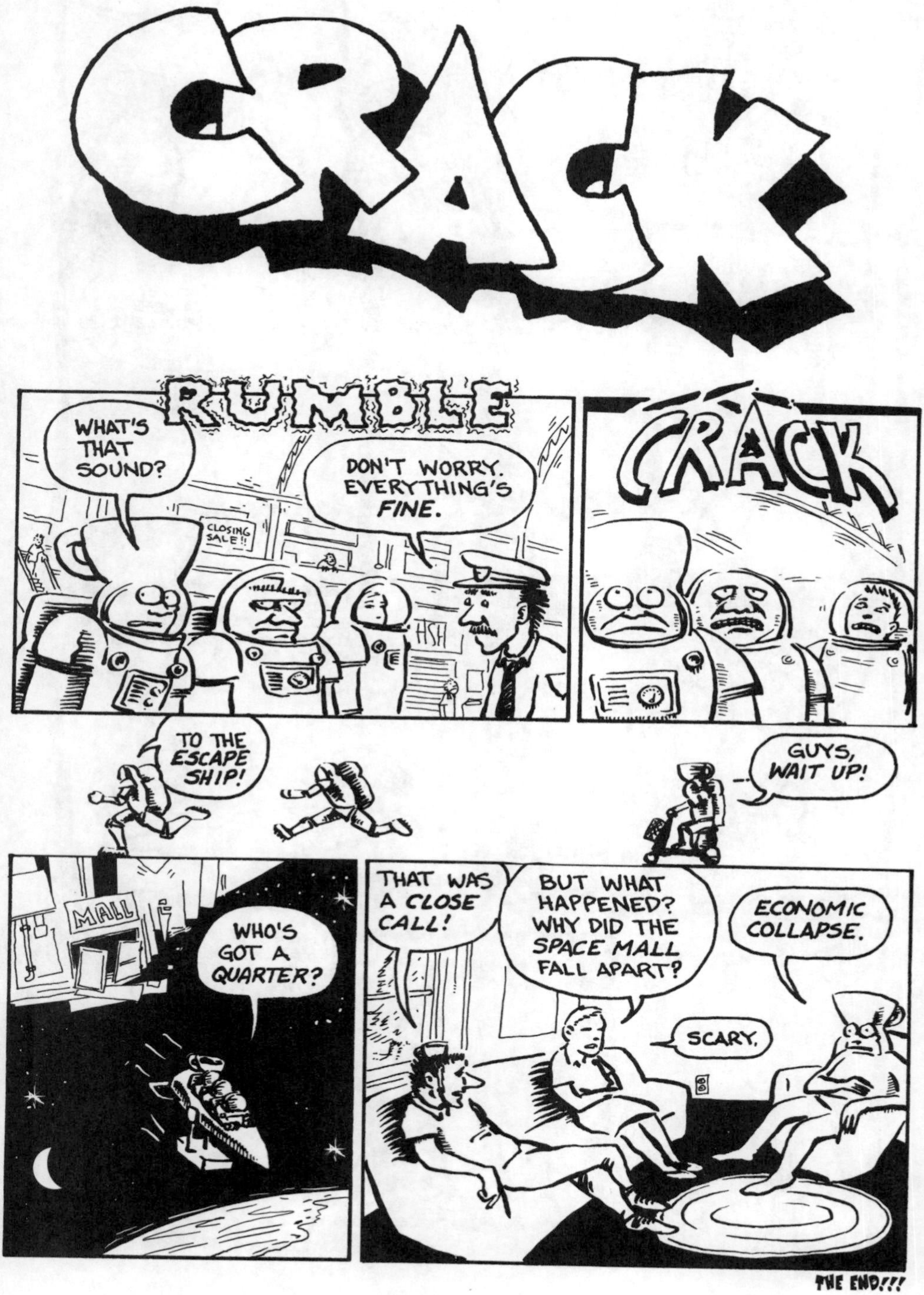
CRACK
RUMBLE
WHAT'S THAT SOUND?
DON'T WORRY. EVERYTHING'S FINE.
CLOSING SALE!!
CRACK
TO THE ESCAPE SHIP!
GUYS, WAIT UP!
MALL
WHO'S GOT A QUARTER?
THAT WAS A CLOSE CALL!
BUT WHAT HAPPENED? WHY DID THE SPACE MALL FALL APART?
ECONOMIC COLLAPSE.
SCARY.
THE END!!!

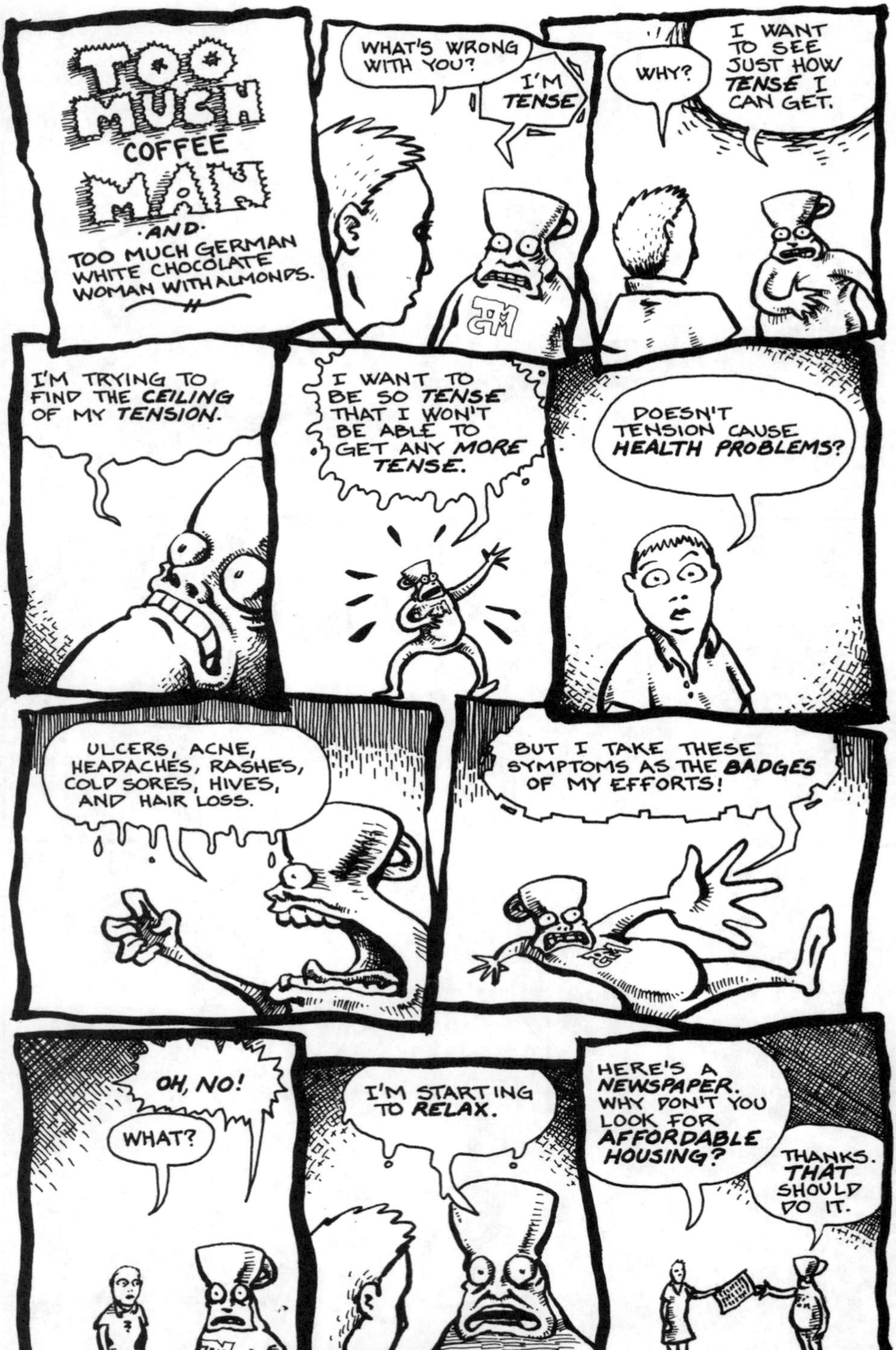
TOO MUCH COFFEE MAN
·AND·
TOO MUCH GERMAN WHITE CHOCOLATE WOMAN WITH ALMONDS.
WHAT'S WRONG WITH YOU?
I'M TENSE
WHY?
I WANT TO SEE JUST HOW TENSE I CAN GET.
I'M TRYING TO FIND THE CEILING OF MY TENSION.
I WANT TO BE SO TENSE THAT I WON'T BE ABLE TO GET ANY MORE TENSE.
DOESN'T TENSION CAUSE HEALTH PROBLEMS?
ULCERS, ACNE, HEADACHES, RASHES, COLD SORES, HIVES, AND HAIR LOSS.
BUT I TAKE THESE SYMPTOMS AS THE BADGES OF MY EFFORTS!
OH, NO!
WHAT?
I'M STARTING TO RELAX.
HERE'S A NEWSPAPER. WHY DON'T YOU LOOK FOR AFFORDABLE HOUSING?
THANKS. THAT SHOULD DO IT.

Too Much Coffee Man

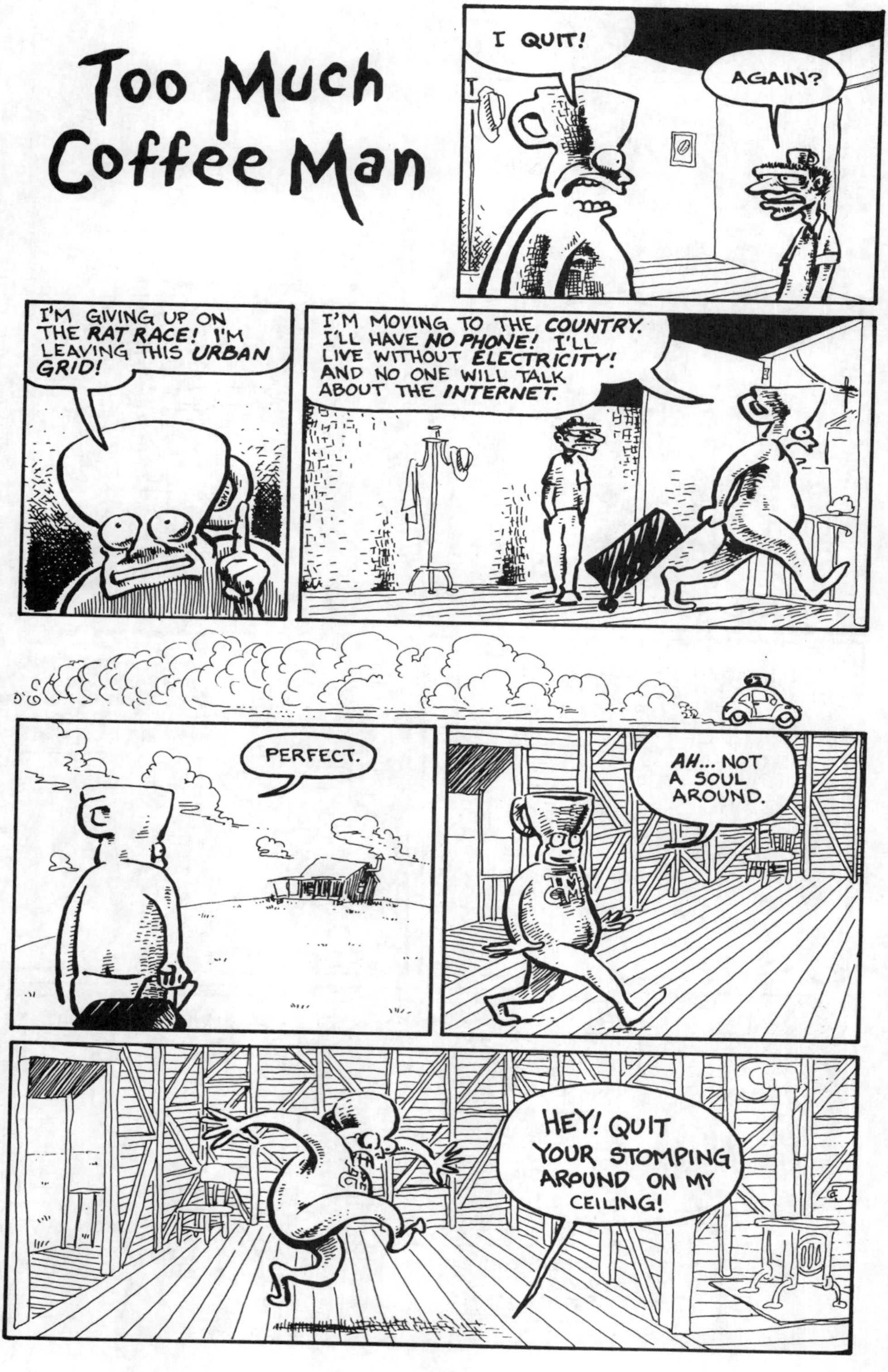
I QUIT!
AGAIN?
I'M GIVING UP ON THE RAT RACE! I'M LEAVING THIS URBAN GRID!
I'M MOVING TO THE COUNTRY. I'LL HAVE NO PHONE! I'LL LIVE WITHOUT ELECTRICITY! AND NO ONE WILL TALK ABOUT THE INTERNET.
PERFECT.
AH... NOT A SOUL AROUND.
HEY! QUIT YOUR STOMPING AROUND ON MY CEILING!

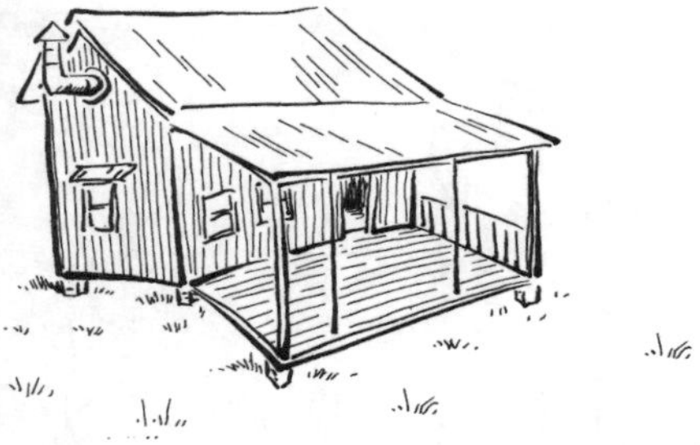

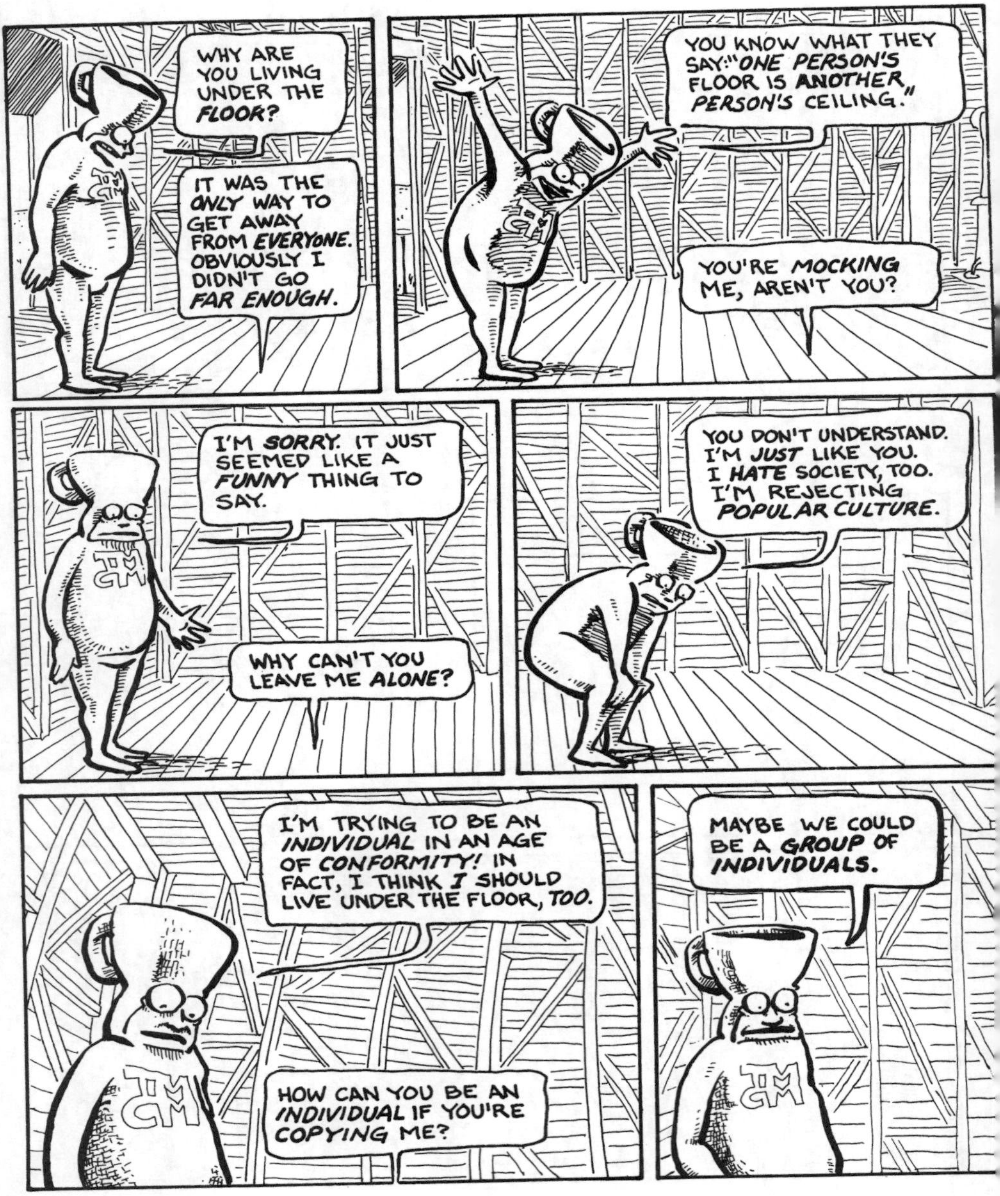
WHY ARE YOU LIVING UNDER THE FLOOR?
IT WAS THE ONLY WAY TO GET AWAY FROM EVERYONE. OBVIOUSLY I DIDN'T GO FAR ENOUGH.
YOU KNOW WHAT THEY SAY: "ONE PERSON'S FLOOR IS ANOTHER PERSON'S CEILING."
YOU'RE MOCKING ME, AREN'T YOU?
I'M SORRY. IT JUST SEEMED LIKE A FUNNY THING TO SAY.
WHY CAN'T YOU LEAVE ME ALONE?
YOU DON'T UNDERSTAND. I'M JUST LIKE YOU. I HATE SOCIETY, TOO. I'M REJECTING POPULAR CULTURE.
I'M TRYING TO BE AN INDIVIDUAL IN AN AGE OF CONFORMITY! IN FACT, I THINK I SHOULD LIVE UNDER THE FLOOR, TOO.
HOW CAN YOU BE AN INDIVIDUAL IF YOU'RE COPYING ME?
MAYBE WE COULD BE A GROUP OF INDIVIDUALS.

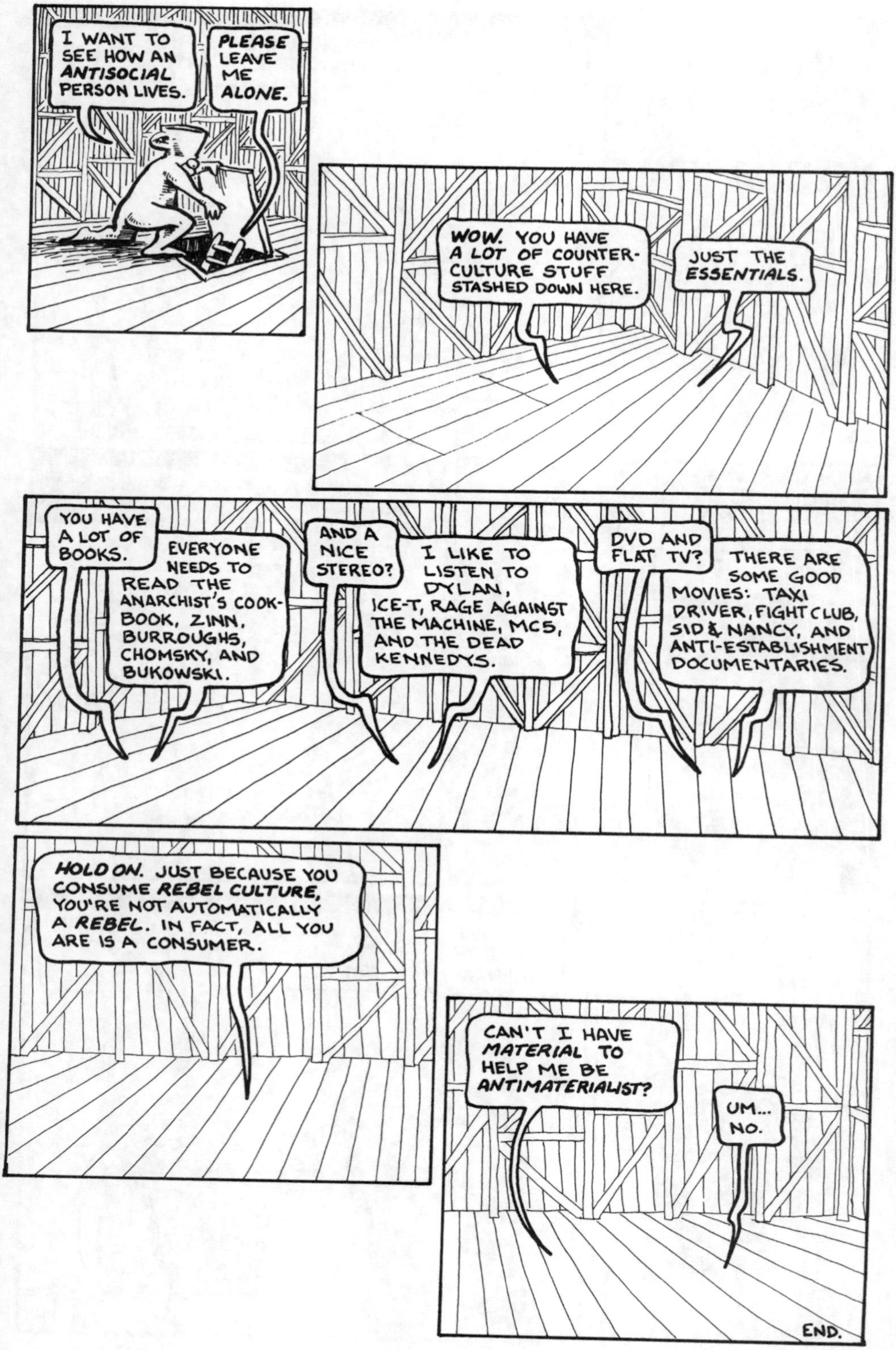
I WANT TO SEE HOW AN ANTISOCIAL PERSON LIVES.
PLEASE LEAVE ME ALONE.
WOW. YOU HAVE A LOT OF COUNTER-CULTURE STUFF STASHED DOWN HERE.
JUST THE ESSENTIALS.
YOU HAVE A LOT OF BOOKS.
EVERYONE NEEDS TO READ THE ANARCHIST'S COOK-BOOK, ZINN, BURROUGHS, CHOMSKY, AND BUKOWSKI.
AND A NICE STEREO?
I LIKE TO LISTEN TO DYLAN, ICE-T, RAGE AGAINST THE MACHINE, MC5, AND THE DEAD KENNEDYS.
DVD AND FLAT TV?
THERE ARE SOME GOOD MOVIES: TAXI DRIVER, FIGHT CLUB, SID & NANCY, AND ANTI-ESTABLISHMENT DOCUMENTARIES.
HOLD ON. JUST BECAUSE YOU CONSUME REBEL CULTURE, YOU'RE NOT AUTOMATICALLY A REBEL. IN FACT, ALL YOU ARE IS A CONSUMER.
CAN'T I HAVE MATERIAL TO HELP ME BE ANTIMATERIALIST?
UM... NO.
END.

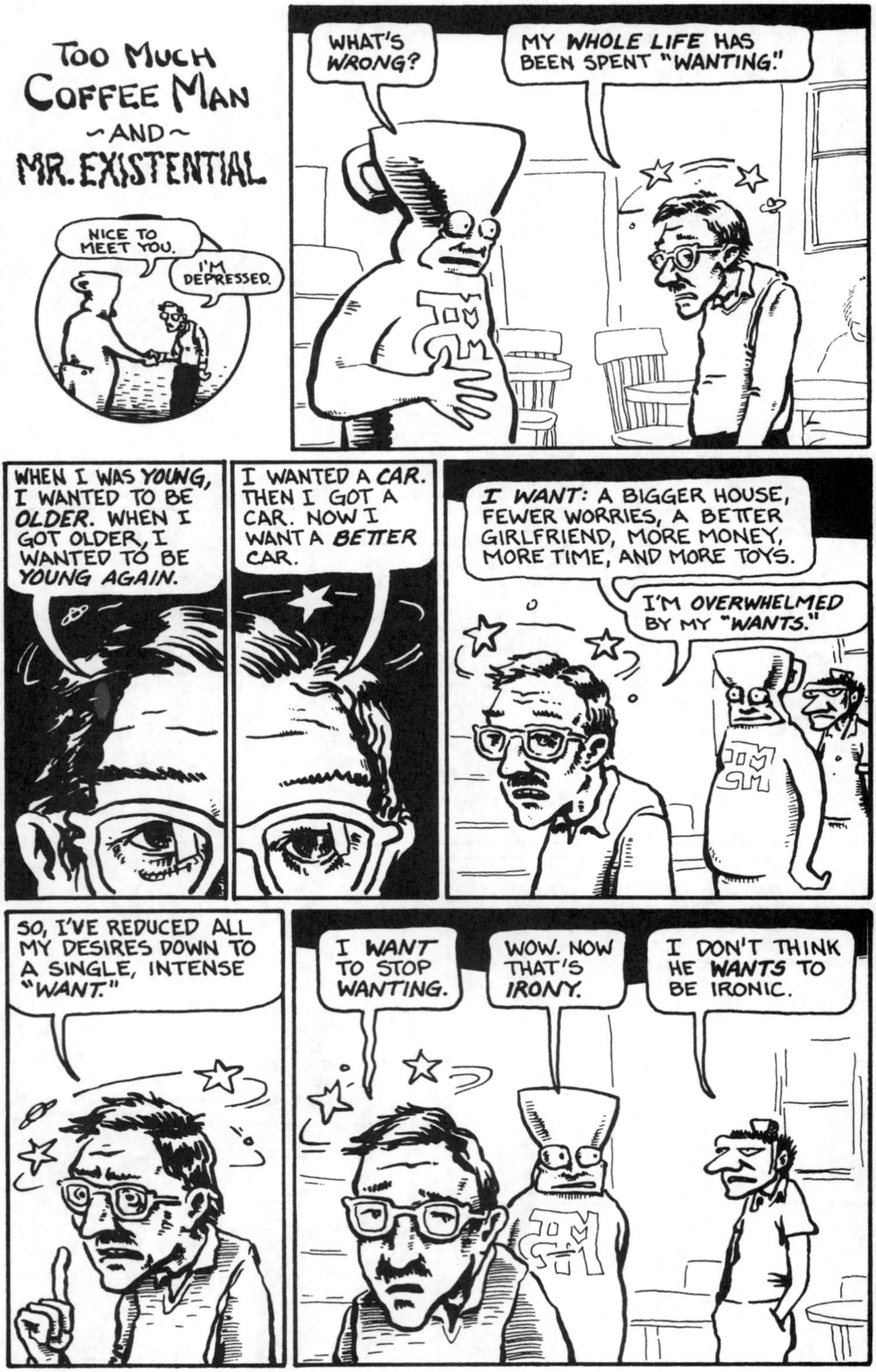
TOO MUCH COFFEE MAN
~AND~
MR. EXISTENTIAL
NICE TO MEET YOU.
I'M DEPRESSED.
WHAT'S WRONG?
MY WHOLE LIFE HAS BEEN SPENT "WANTING."
WHEN I WAS YOUNG, I WANTED TO BE OLDER. WHEN I GOT OLDER, I WANTED TO BE YOUNG AGAIN.
I WANTED A CAR. THEN I GOT A CAR. NOW I WANT A BETTER CAR.
I WANT: A BIGGER HOUSE, FEWER WORRIES, A BETTER GIRLFRIEND, MORE MONEY, MORE TIME, AND MORE TOYS.
I'M OVERWHELMED BY MY "WANTS."
SO, I'VE REDUCED ALL MY DESIRES DOWN TO A SINGLE, INTENSE "WANT."
I WANT TO STOP WANTING.
WOW. NOW THAT'S IRONY.
I DON'T THINK HE WANTS TO BE IRONIC.

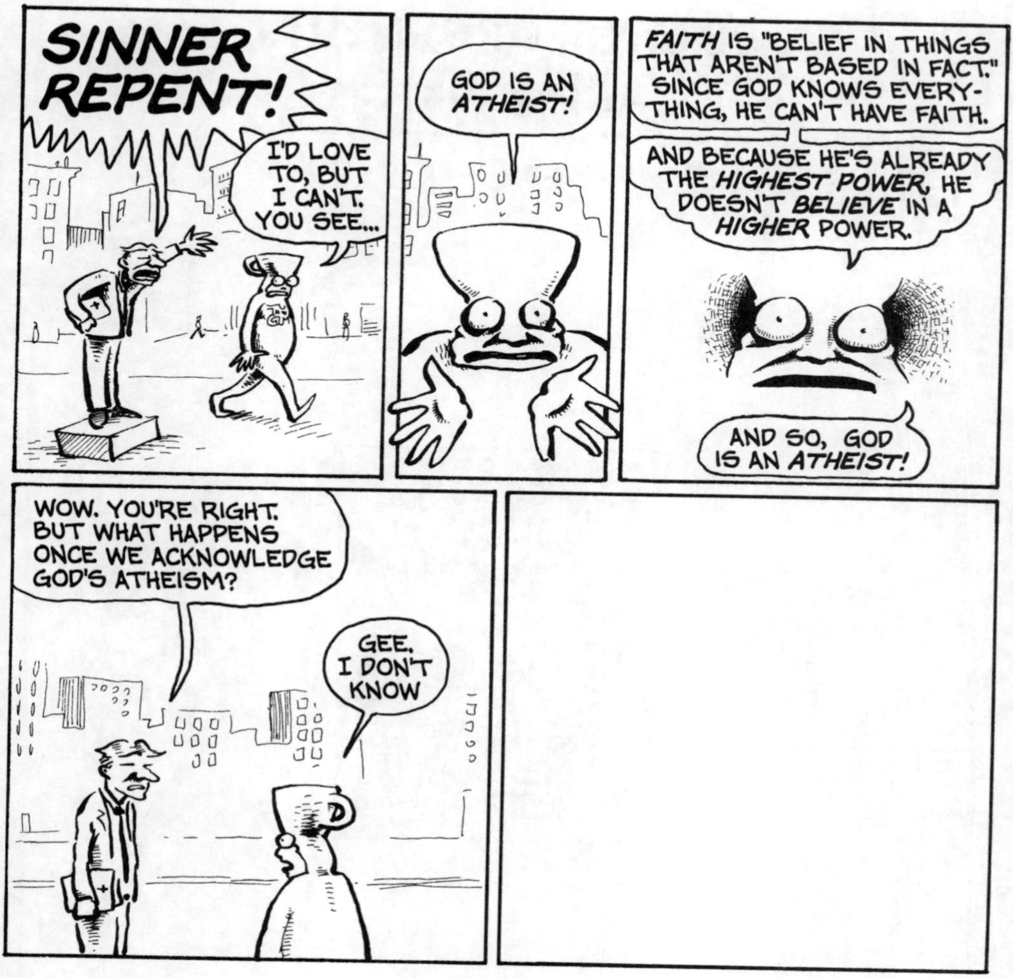
SINNER REPENT!
I'D LOVE TO, BUT I CAN'T. YOU SEE...
GOD IS AN *ATHEIST!*
FAITH IS "BELIEF IN THINGS THAT AREN'T BASED IN FACT." SINCE GOD KNOWS EVERY-THING, HE CAN'T HAVE FAITH.
AND BECAUSE HE'S ALREADY THE *HIGHEST POWER,* HE DOESN'T *BELIEVE* IN A *HIGHER* POWER.
AND SO, GOD IS AN *ATHEIST!*
WOW. YOU'RE RIGHT. BUT WHAT HAPPENS ONCE WE ACKNOWLEDGE GOD'S ATHEISM?
GEE. I DON'T KNOW

chapter 7

DEBATES, ARGUMENTS, AND STORIES

Money is a placebo, and other thoughts

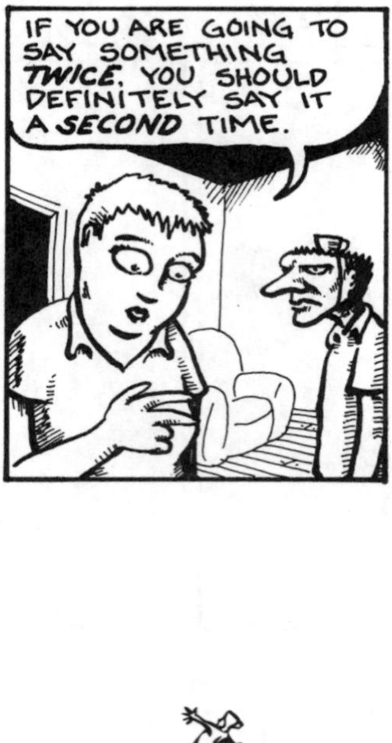
IF YOU ARE GOING TO SAY SOMETHING *TWICE*, YOU SHOULD DEFINITELY SAY IT A *SECOND* TIME.

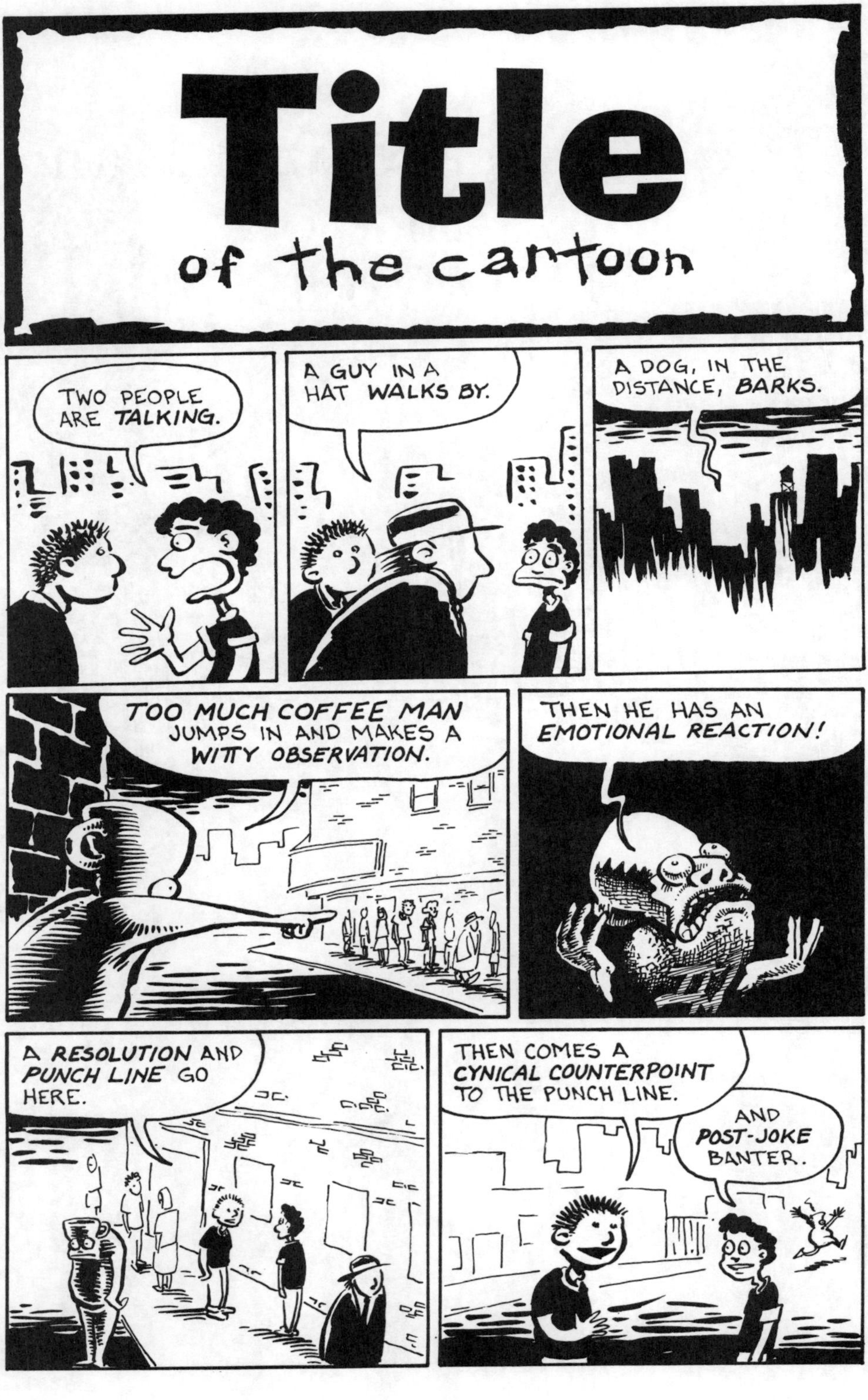
Title
of the cartoon
TWO PEOPLE ARE TALKING.
A GUY IN A HAT WALKS BY.
A DOG, IN THE DISTANCE, BARKS.
TOO MUCH COFFEE MAN JUMPS IN AND MAKES A WITTY OBSERVATION.
THEN HE HAS AN EMOTIONAL REACTION!
A RESOLUTION AND PUNCH LINE GO HERE.
THEN COMES A CYNICAL COUNTERPOINT TO THE PUNCH LINE.
AND POST-JOKE BANTER.

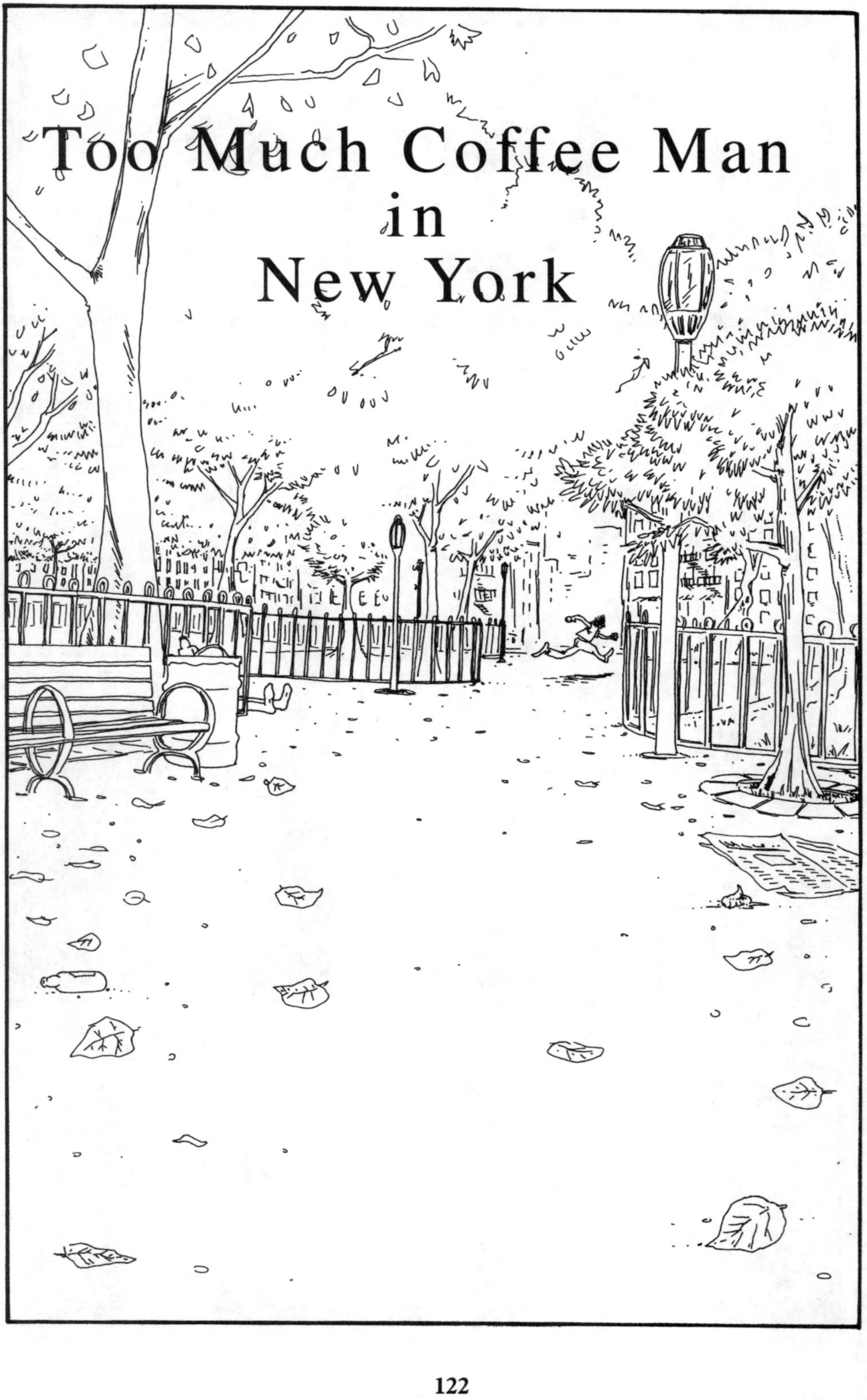
Too Much Coffee Man
in
New York

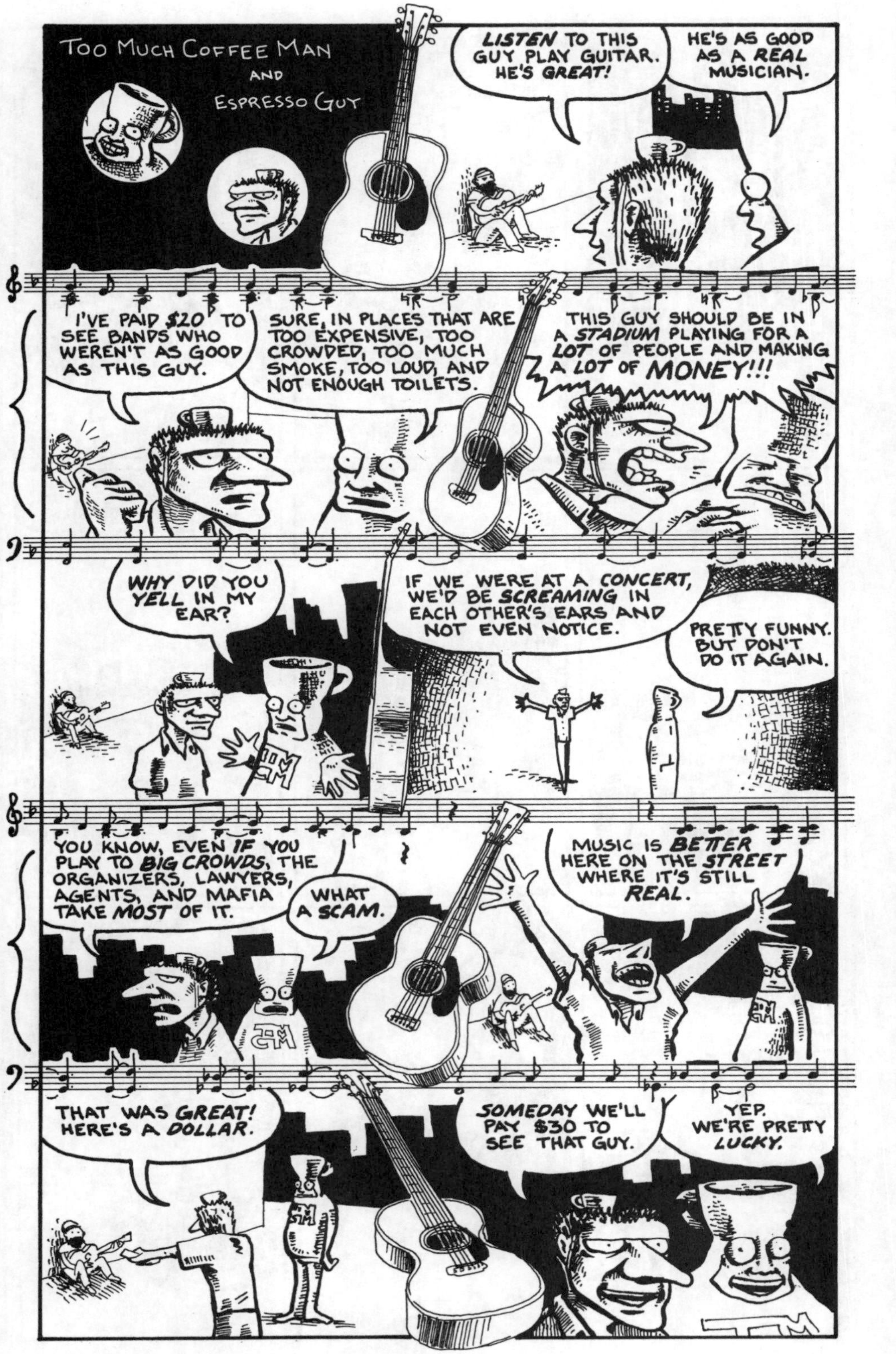

Too Much Coffee Man
and
Espresso Guy
LISTEN TO THIS GUY PLAY GUITAR. HE'S GREAT!
HE'S AS GOOD AS A REAL MUSICIAN.
I'VE PAID $20 TO SEE BANDS WHO WEREN'T AS GOOD AS THIS GUY.
SURE, IN PLACES THAT ARE TOO EXPENSIVE, TOO CROWDED, TOO MUCH SMOKE, TOO LOUD, AND NOT ENOUGH TOILETS.
THIS GUY SHOULD BE IN A STADIUM PLAYING FOR A LOT OF PEOPLE AND MAKING A LOT OF MONEY!!!
WHY DID YOU YELL IN MY EAR?
IF WE WERE AT A CONCERT, WE'D BE SCREAMING IN EACH OTHER'S EARS AND NOT EVEN NOTICE.
PRETTY FUNNY. BUT DON'T DO IT AGAIN.
YOU KNOW, EVEN IF YOU PLAY TO BIG CROWDS, THE ORGANIZERS, LAWYERS, AGENTS, AND MAFIA TAKE MOST OF IT.
WHAT A SCAM.
MUSIC IS BETTER HERE ON THE STREET WHERE IT'S STILL REAL.
THAT WAS GREAT! HERE'S A DOLLAR.
SOMEDAY WE'LL PAY $30 TO SEE THAT GUY.
YEP. WE'RE PRETTY LUCKY.

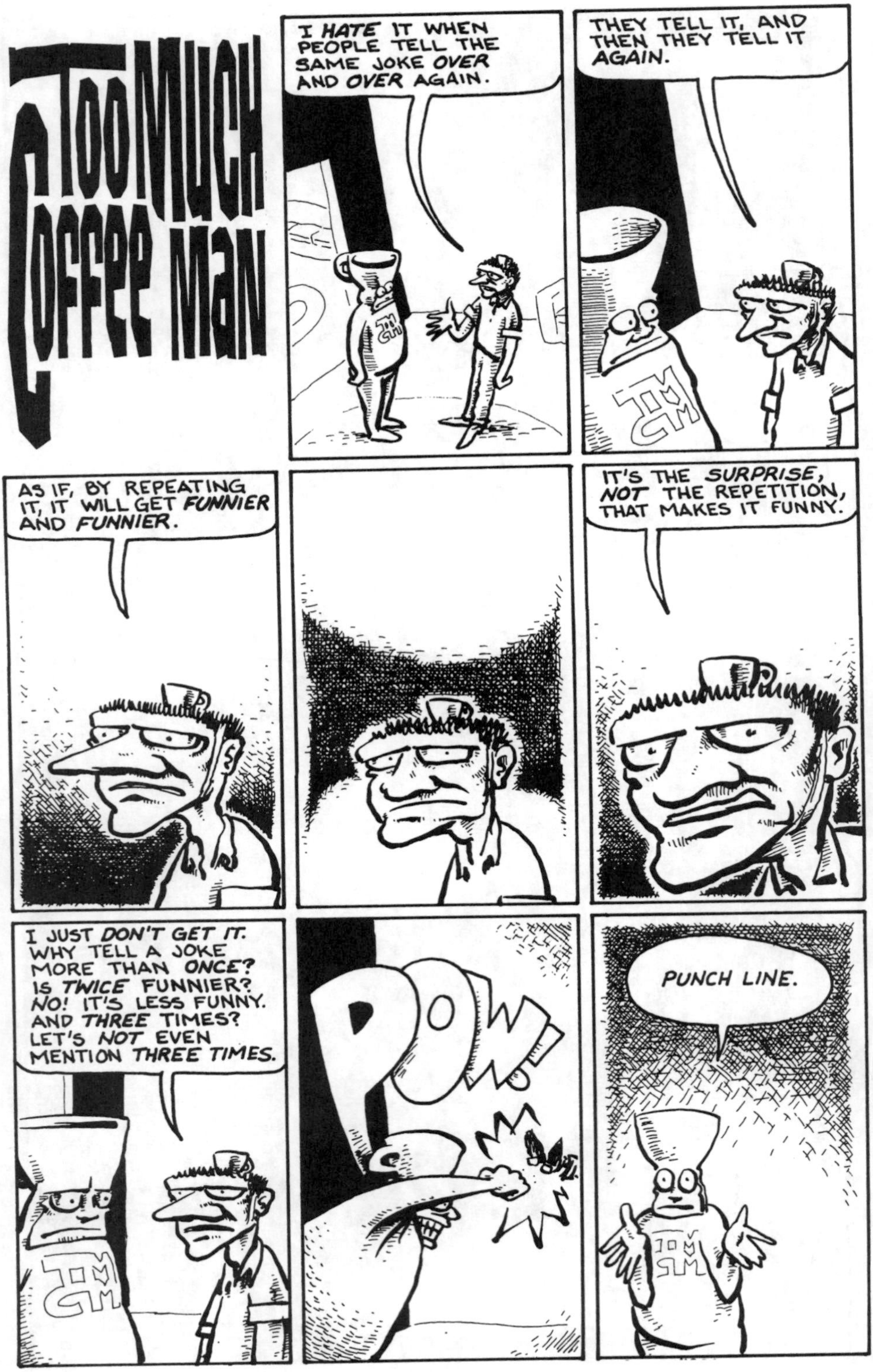
A TOO MUCH COFFEE MAN
I HATE IT WHEN PEOPLE TELL THE SAME JOKE OVER AND OVER AGAIN.
THEY TELL IT, AND THEN THEY TELL IT AGAIN.
AS IF, BY REPEATING IT, IT WILL GET FUNNIER AND FUNNIER.
IT'S THE SURPRISE, NOT THE REPETITION, THAT MAKES IT FUNNY.
I JUST DON'T GET IT. WHY TELL A JOKE MORE THAN ONCE? IS TWICE FUNNIER? NO! IT'S LESS FUNNY. AND THREE TIMES? LET'S NOT EVEN MENTION THREE TIMES.
POW!
PUNCH LINE.

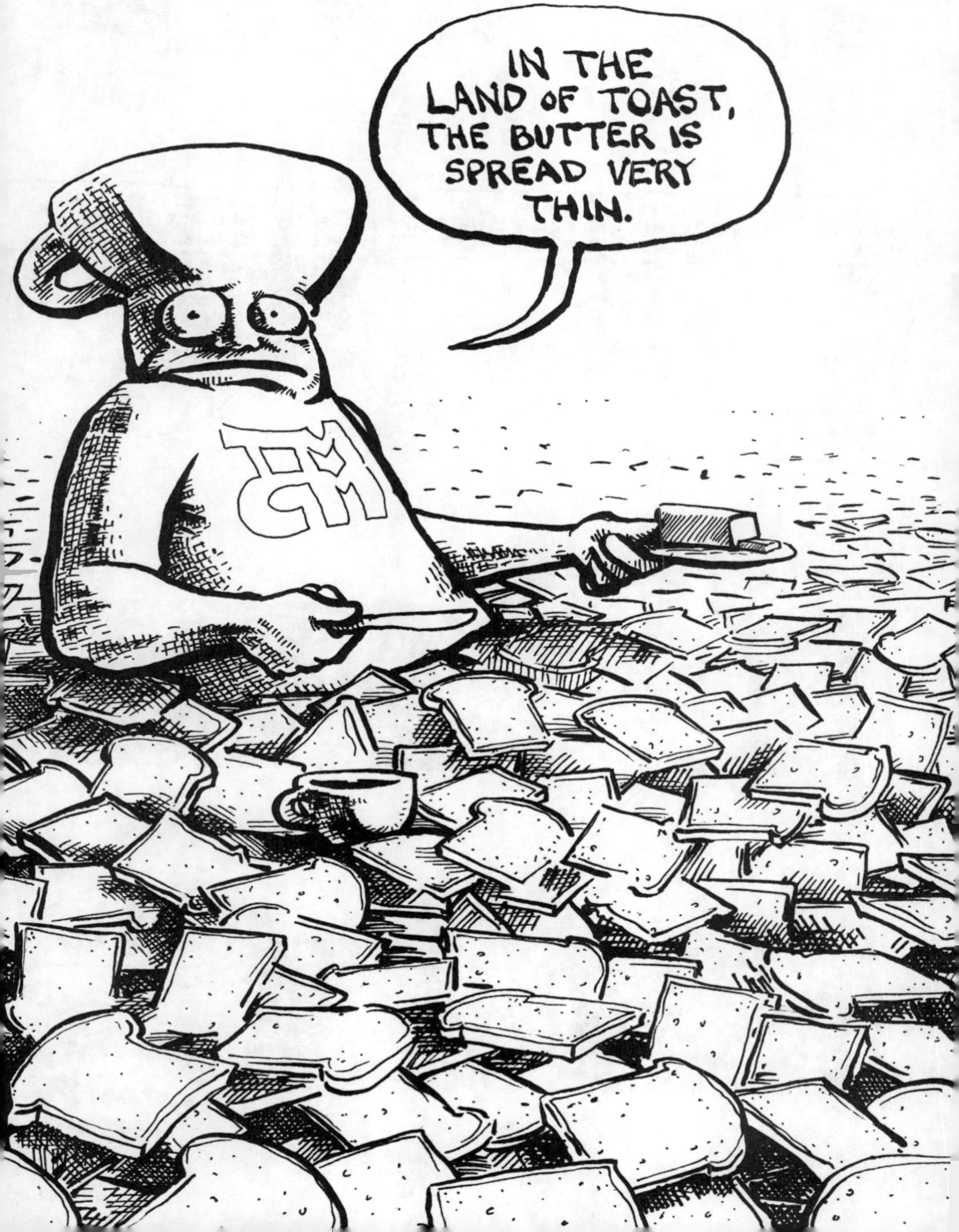
IN THE LAND OF TOAST, THE BUTTER IS SPREAD VERY THIN.

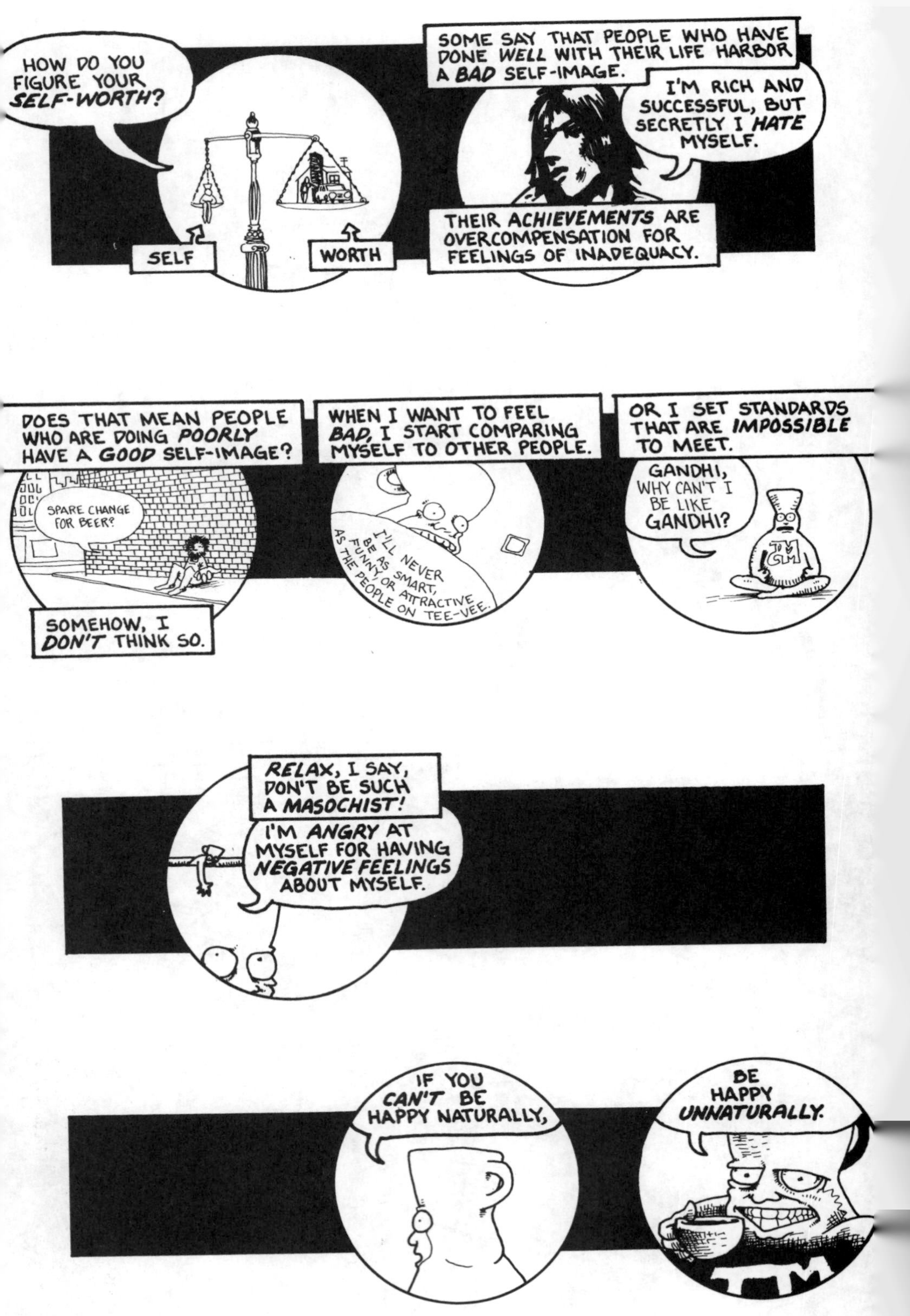
HOW DO YOU FIGURE YOUR *SELF-WORTH*?
SELF
WORTH
SOME SAY THAT PEOPLE WHO HAVE DONE *WELL* WITH THEIR LIFE HARBOR A *BAD* SELF-IMAGE.
I'M RICH AND SUCCESSFUL, BUT SECRETLY I *HATE* MYSELF.
THEIR *ACHIEVEMENTS* ARE OVERCOMPENSATION FOR FEELINGS OF INADEQUACY.
DOES THAT MEAN PEOPLE WHO ARE DOING *POORLY* HAVE A *GOOD* SELF-IMAGE?
SPARE CHANGE FOR BEER?
SOMEHOW, I *DON'T* THINK SO.
WHEN I WANT TO FEEL *BAD*, I START COMPARING MYSELF TO OTHER PEOPLE.
I'LL NEVER BE AS SMART, FUNNY, OR ATTRACTIVE AS THE PEOPLE ON TEE-VEE.
OR I SET STANDARDS THAT ARE *IMPOSSIBLE* TO MEET.
GANDHI, WHY CAN'T I BE LIKE GANDHI?
RELAX, I SAY, DON'T BE SUCH A *MASOCHIST*!
I'M *ANGRY* AT MYSELF FOR HAVING *NEGATIVE FEELINGS* ABOUT MYSELF.
IF YOU *CAN'T* BE HAPPY NATURALLY,
BE HAPPY *UNNATURALLY*.
TM

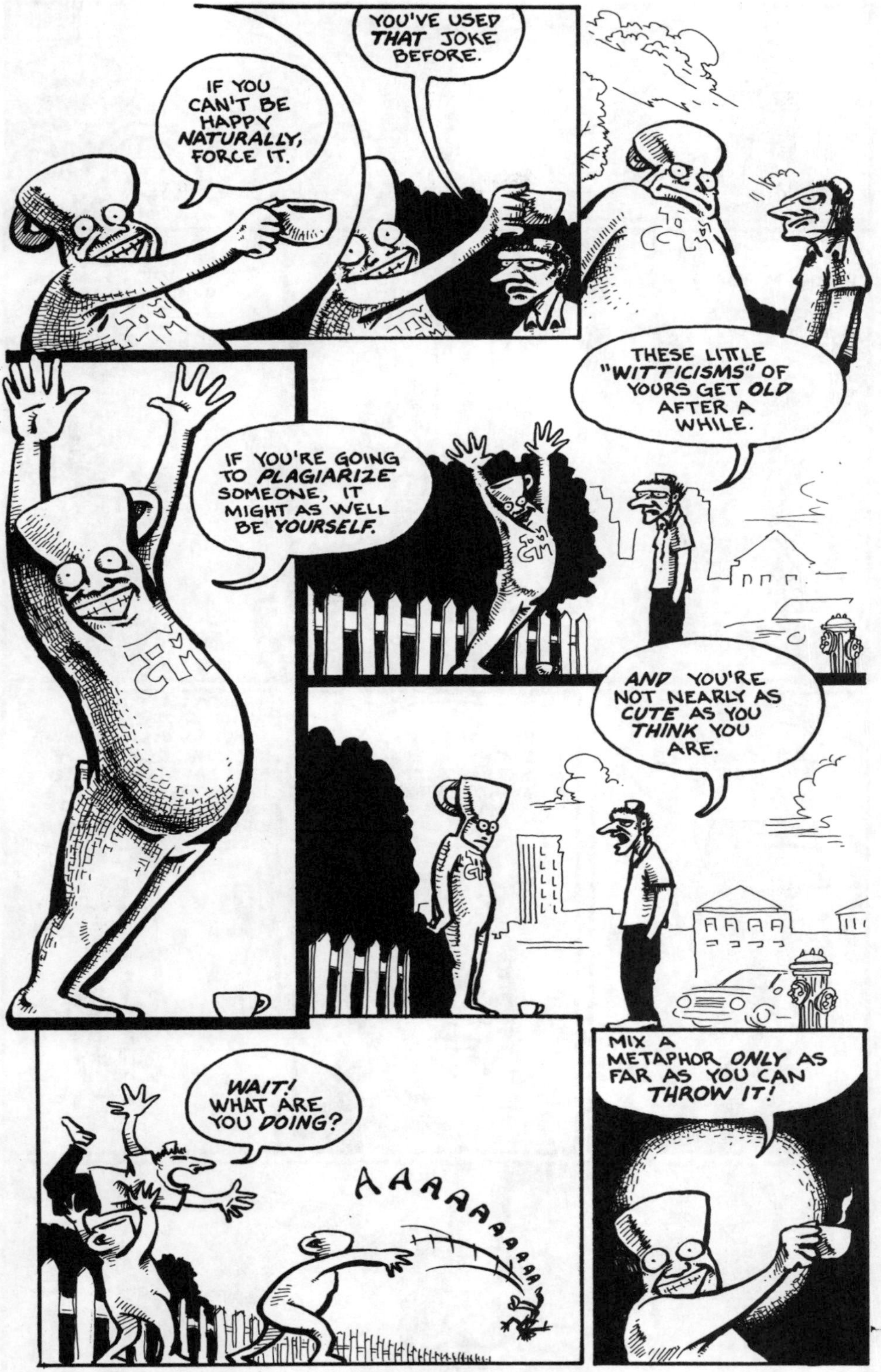
IF YOU CAN'T BE HAPPY NATURALLY, FORCE IT.
YOU'VE USED THAT JOKE BEFORE.
THESE LITTLE "WITTICISMS" OF YOURS GET OLD AFTER A WHILE.
IF YOU'RE GOING TO PLAGIARIZE SOMEONE, IT MIGHT AS WELL BE YOURSELF.
AND YOU'RE NOT NEARLY AS CUTE AS YOU THINK YOU ARE.
WAIT! WHAT ARE YOU DOING?
AAAAAAAAAAAA
MIX A METAPHOR ONLY AS FAR AS YOU CAN THROW IT!

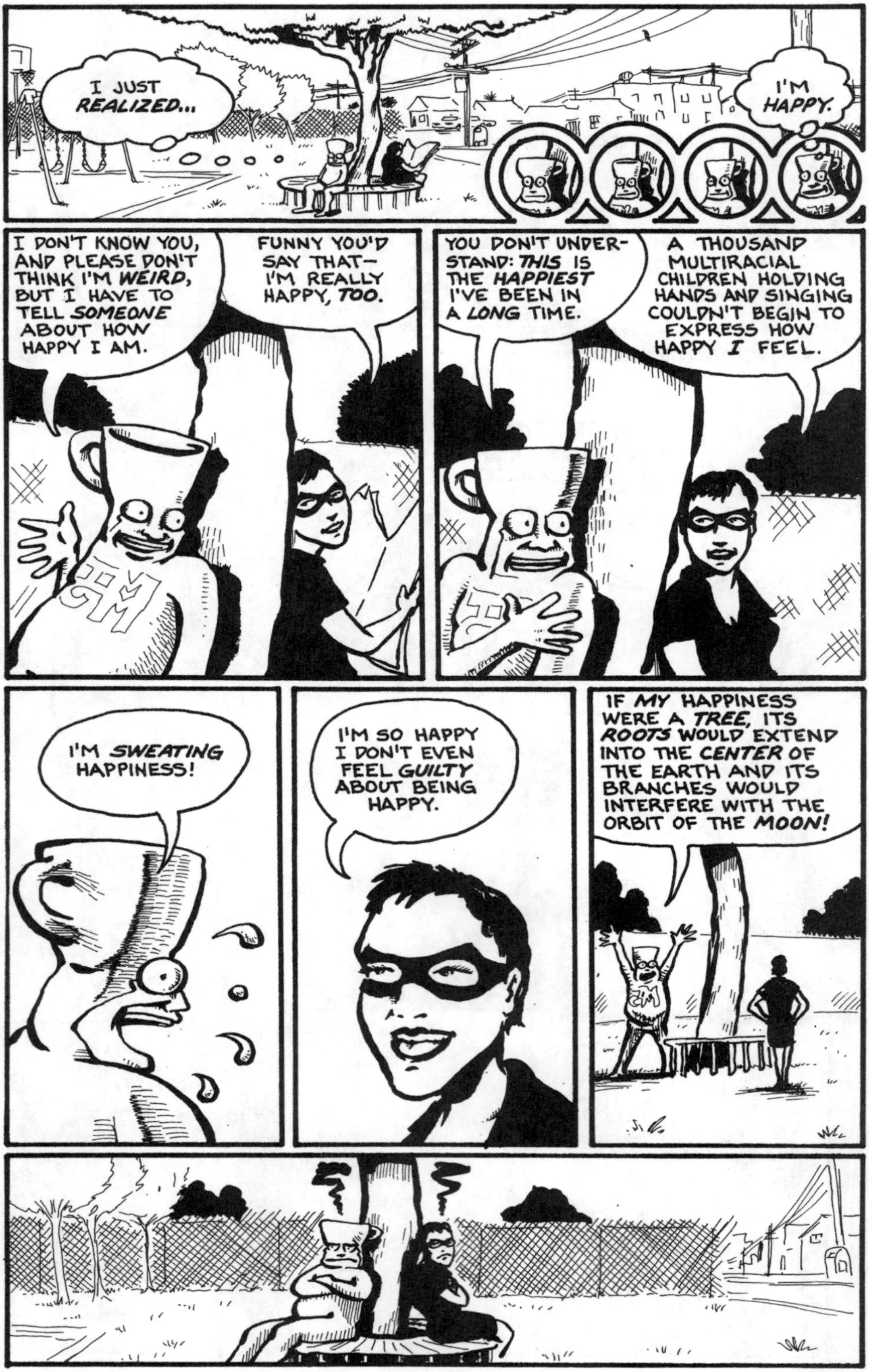
I JUST REALIZED...
I'M HAPPY.
I DON'T KNOW YOU, AND PLEASE DON'T THINK I'M WEIRD, BUT I HAVE TO TELL SOMEONE ABOUT HOW HAPPY I AM.
FUNNY YOU'D SAY THAT— I'M REALLY HAPPY, TOO.
YOU DON'T UNDERSTAND: THIS IS THE HAPPIEST I'VE BEEN IN A LONG TIME.
A THOUSAND MULTIRACIAL CHILDREN HOLDING HANDS AND SINGING COULDN'T BEGIN TO EXPRESS HOW HAPPY I FEEL.
I'M SWEATING HAPPINESS!
I'M SO HAPPY I DON'T EVEN FEEL GUILTY ABOUT BEING HAPPY.
IF MY HAPPINESS WERE A TREE, ITS ROOTS WOULD EXTEND INTO THE CENTER OF THE EARTH AND ITS BRANCHES WOULD INTERFERE WITH THE ORBIT OF THE MOON!

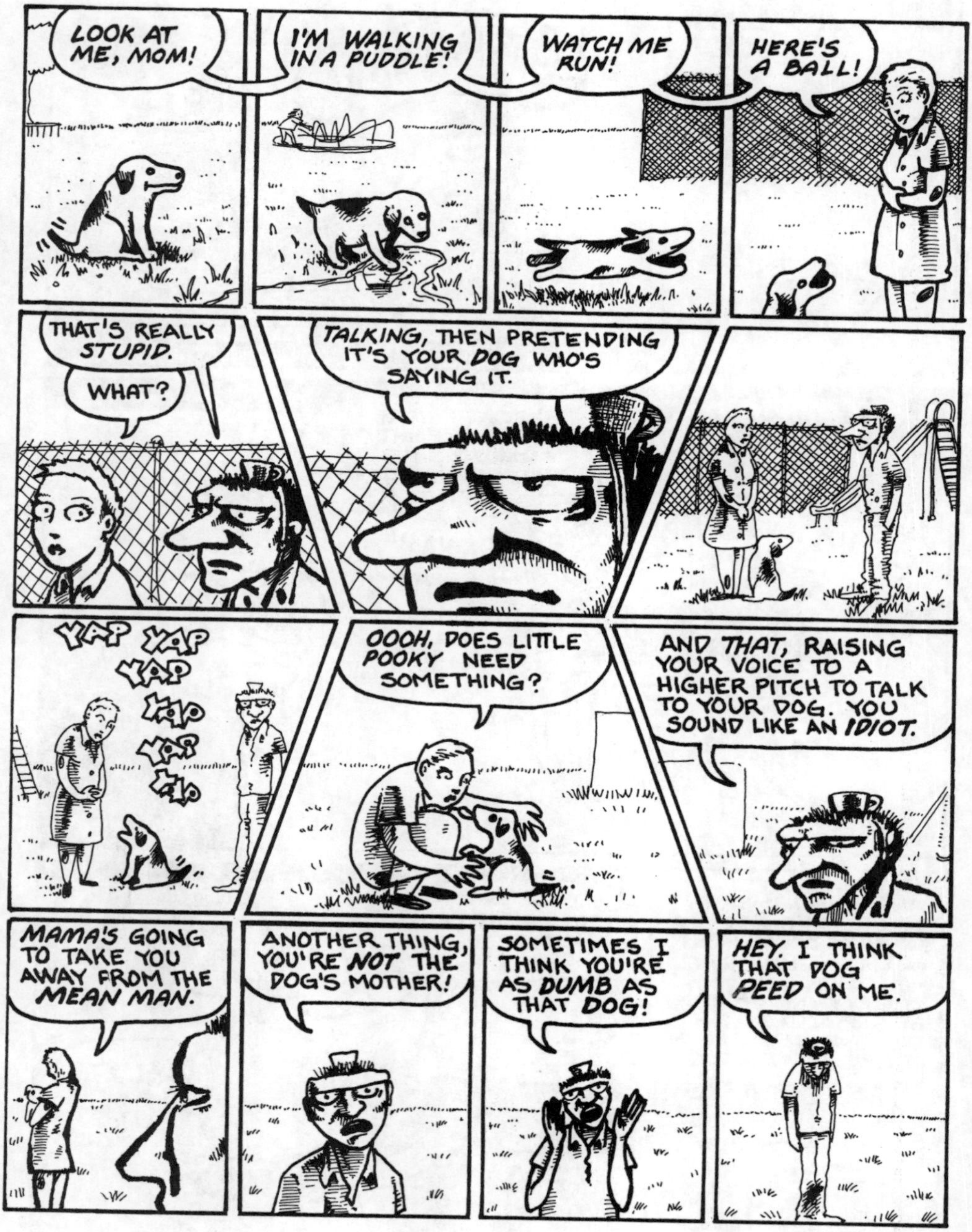
LOOK AT ME, MOM!
I'M WALKING IN A PUDDLE!
WATCH ME RUN!
HERE'S A BALL!
THAT'S REALLY STUPID.
WHAT?
TALKING, THEN PRETENDING IT'S YOUR DOG WHO'S SAYING IT.
YAP YAP YAP YAP YAP YAP
OOOH, DOES LITTLE POOKY NEED SOMETHING?
AND THAT, RAISING YOUR VOICE TO A HIGHER PITCH TO TALK TO YOUR DOG. YOU SOUND LIKE AN IDIOT.
MAMA'S GOING TO TAKE YOU AWAY FROM THE MEAN MAN.
ANOTHER THING, YOU'RE NOT THE DOG'S MOTHER!
SOMETIMES I THINK YOU'RE AS DUMB AS THAT DOG!
HEY. I THINK THAT DOG PEED ON ME.

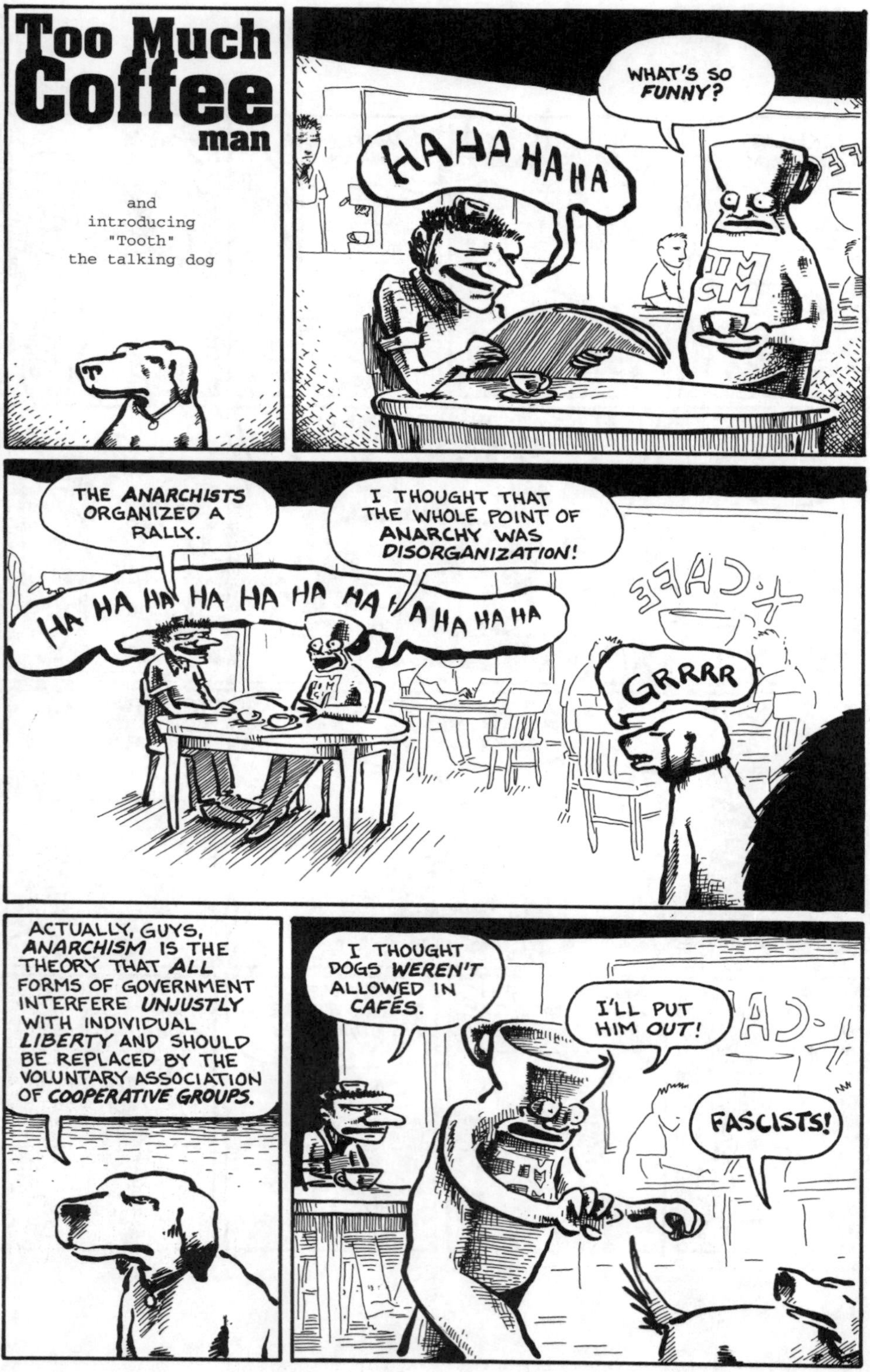
Too Much Coffee man
and introducing "Tooth" the talking dog
WHAT'S SO FUNNY?
HAHAHAHAHA
THE ANARCHISTS ORGANIZED A RALLY.
I THOUGHT THAT THE WHOLE POINT OF ANARCHY WAS DISORGANIZATION!
HA HA HA HA HA HA HA HA HA HA HA HA
GRRRR
ACTUALLY, GUYS, ANARCHISM IS THE THEORY THAT ALL FORMS OF GOVERNMENT INTERFERE UNJUSTLY WITH INDIVIDUAL LIBERTY AND SHOULD BE REPLACED BY THE VOLUNTARY ASSOCIATION OF COOPERATIVE GROUPS.
I THOUGHT DOGS WEREN'T ALLOWED IN CAFÉS.
I'LL PUT HIM OUT!
FASCISTS!

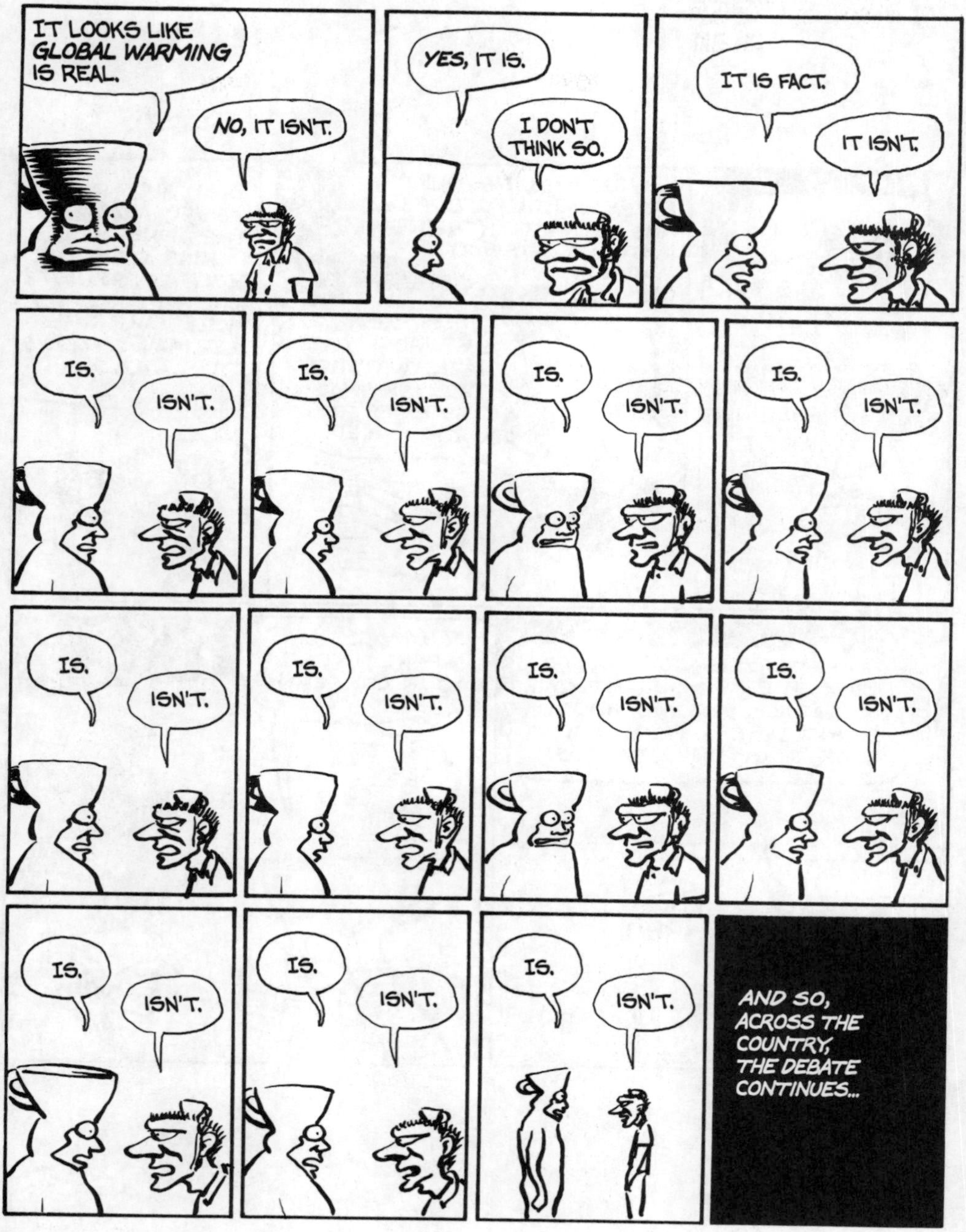
IT LOOKS LIKE GLOBAL WARMING IS REAL.
NO, IT ISN'T.
YES, IT IS.
I DON'T THINK SO.
IT IS FACT.
IT ISN'T.
IS.
ISN'T.
IS.
ISN'T.
IS.
ISN'T.
IS.
ISN'T.
IS.
ISN'T.
IS.
ISN'T.
IS.
ISN'T.
IS.
ISN'T.
IS.
ISN'T.
IS.
ISN'T.
IS.
ISN'T.
AND SO, ACROSS THE COUNTRY, THE DEBATE CONTINUES...

WE'RE ALL *NAZIS.*

WE'RE *KILLING* OUR PLANET WITH *POLLUTION,* AND ULTIMATELY WE'RE JUST WATCHING IT HAPPEN.

IT'S JUST LIKE HOW THE *NAZIS* WATCHED THE *JEWS* BE LED OFF TO BE KILLED.

BUT THE NAZIS ACTIVELY *MURDERED* THE JEWS. YOU'RE TALKING ABOUT THE *GUILT OF PASSIVITY* WHICH MAKES US MORE LIKE THE GERMAN *CITIZENS* THAN *NAZIS.*

YOU *MIGHT* HAVE A *VALID IDEA,* BUT IF YOU GET YOUR METAPHOR *WRONG,* YOU'LL SOUND LIKE A *FOOL* AND YOUR POINT WILL BE *LOST.*

THANKS. I APPRECIATE YOUR CONCERN.

JERK.

FOOL.

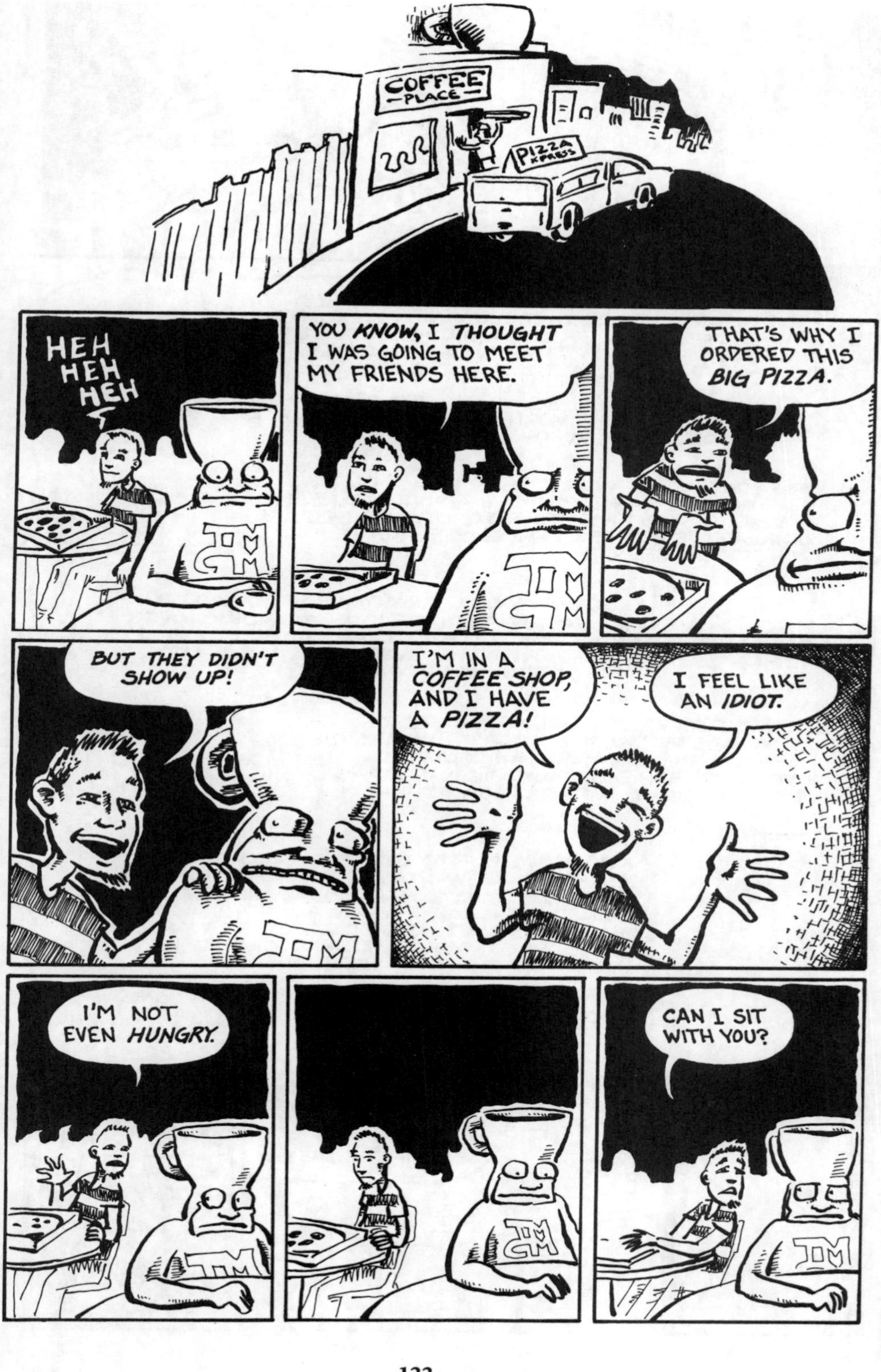
COFFEE PLACE
PIZZA XPRESS
HEH HEH HEH
YOU KNOW, I THOUGHT I WAS GOING TO MEET MY FRIENDS HERE.
THAT'S WHY I ORDERED THIS BIG PIZZA.
BUT THEY DIDN'T SHOW UP!
I'M IN A COFFEE SHOP, AND I HAVE A PIZZA!
I FEEL LIKE AN IDIOT.
I'M NOT EVEN HUNGRY.
CAN I SIT WITH YOU?

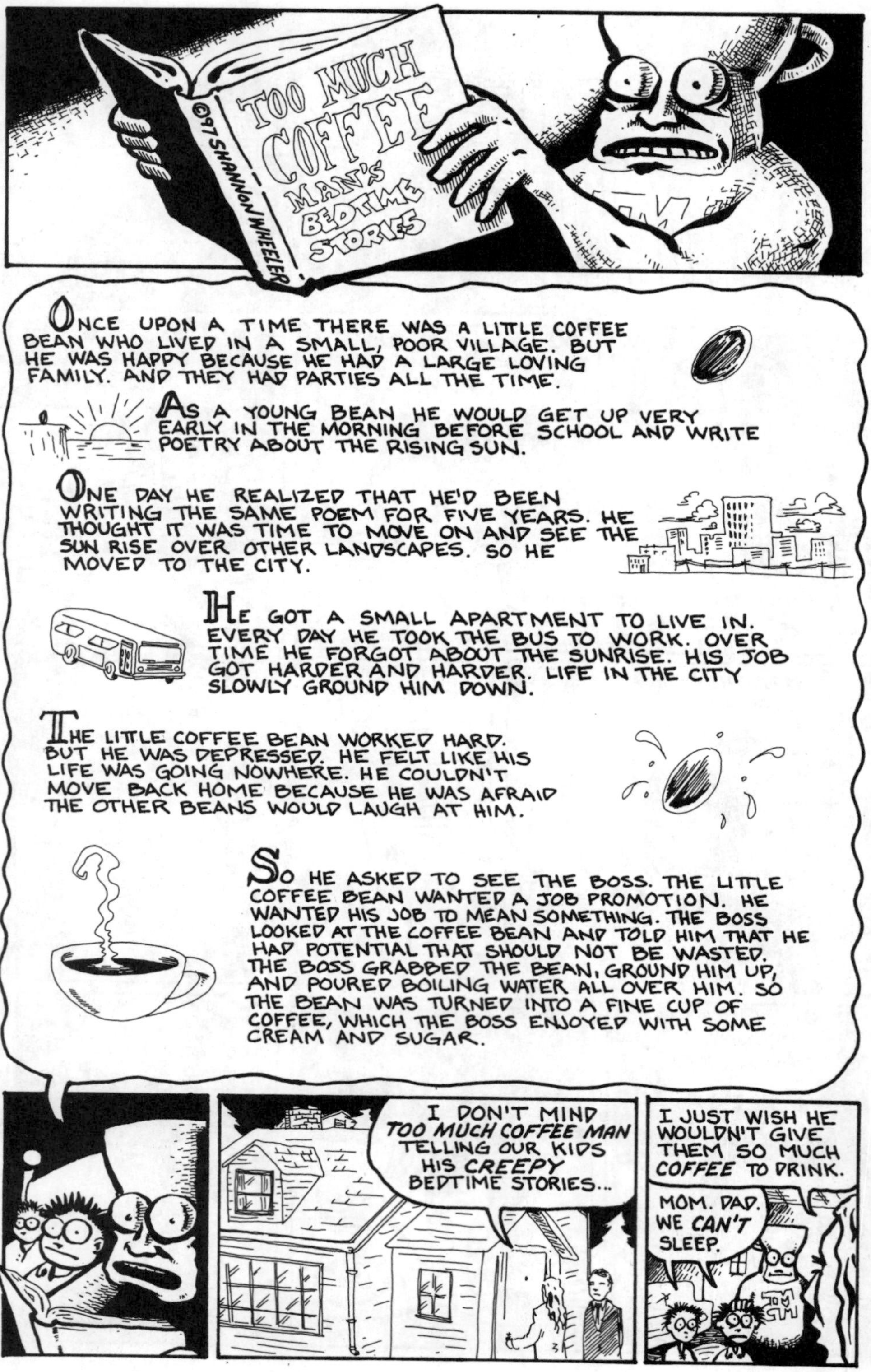
TOO MUCH COFFEE MAN'S BEDTIME STORIES
©97 SHANNON WHEELER
ONCE UPON A TIME THERE WAS A LITTLE COFFEE BEAN WHO LIVED IN A SMALL, POOR VILLAGE. BUT HE WAS HAPPY BECAUSE HE HAD A LARGE LOVING FAMILY. AND THEY HAD PARTIES ALL THE TIME.
AS A YOUNG BEAN HE WOULD GET UP VERY EARLY IN THE MORNING BEFORE SCHOOL AND WRITE POETRY ABOUT THE RISING SUN.
ONE DAY HE REALIZED THAT HE'D BEEN WRITING THE SAME POEM FOR FIVE YEARS. HE THOUGHT IT WAS TIME TO MOVE ON AND SEE THE SUN RISE OVER OTHER LANDSCAPES. SO HE MOVED TO THE CITY.
HE GOT A SMALL APARTMENT TO LIVE IN. EVERY DAY HE TOOK THE BUS TO WORK. OVER TIME HE FORGOT ABOUT THE SUNRISE. HIS JOB GOT HARDER AND HARDER. LIFE IN THE CITY SLOWLY GROUND HIM DOWN.
THE LITTLE COFFEE BEAN WORKED HARD. BUT HE WAS DEPRESSED. HE FELT LIKE HIS LIFE WAS GOING NOWHERE. HE COULDN'T MOVE BACK HOME BECAUSE HE WAS AFRAID THE OTHER BEANS WOULD LAUGH AT HIM.
SO HE ASKED TO SEE THE BOSS. THE LITTLE COFFEE BEAN WANTED A JOB PROMOTION. HE WANTED HIS JOB TO MEAN SOMETHING. THE BOSS LOOKED AT THE COFFEE BEAN AND TOLD HIM THAT HE HAD POTENTIAL THAT SHOULD NOT BE WASTED. THE BOSS GRABBED THE BEAN, GROUND HIM UP, AND POURED BOILING WATER ALL OVER HIM. SO THE BEAN WAS TURNED INTO A FINE CUP OF COFFEE, WHICH THE BOSS ENJOYED WITH SOME CREAM AND SUGAR.
I DON'T MIND *TOO MUCH COFFEE MAN* TELLING OUR KIDS HIS *CREEPY* BEDTIME STORIES...
I JUST WISH HE WOULDN'T GIVE THEM SO MUCH *COFFEE* TO DRINK.
MOM. DAD. WE *CAN'T* SLEEP.

TELL ME
TOO MUCH COFFEE MAN
WHAT IS YOUR FAMILY LIKE?
IT'S A TRAGIC STORY.
BUT IT'S ALSO A FUNNY STORY.
AAAAH... THE MEMORIES.
THERE WAS A BEAST WHO WAS VERY LONELY.
IT WENT TO LOOK FOR LOVE!
IT CAME TO A STREAM IT COULD NOT CROSS.
THE SUN WAS HOT, BUT IT FELT GOOD.
THE BEAST BEGAN TO SING.
A FISH HEARD THE SONG AND FELL IN LOVE.
THE BEAST AND THE FISH SANG TOGETHER, AND THE BEAST FELL IN LOVE, TOO.
THE FISH CARRIED THE BEAST ACROSS THE WATER.
THE BEAST LEFT THE FISH AND WENT TO LOOK FOR MORE LOVE.
WHAT WAS THE QUESTION AGAIN?
NEVER MIND.

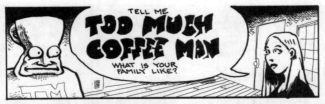

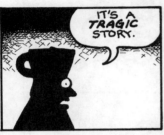

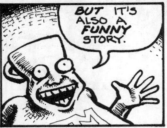

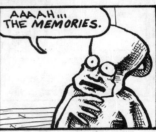

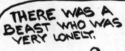

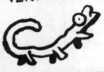

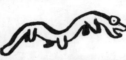

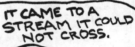

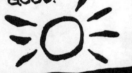

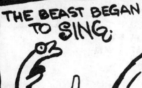

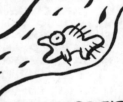

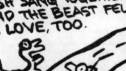

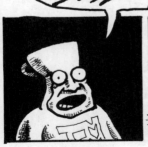

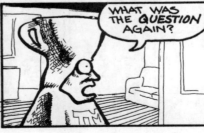

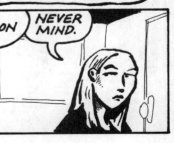

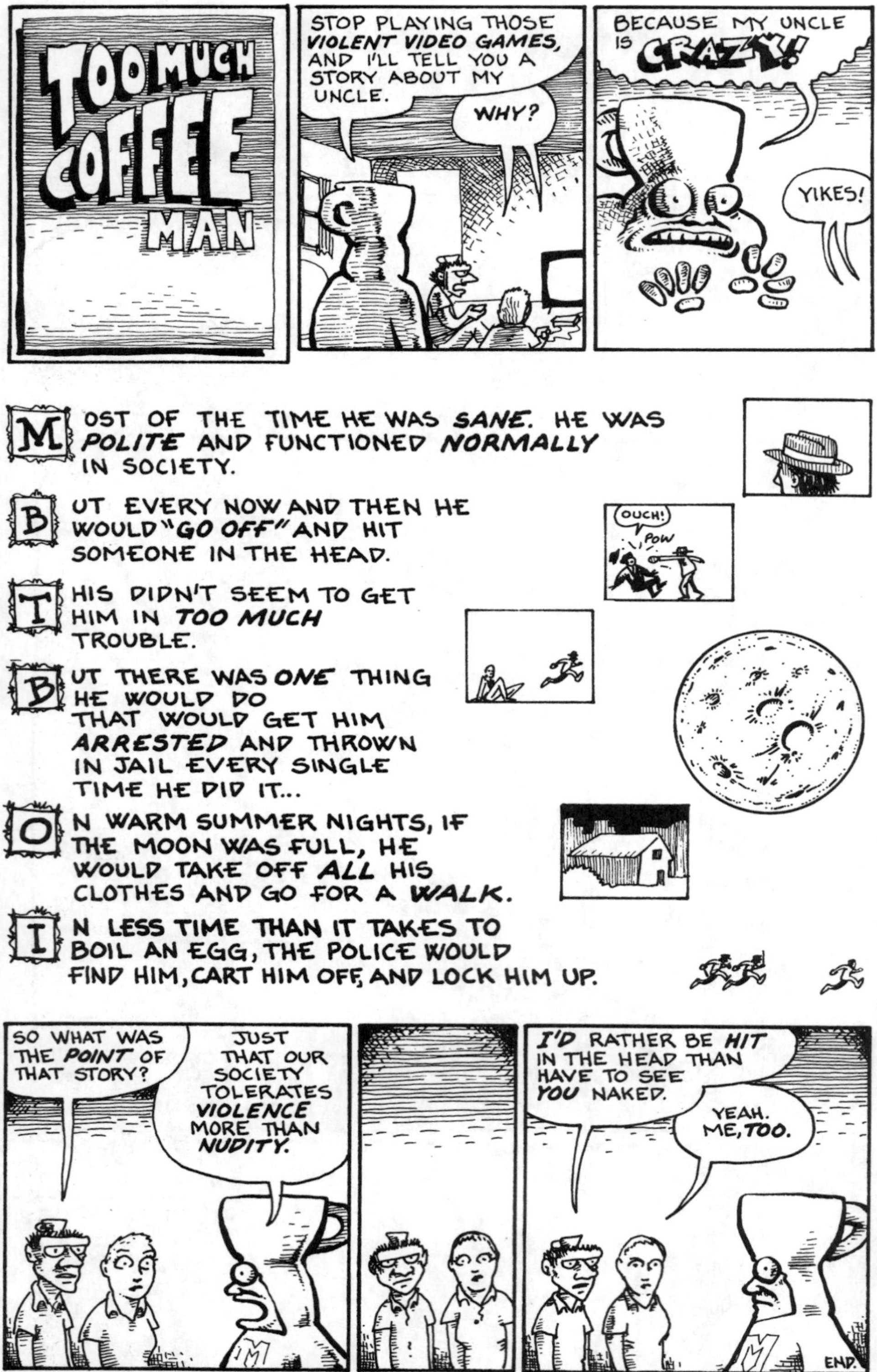
TOO MUCH COFFEE MAN
STOP PLAYING THOSE VIOLENT VIDEO GAMES, AND I'LL TELL YOU A STORY ABOUT MY UNCLE.
WHY?
BECAUSE MY UNCLE IS CRAZY!
YIKES!
MOST OF THE TIME HE WAS SANE. HE WAS POLITE AND FUNCTIONED NORMALLY IN SOCIETY.
BUT EVERY NOW AND THEN HE WOULD "GO OFF" AND HIT SOMEONE IN THE HEAD.
OUCH!
POW
THIS DIDN'T SEEM TO GET HIM IN TOO MUCH TROUBLE.
BUT THERE WAS ONE THING HE WOULD DO THAT WOULD GET HIM ARRESTED AND THROWN IN JAIL EVERY SINGLE TIME HE DID IT...
ON WARM SUMMER NIGHTS, IF THE MOON WAS FULL, HE WOULD TAKE OFF ALL HIS CLOTHES AND GO FOR A WALK.
IN LESS TIME THAN IT TAKES TO BOIL AN EGG, THE POLICE WOULD FIND HIM, CART HIM OFF, AND LOCK HIM UP.
SO WHAT WAS THE POINT OF THAT STORY?
JUST THAT OUR SOCIETY TOLERATES VIOLENCE MORE THAN NUDITY.
I'D RATHER BE HIT IN THE HEAD THAN HAVE TO SEE YOU NAKED.
YEAH. ME, TOO.
END.

THANKS TO MR. ELLIS FOR THE TRUE STORY.

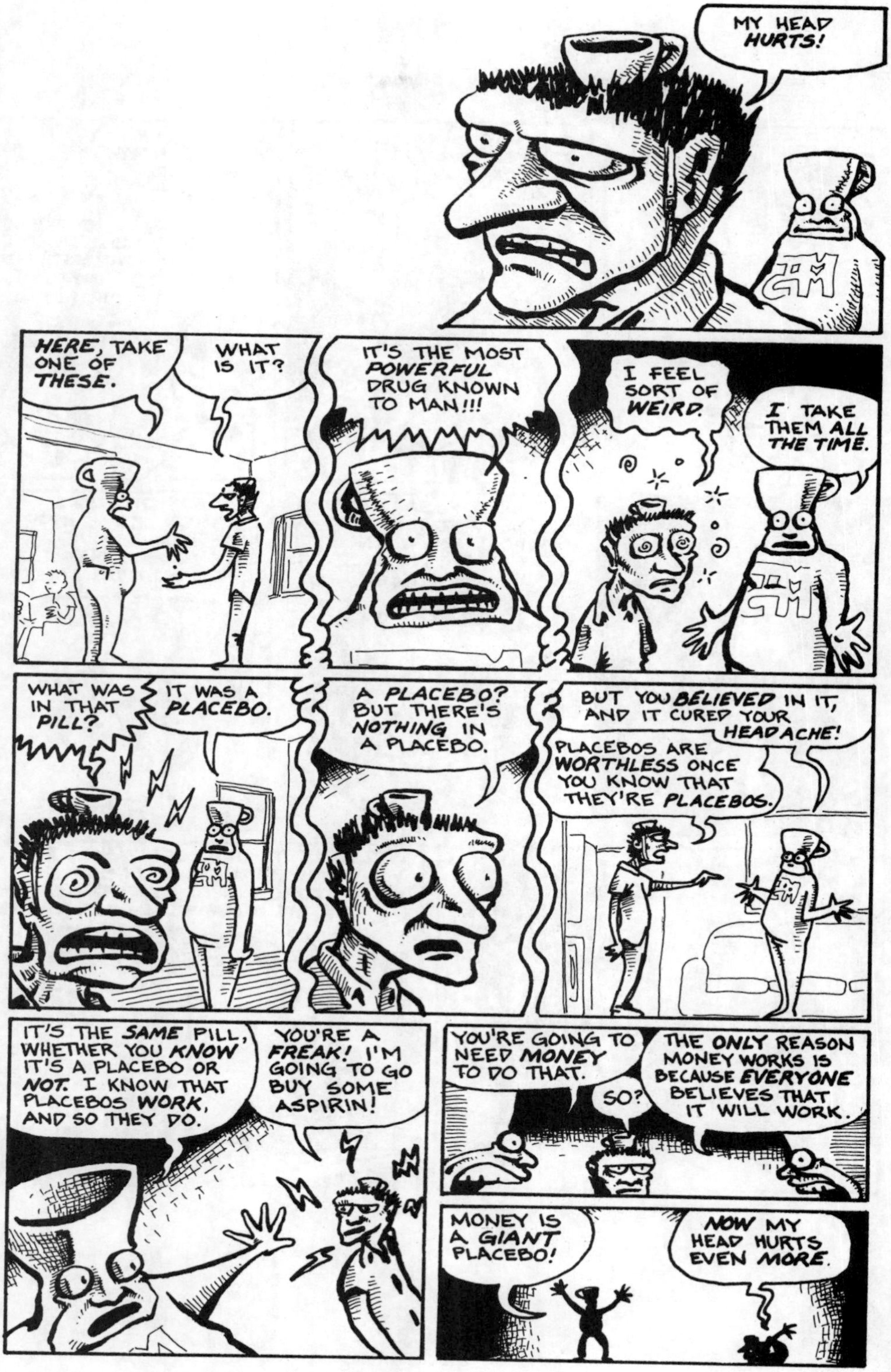
MY HEAD HURTS!
HERE, TAKE ONE OF THESE.
WHAT IS IT?
IT'S THE MOST POWERFUL DRUG KNOWN TO MAN!!!
I FEEL SORT OF WEIRD.
I TAKE THEM ALL THE TIME.
WHAT WAS IN THAT PILL?
IT WAS A PLACEBO.
A PLACEBO? BUT THERE'S NOTHING IN A PLACEBO.
BUT YOU BELIEVED IN IT, AND IT CURED YOUR HEADACHE!
PLACEBOS ARE WORTHLESS ONCE YOU KNOW THAT THEY'RE PLACEBOS.
IT'S THE SAME PILL, WHETHER YOU KNOW IT'S A PLACEBO OR NOT. I KNOW THAT PLACEBOS WORK, AND SO THEY DO.
YOU'RE A FREAK! I'M GOING TO GO BUY SOME ASPIRIN!
YOU'RE GOING TO NEED MONEY TO DO THAT.
SO?
THE ONLY REASON MONEY WORKS IS BECAUSE EVERYONE BELIEVES THAT IT WILL WORK.
MONEY IS A GIANT PLACEBO!
NOW MY HEAD HURTS EVEN MORE.

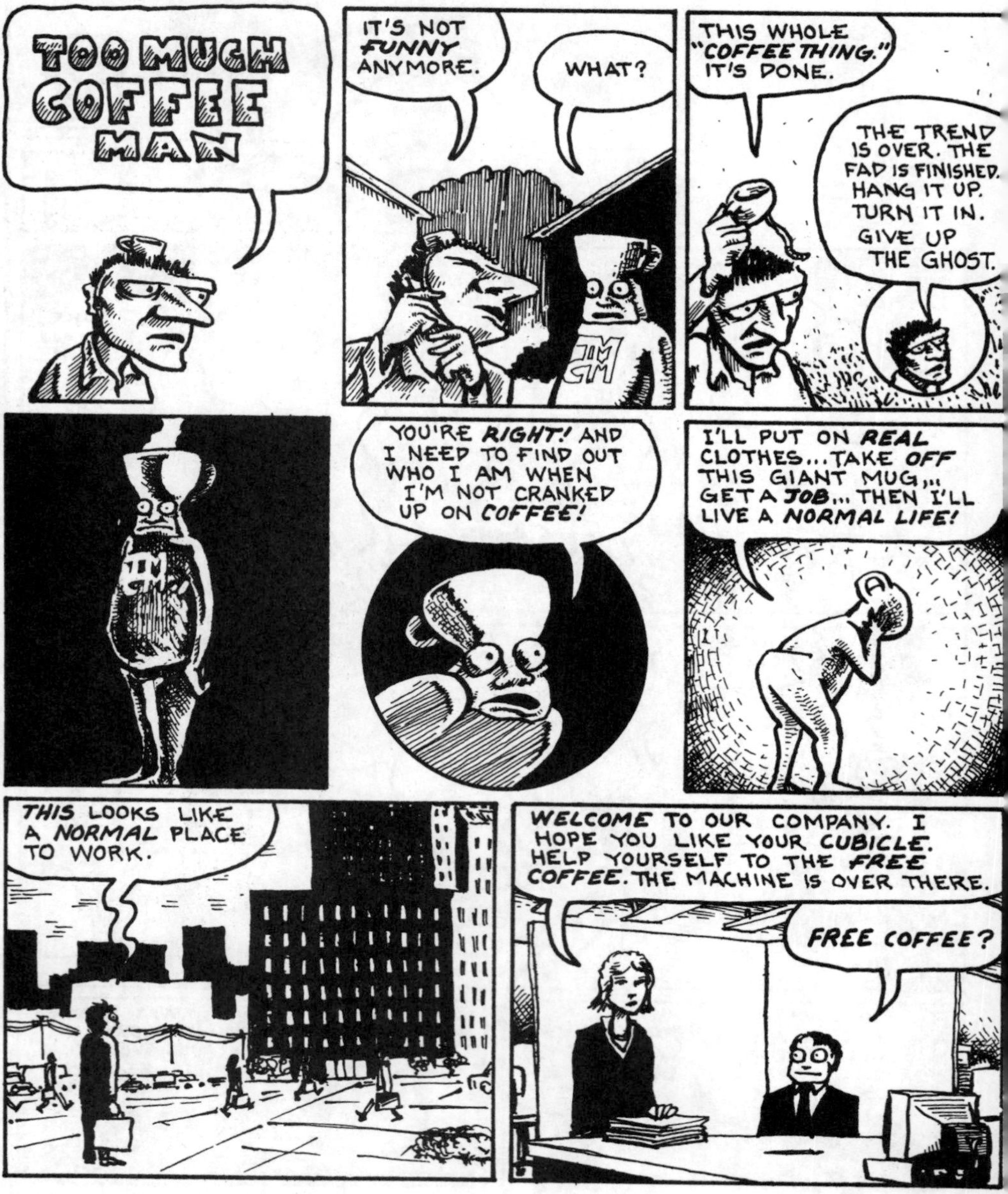
TOO MUCH COFFEE MAN
IT'S NOT FUNNY ANYMORE.
WHAT?
THIS WHOLE "COFFEE THING." IT'S DONE.
THE TREND IS OVER. THE FAD IS FINISHED. HANG IT UP. TURN IT IN. GIVE UP THE GHOST.
YOU'RE RIGHT! AND I NEED TO FIND OUT WHO I AM WHEN I'M NOT CRANKED UP ON COFFEE!
I'LL PUT ON REAL CLOTHES... TAKE OFF THIS GIANT MUG... GET A JOB... THEN I'LL LIVE A NORMAL LIFE!
THIS LOOKS LIKE A NORMAL PLACE TO WORK.
WELCOME TO OUR COMPANY. I HOPE YOU LIKE YOUR CUBICLE. HELP YOURSELF TO THE FREE COFFEE. THE MACHINE IS OVER THERE.
FREE COFFEE?

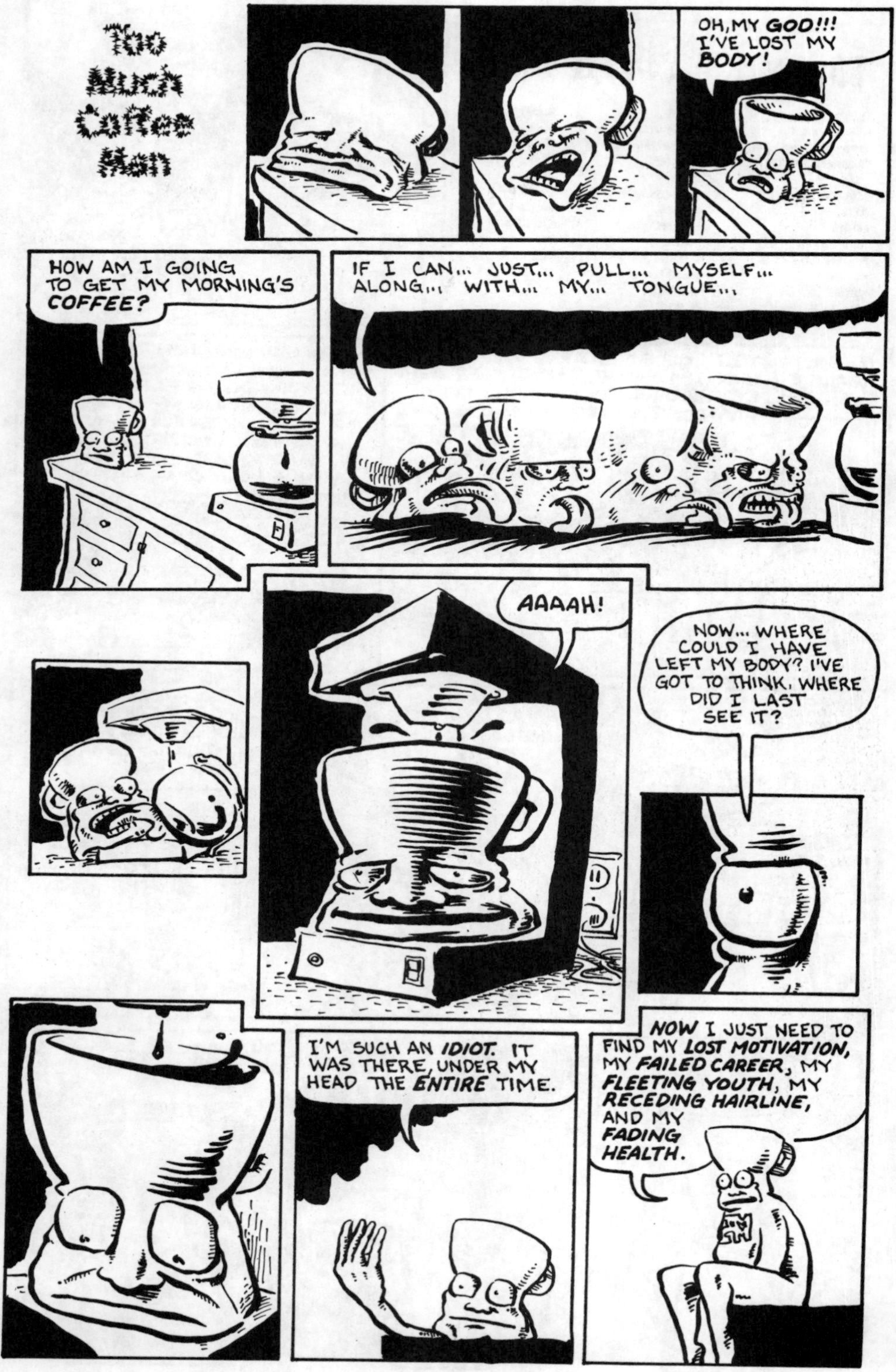

Too Much Coffee Man
OH, MY GOD!!! I'VE LOST MY BODY!
HOW AM I GOING TO GET MY MORNING'S COFFEE?
IF I CAN... JUST... PULL... MYSELF... ALONG... WITH... MY... TONGUE...
AAAAH!
NOW... WHERE COULD I HAVE LEFT MY BODY? I'VE GOT TO THINK. WHERE DID I LAST SEE IT?
I'M SUCH AN IDIOT. IT WAS THERE, UNDER MY HEAD THE ENTIRE TIME.
NOW I JUST NEED TO FIND MY LOST MOTIVATION, MY FAILED CAREER, MY FLEETING YOUTH, MY RECEDING HAIRLINE, AND MY FADING HEALTH.

TOO MUCH COFFEE MAN

BY SHANNON WHEELER

UNDERWATER GUY
TOO MUCH GERMAN WHITE CHOCOLATE WOMAN WITH ALMONDS
TRADEMARK COPYRIGHT MAN
ATLAS
CIGGY, THE NICOTEENAGER
CLICHÉ
ROBOTS
TOO MUCH COFFEE WOMAN
BUSINESS GUY
MY BANKER
WRITERS
CIGARETTE COMPANIES

MR. AGENT
THE HAPPY GIRL
BRINE SHRIMP
COPS
STREET MUSICIAN
CAFÉ POETS
WAIF SUPERMODEL
INTERNET MAN
STINKY HOMELESS GUY
WORKING-SUIT ZOMBIES
TRENDY PEOPLE
BOX BOY

MONKEY BOYS
STUDENTS
CAR DRIVERS
RELIGIOUS PEOPLE
BAD TV
SHOPPERS
MR. GEEKY
SALESMAN
ETC.
ETC.
ETC.

WHAT ARE YOU DOING?

I'M MAKING A LIST OF ALL THE PEOPLE WHO HAVE PISSED ME OFF.

UNFORTUNATELY, ONCE I STARTED, I REALIZED THAT I'M MAD AT ALMOST EVERYONE. EVERYONE, EITHER DIRECTLY OR INDIRECTLY, HAS DONE SOMETHING WRONG TO ME.

I LOANED UNDERWATER GUY FIVE BUCKS AND HE HASN'T PAID ME BACK, THE COFFEE SHOP GIRL DOESN'T RETURN MY AFFECTIONS, MY DRY CLEANER RUINED MY SUIT, THE PHONE COMPANY IS FILLED WITH JERKS AND THEY DON'T EVEN HAVE A COMPLAINT DEPT.

THEY CLOG THE TOILETS IN PUBLIC RESTROOMS AND OVERPOPULATE... SEND ME JUNK... BILLS... ROTTING V... AND... TAX MY PA... EN... SHOP AT M... JUNK MAIL... UGLY PEOPLE... TRY TO TALK TO... IC, ATTRACTIVE PEOPLE AVOID ME.

HEY! HOW COME I'M NOT ON THE LIST?

WHAT'S WRONG WITH ME? AREN'T I GOOD ENOUGH FOR YOUR LIST? AREN'T I MEAN ENOUGH?

I'VE BEEN CRUEL TO YOU FOR YEARS! I DESERVE A SPOT MORE THAN YOUR... YOUR... BUS DRIVER!

SORRY, I'M JUST NOT ANGRY WITH YOU.

I HATE YOU.

YOUR ANGER MAKES ME HAPPY. IRONIC, ISN'T IT?

140

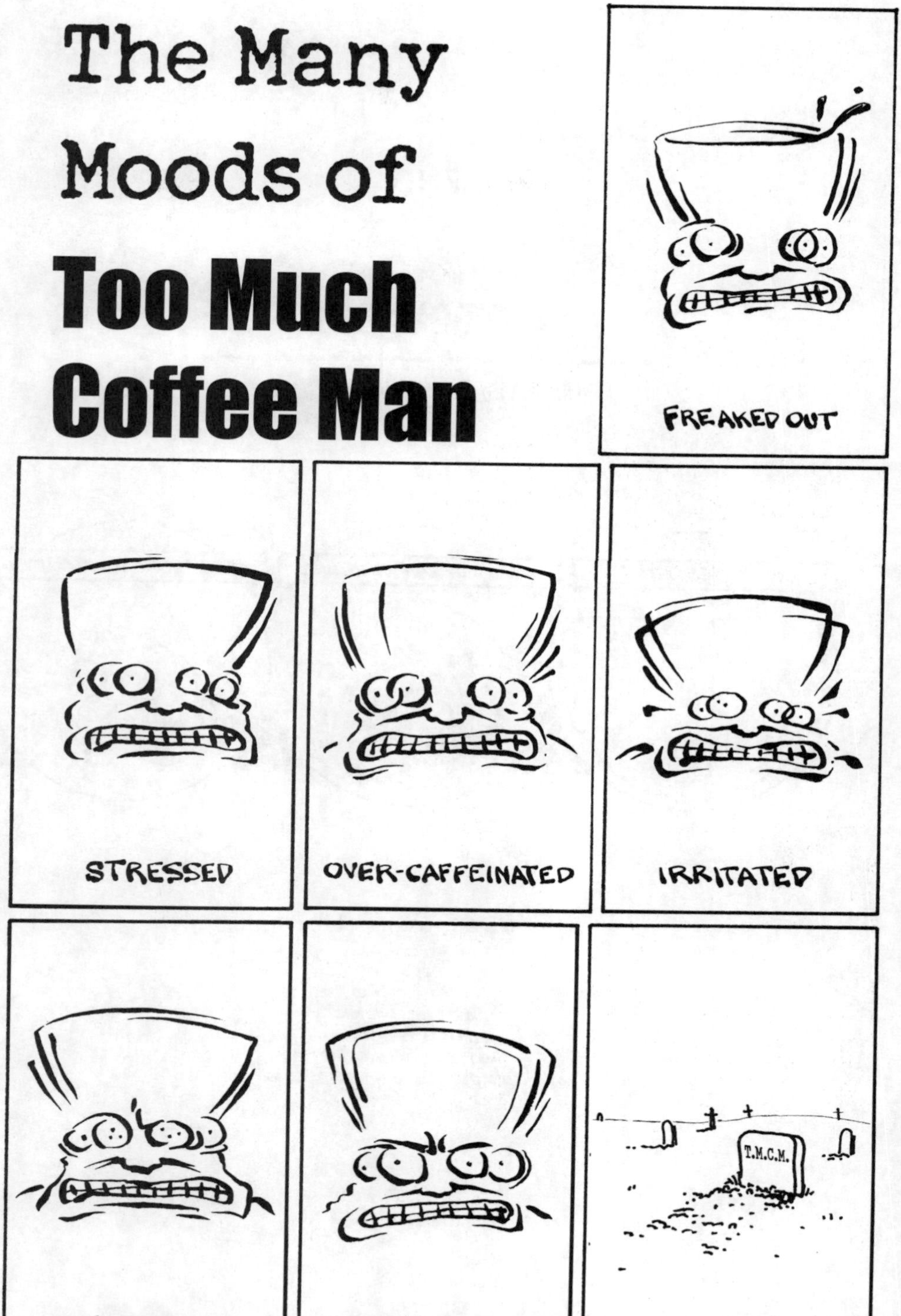
The Many Moods of Too Much Coffee Man
FREAKED OUT
STRESSED
OVER-CAFFEINATED
IRRITATED
HOSTILE
ANGRY
T.M.C.M.
RELAXED

END

AFTERWORD

Thank you for reading my book.

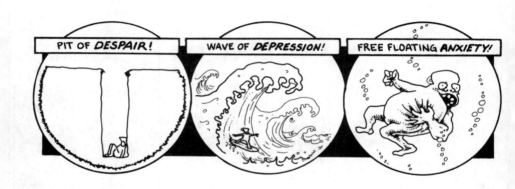

PIT OF *DESPAIR*! · WAVE OF *DEPRESSION*! · FREE FLOATING *ANXIETY*!

Other titles considered for this book:
Motionless Pictures
Caffeine is a Drug
Reflections in Coffee
Dancing in my Mind Field
Too Much Coffee Man A-Go-Go
I am not Too Much Coffee Man
Too Much Coffee Man - Paranoia, and other Popular Notions

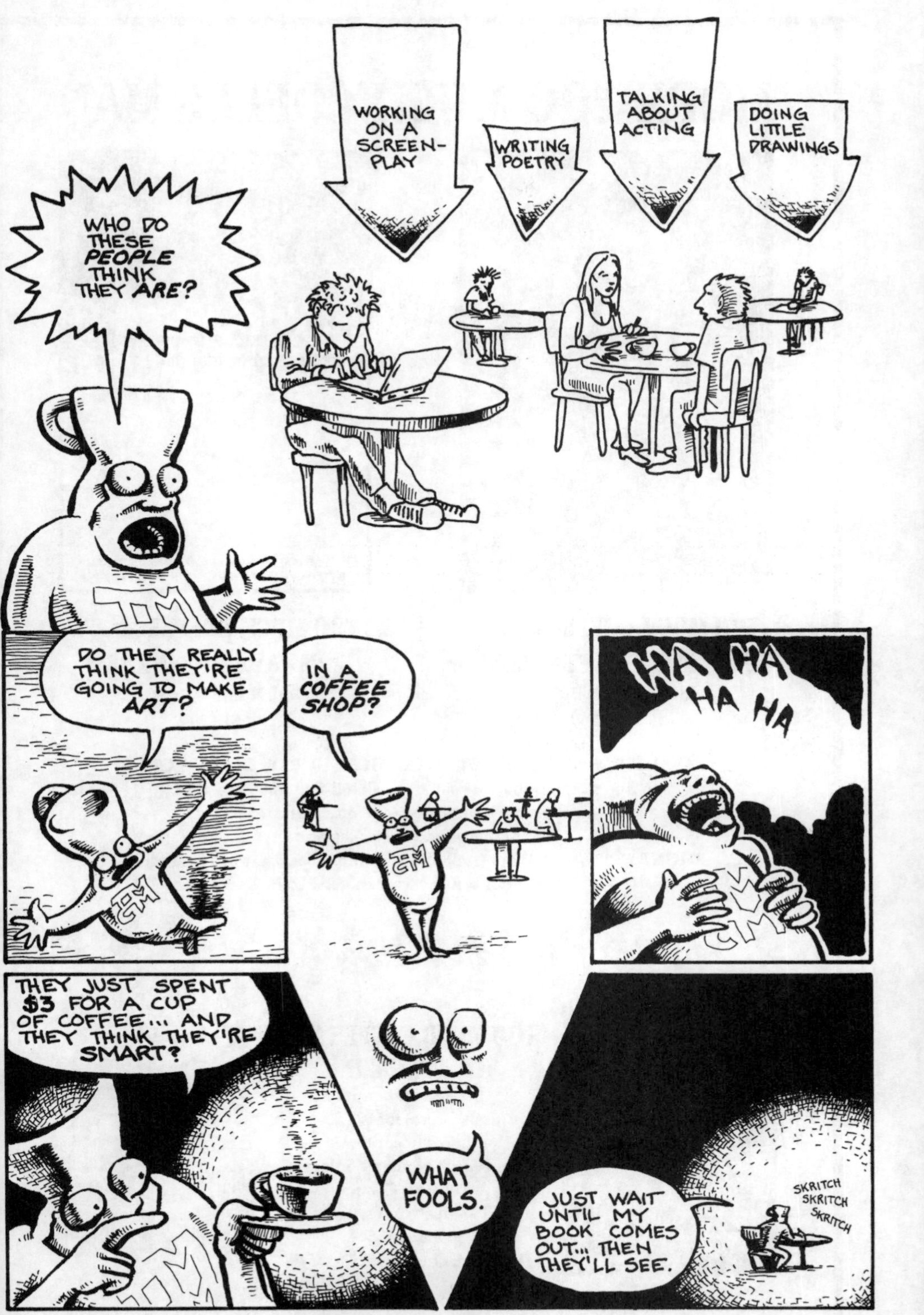
WORKING ON A SCREEN-PLAY
WRITING POETRY
TALKING ABOUT ACTING
DOING LITTLE DRAWINGS
WHO DO THESE *PEOPLE* THINK THEY *ARE*?
DO THEY REALLY THINK THEY'RE GOING TO MAKE *ART*?
IN A *COFFEE SHOP*?
HA HA HA HA
THEY JUST SPENT $3 FOR A CUP OF COFFEE... AND THEY THINK THEY'RE SMART?
WHAT FOOLS.
JUST WAIT UNTIL MY BOOK COMES OUT... THEN THEY'LL SEE.
SKRITCH SKRITCH SKRITCH

MORE TOO MUCH COFFEE MAN

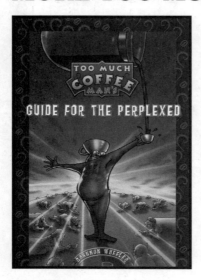 

TOO MUCH COFFEE MAN'S
GUIDE FOR THE PERPLEXED
ISBN 1-56971-289-1
$10.95

TOO MUCH COFFEE MAN'S
PARADE OF TIRADE
ISBN 1-56971-437-1
$12.95

AVAILABLE AT YOUR LOCAL COMICS SHOP OR BOOKSTORE
To find a comics shop in your area, call toll-free 1-888-266-4226.
For more information or to order direct:
E-MAIL: mailorder@darkhorse.com
PHONE: 1-800-862-0052 or (503) 652-9701 Mon.-Sat. 9 A.M. to 5 P.M. Pacific
ON THE WEB: www.darkhorse.com

TOO MUCH COFFEE MAN
THE MAGAZINE
One-year subscription
(six issues) for $24.95
info@tmcm.com
Send check or money order to:
Adhesive Comics
Too Much Coffee Man
P.O. Box 14549
Portland, Oregon 97293-14549